ALLEN&UNWIN

SYDNEY • MELBOURNE • AUCKLAND • LONDON

THE
WRITER'S
ROOM

Published by Allen & Unwin in 2016

Copyright © Charlotte Wood 2016

Allen & Unwin
Sydney, Melbourne, Auckland, London

83 Alexander Street
Crows Nest NSW 2065
Australia
Phone: (61 2) 8425 0100
Email: info@allenandunwin.com
Web: www.allenandunwin.com

Cataloguing-in-Publication details are available
from the National Library of Australia
trove.nla.gov.au

ISBN 978 1 76029 334 5

Text design by Design by Committee
Set in 12/18.25 pt Electra LT Std by Bookhouse, Sydney
Printed and bound in Australia by Griffin Press

10 9 8 7 6 5 4 3 2 1

CONTENTS

INTRODUCTION

When in 2012 I read an insightful conversation between two painters, Steve Lopes and Euan Macleod, in *Artist Profile* magazine I found myself wishing there was something like it for Australian writers.

I had always loved *The Paris Review*'s 'on writing' interviews. As a young woman I'd devoured Candida Baker's *Yacker* book series of the 1980s and early '90s, while Kate Grenville's and Sue Woolfe's *Making Stories* became my bible as a young writer. But a magazine would be something different—and besides, it had been more than two decades since a significant collection of long-form interviews with writers had appeared in our country. I realised that my mid-career novelist's experience, together with my background in journalism and the distribution now allowed by the internet, put me in an ideal position to create what I wanted.

In 2013 *The Writer's Room Interviews* was born: a bimonthly digital magazine, each issue featuring a long Q&A with an established Australian author.

From the start I knew I'd adopt *The Paris Review* model,

where the writer has a chance to review and change the edited transcript of the interview. Having been interviewed about my own work so many times and then been embarrassed by my awkward words in print, I wanted 'my' writers to know they would have complete and final control over anything that appeared in the magazine. Invariably, they changed nothing. Or, more accurately, they sometimes made small but important clarifications, or expanded on an area they'd been oblique about, or made their opinion on something more definite. I have a hunch that knowing they had a chance to retract or change things later actually allowed them to be more expansive at the time of the interview. More open, less defended, more generous. And because they were word people, their care with language was a joy: we worked together to make their words as precise, as shimmeringly perfect as possible.

I also knew I wanted to talk with writers as far away from 'publication time' as possible. The point of *The Writer's Room Interviews* was not celebrity or accolades or life stories, but a deeper sharing of the creative experience among writers working in different genres. While most author interviews focus on promoting new books, I wanted these to feel slower, calmer and deeper. I wanted them to illuminate something of the *way* a writer works—the hows and whys and mysteries and surprises of the creative process. I found talking with writers at a time when they were generally away from the public gaze meant they were more reflective, opening up in deeper ways about how and why they worked as they did. Usually they were in the middle of a book, grappling with new discoveries about character or research or structure, and these things were in the forefront of their minds. Quite often, indeed, they seemed to be discovering their opinions as they spoke.

For me, it was an extraordinary privilege to sit with each of these writers in a private masterclass of my own, asking really quite intimate questions about their imaginative processes. The magazine's lifespan, I later realised, almost exactly matched the duration of the writing of my novel *The Natural Way of Things*, and in each interview I can pinpoint the precise lessons I took into the creation of that book. For the interviewee, I hoped the experience might feel like a calm, clear light falling over their body of work. At a time when public discussion of literature seems so focused on the turnover of product and prizes and promotion, I hope these conversations will stand, over time, as a record of how Australian literature is made—honouring the writers, their work and each of their particular creative tracks.

The magazine continued for three years, until December 2015. This book contains just a selection of those interviews; my hope is that in time, a second volume will allow me to present the others, and even to have new conversations with authors whose work continues to inspire and teach me.

Charlotte Wood, 2016

Photo: Bette Misfud

TEGAN BENNETT DAYLIGHT is the author of three novels for adults, several books for children and teenagers and a forthcoming collection of short stories. She is also a literary critic and a teacher.

Then writing as Tegan Bennett, her first novel, *Bombora*, was shortlisted for the Vogel's Literary Award and published to acclaim in 1996, when she was just twenty-six. She was hailed as 'a fresh, confident and engaging new literary voice' and novelist James Bradley described her prose as 'at its best the equal of Helen Garner or Penelope Lively'. Five years later, her second novel, *What Falls Away*, was named book of the year in the annual *Sydney Morning Herald* Best Young Novelists list, and the third, *Safety* (2004), was widely praised for its deft portrayal of a marriage under strain, and for the clarity and insight of its prose.

Throughout her writing life, Daylight (whose new name arrived with her marriage) has been a university tutor and lecturer, first teaching creative writing at the University of Technology, Sydney for many years, and now lecturing in English at Charles Sturt University in Bathurst.

When I was invited by Allen & Unwin to commission pieces from twelve Australian writers for an anthology about siblings in 2009, Daylight was one of the first I asked. The resulting story, 'Trouble', about two Australian sisters in London, was among the best in the *Brothers & Sisters* collection. As it turned out, this commission also prompted her to devote serious attention to short stories for the first time.

While she did some reviewing when she was young— arguably too young—it was not until she reached her forties that Daylight began publishing long-form criticism and literary essays, a form of writing in which she has been pleased to find a new 'vocation'. Her essays for *The Australian* and others on Alice Munro and Helen Garner, Kazuo Ishiguro and George Saunders are elegant and well-argued, both entertaining and intellectually muscular. Out of this work, too, has grown her reputation as a skilled live interviewer of writers. In recent years she has appeared on stage in conversation with some of Australia's biggest names, including Tim Winton, Helen Garner and David Malouf, as well as international writers such as Jonathan Franzen and the critic James Wood, whom she greatly admires.

In July 2015 she published her first book in nine years: *Six Bedrooms*, a collection of acute, moving, often excruciatingly insightful stories about young people on the cusp of adulthood. In writing these stories—slowly, as her own children have grown from toddlers into teenagehood—Daylight believes she has reached a new level of artistic skill, and experienced a welcome return of the excitement and pleasure in work she had not felt since writing her first novel.

I came to know Daylight after I read *What Falls Away* and wrote her a fan letter; to my delight she responded instantly, and we quickly became close friends. I still remember the image that made me start my letter—the flight of a white cockatoo, its silver movement 'like a flipped coin'—and the feeling I had (and still do) when I read her work, of being torn between a need to stay very still and read, and to rush off and write myself. We have grown up as writers together, in a sense, and our conversations have been some of the richest of my life. She is often the first reader of my fiction, which I send to her with a mix of fear and gratitude; she won't protect you or herself with dishonest praise, and it would not occur to her to shy away from difficult questions. But while her reading may be driven by a fiercely questing intellect, her response is always delivered with respect and a deep kindness. It is this drive for intellectual inquiry and self-examination, combined with a profoundly compassionate understanding of human relationships, that makes Daylight such a compelling writer, and such a perceptive interviewee. Our conversation took place in the blue-walled living room of her home in the Blue Mountains, where she lives with her husband Russell, and their children Alice and Paddy.

– Charlotte Wood

CW: Tell me what it was like to start publishing so young. Did you do a writing degree at university?

TBD: I tell people I did a writing degree but in fact I only did about three writing subjects and the rest were all 'Film, Gender and Desire' type things. But at that time I was also friends with the sister of the *Dolly* magazine editor, and they were looking for people to write those *Dolly* fiction books. So, I first got published at about twenty, simultaneously with the *Dolly* fiction and a children's book with Mark Macleod at Random House.

CW: A picture book?

TBD: No, a little novelette. It was about fifteen thousand words, called *Sean Twigg and the Witch*. And I wrote it when I was about nineteen I guess. I got out the *Yellow Pages* and I sent it to all the publishers who had the biggest ads. HarperCollins, Penguin, Random House, and a couple of others.

Penguin wanted it. They took it off the slush pile and wanted it but asked if I would rewrite it. I did rewrite it and then they didn't want it—which was salutary. But then a few months later I got a call from Random House; they had seen it on the slush pile, and wanted it. So that was my first 'proper' book. I was really pleased with myself, and unfortunately I can still recall my first meeting with Mark Macleod. The sound of myself showing off just carries down the years.

CW: But you should have been pleased with yourself. That's a pretty serious level of professionalism for a twenty-year-old.

TBD: I guess so. It sort of seems so now. At the time, it didn't. I think it was really just drivenness. Not a drive for *success*, although I had that as well. But I just couldn't stop writing. I was filling books and books and books of journals and I was sitting up at night, writing.

CW: Had you always written when you were a child?

TBD: Yeah, always. Always. I've recently been sorting books and finding some old diaries, which is just scarifying. I am waiting to have the bonfire. But at a really young age I was writing sentences and rewriting them, to shape them. So I was interested in words. I didn't ever think, 'I want to be a writer', because that doesn't make any sense when you don't know what a writer does or what they are. It was just that I had—and I think you have this as well—an incredible need to *communicate*, to tell people what you've seen.

So I wrote a lot of letters; I was always writing letters to people, always firing things off, and I think that was what made me finish a book. And getting something finished, the finicky work of editing and making a story work and all that kind of stuff, I just loved it.

But I was always trying to write something serious all that time. I kept trying to write a novel, but I didn't have any idea how to do it. *Bombora* was the first thing that started to take hold, when I was about twenty-three; the first thing where I was writing scenes that made sense with other scenes, and I could see that I was actually starting to form something.

Bombora was published when I was twenty-six. I entered it in the Vogel a couple of years earlier and it took them a while to decide to publish it, because it was so short they didn't quite know what to do with it. I had finished uni by then and I had had enough success—I'd written another kids' book and another *Dolly* fiction by then, so I'd had just enough success to keep me doing it. And also I still had that obsession.

When I think about it now, I realise I always felt terrible because I was one of the few people I knew who didn't have a boyfriend. I had a lot of short-term lovers and that kind of stuff, but I didn't have a proper boyfriend and I knew all these . . . *settled* women, around my age. I knew young women who were like older women. You know—they *cooked*. [*laughs*]

But I was just living with my best friend Patrick and I used to get up at two in the morning, or get home at two in the morning, pissed, and do some more writing. I was really free. At the time, of course, I was so unhappy and alone, but I now see it as a really exciting time.

I think being alone for much of that time really made a difference, actually. I just had more time to form myself, as a thinker and a writer. So it doesn't feel like a coincidence that I started seeing Russell just as *Bombora* was being published. I was sort of ready to be more adult and to be myself with someone else. It was a completely different relationship to all the other ones.

CW: That impulse that you talked about, the driving need to communicate, is it still your impulse now?

TBD: Yeah. The impulse hasn't changed but the form changes as you get older, doesn't it? I try not to overuse the impulse because I need it for the writing, but I get a lot of pleasure out of communicating with my writing friends. Writing letters, put it that way.

But once you have kids, you don't have the mental space any more to go on describing things in your head as you have been until then. That's what I was doing the whole time: I was looking at things. In the diaries I was keeping at sixteen, I've described the way someone looked on the train, and then I've described them again, tried to rewrite it and to shape it. I mean it's all just excruciating to read now because my attitudes were such a weird mixture of stupid and radical and conservative and just horrible. But you go round describing the world to yourself, and then you have kids and they colonise that part of you.

It's taken a long time for me to come back to that impulse, I think.

CW: You've said that when you look back it feels that you wrote *Bombora* in a kind of dream.

TBD: Jesus, yes. It really was totally like a love affair. I just couldn't wait to get back to it, I thought about it all the time. It was a sort of private beauty, you know. And everything I did on it felt blessed.

Near the end of writing it, I was in my bed upstairs in Hordern Street in Newtown and I just woke up in the night and thought, 'I know what needs to be done.' I got up and I switched on the Mac Classic and I just moved everything around. I had written it in scenes, without any real structure. But now I suddenly realised what the order of it was. It felt as though all of the scenes were in front of me, hanging in the air in a kind of shivering, glittering way, and I just moved everything around. Then it was like, 'And now I am done.'

Then I entered it into the Vogel and the rest is history. Not a very glamorous history. [*laughs*]

CW: What happened after that?

TBD: I tried to write another novel, and I wrote about forty or fifty thousand words of it, but it was really dead, so I had to put it to one side. It was no good. I had to start writing again because I was just desperate to get something done, so I started writing *What Falls Away* and then, later, *Safety*. I'm pleased with those books, but they didn't have that beautiful driven feeling. They have moments, but I never felt that quickening. I had lovely moments where I would go for walks and it would occur to me how to fix a scene and all that kind of thing, but I just didn't feel that beautiful feeling.

CW: Do you think it's possible to ever recover that beautiful first-novel feeling?

TBD: Probably not. But the short stories have started to give it back, that's the thing. For me, when it's really happening, writing feels like this hilarious private conversation you're having with yourself. It makes you laugh and makes you feel bad in all the goodest ways. It makes you feel sort of naughty but in a joyous way. [*laughs*]

CW: I'm going to come back to that idea about laughter in a little while. But tell me what made you turn to short stories as opposed to writing another novel.

TBD: Well, the first short story I wrote was for *Brothers & Sisters*, that was the first proper short story. I did publish one before that, 'Chemotherapy Bay', in 2002 *Best Australian Stories*. I was writing the novel which became *Safety* and I had this adjunct character, Martin, based on my friend Steve who had died when we were young. I tried to fit the story of his illness and death into *Safety*, but every time I tried to push it in, it popped out again. I would force it in again and it would pop out, and then I got a phone call from Peter Craven saying he was interested in me submitting something for *Best Australian Stories*, and did I have something?

So I went to the manuscript and I could just lift the Martin stuff out, like a cake out of a tin. They just came straight out, all those Martin sections, and then I joined them together and wrote a few bridging things and that was it. So, it really was a short story that was living inside a novel without me realising it.

CW: Well, it reads like a completely whole story.

TBD: When I reread it I am happy with it, but . . . there's a flow of thought in the later short stories, I can see they've got a direction, I know where they're going. Whereas that one, it's just a series of powerful impressions ending in a death. So I'm pleased with it, but I know it doesn't have the muscle that the other ones do.

The first one that had a genuine short-story muscle was 'Trouble'. In fact, I think I've written purer narrative and plot-driven stuff in the short stories than I've ever written in a novel. They turned out to be really about structure and narrative in a way the novel wasn't. And it was being asked to write for *Brothers & Sisters* that made me try to write a proper short story, one that wasn't just a collection of pleasantly-put-together scenes, but had narrative movement and purpose and an idea, in which you might feel as though you had reached somewhere when you got to the end of it instead of it actually being tonally all the same, which I do think 'Chemotherapy Bay' is.

CW: But readers have loved that story, it's very powerful.

TBD: I sometimes think people are a bit mesmerised by it because it's a cancer story, so they don't notice that it is tonally quite similar. Nothing really happens. I mean, he does die, but nothing really changes.

CW: We've talked before about how there's a certain slightly unpleasant ease in this kind of thing. You can get away with a lot if you kill someone. Especially a young person. And it can be a little bit suspect.

TBD: Yeah, that's right. That's what I mean about people being mesmerised. It's like, 'Oh, my god! He's so sick and he's dying. Chemotherapy!'

CW: I've done that—killed babies, a couple of times. In a horrible way it's a sort of guaranteed crowd-pleaser.

TBD: It's a bit of a cheap trick, isn't it? [*laughs*] Oh god.

CW: But I think doing that is perhaps a part of learning to write, don't you? Slowly learning to resist the easy manipulation of readers' feelings.

TBD: You know what it is? It's this: darkness is what really vivifies fiction, what makes it exciting. But when you're young, you think darkness equals death and that kind of thing. But darkness is actually just nasty impulse: cruelty, selfishness, greed, jealousy, all of those sorts of things. Those are the really interesting feelings. That's the really animating stuff, to me. And that was what the short stories gave me. A possibility to express a self that felt like it was a failure, but was going to come out swinging anyway.

CW: It seems to me you started writing long-form criticism at around the same time you turned to the short stories. Is that right?

TBD: That's not strictly true because the criticism actually grew out of doing my doctoral exegesis—which was thirty thousand words about reading and influence—and it forced me to articulate some of the things I'd been privately thinking about writing for such a long time. So the first couple of long-form critical pieces that I published were actually plundered from the exegesis. The piece on Helen Garner, for example, came from there. But I didn't realise what was happening—it was Russell who pointed it out to me. About three-quarters of the way through my writing the exegesis, he said, 'Something is changing for you, you're finding a really good voice in this stuff.'

CW: You seemed to claim an authority that was new to you, rather than writing out of what we've both had in the past, a slightly—this is a terrible word, but *girlish* sensibility.

TBD: Oh yes, sort of apologetic. It was like having strong *feelings* was all you needed to give something validity. Absolutely.

CW: So the criticism shifted something in you—it had to be about the intellect.

TBD: Yes. And you had to take a stand; not just about a certain book, but a stand about your reading. I think I started to recognise that all my life I'd been reading but I'd never valued it. I'm sort of glad I'd never thought to value it, it was just what I was doing. But with this critical writing I suddenly realised that I'd read a lot and I seemed to have accumulated a certain amount of knowledge. I'd never realised that it wasn't just evanescent, but that it was actually piling up. I was actually learning something.

I mean, I'd been pouring it into my fiction all the time, but I now understood that from reading I'd learned so much about the way words work, and I could also write about that.

All this time I'd also been teaching. I divided my class time into reading great works of fiction with the students, and then reading their works, which were not great works of fiction. The bit I loved most was actually just talking about literature with them. That was when I realised I was starting to see patterns and understand the development of the novel and see pools of interesting influence, and all sorts of things started to happen. It was exciting.

In 2000, I think it was, one of my oldest friends gave me *The Broken Estate*, the James Wood book. I'd been reading the *London Review of Books* for years because my mum and dad subscribed to it, and James Wood was starting to turn up in the nineties. There was something just so compelling about the way he wrote. I read him to learn how to write about books—he has that beautiful mix of authority and absolute vulnerability to the text.

CW: It's interesting that teaching has been a part of all this. You are one of the few writers I know who actually gets something from teaching. What has it given you?

TBD: Well, I liked it at the start because I seemed to have a knack for it, and you always like things you are good at. I seemed to enjoy communicating. I liked being with students, making them laugh, all that kind of stuff. So for the first five years, that was really what it was about. I really was not all that interested in their work, but I was interested in *them* and what they showed me.

But then I started to go deeper and I began to be really interested in the way they were learning to write. I started to take proper notice of the texts I was teaching them and I got a bit more agency, so I was allowed to choose those texts. So all of a sudden I was putting together subjects and really enjoying bringing alive a text for them.

The other thing is that I just can't get enough of twenty-year-olds. They're just bristling with life, it's lovely to be with them. I think I've realised that I've got a triple vocation, and I feel really happy about it. Well, quadruple vocation, actually:

teaching, writing criticism, writing fiction and my kids. And it all makes sense, you know?

CW: You have a couple of favourite expressions about writing that partly came out of your teaching. One of them is Martin Amis's remark about 'propaganda, aimed at the self'. What does that mean, and why do you like it?

TBD: Look, everyone should read Martin Amis, a few of his books at least. He's not a very grown-up human being but he is a very, very sophisticated writer. This phrase comes from *The Information*—which, by the way, is where his work, for me, really started to snap in two, because he was trying to be more human and in fact he's not that human, really. He was better off staying with the wordplay. That's not actually giving him his due, but anyway . . . In the novel is this writer who's coming apart, and he has to work at a vanity press. He keeps getting these hilarious manuscripts and Amis describes them as 'propaganda, aimed at the self'.

When you're teaching, so much of the work you read is somebody trying to convince themselves of their position. It's like they're talking to themselves, and it's only the really good new writers who begin to break out of that, they start to break out of their notion of themselves as a victim or their notion of themselves as a favourite or as unloved. Having said that, if I took some time off teaching I'd be perfectly happy because you still have to do marking and that kind of stuff. But the actual being in the classroom, it's mostly just *fun*. If you get it right, it's fun! [*laughs*] You're shaking your head.

CW: Or students write to their pretentious fantasy selves. When I used to teach, everyone was a lighting designer living in a loft in New York.

TBD: Yes! When you're a young writer you have a few obsessions and you kind of write at them as hard as you can, and before you know it you're casting yourself as a victim or as a lighting designer, whatever it is. I saw that over and over and over again, and what is funny is that it's even worse in the older students. You get fifty-five-year-olds and their propaganda has *hardened*. It's solid, this idea of who they reckon they are and what they reckon the world did to them. So that epigram from Amis—it's one of the things he's so brilliant at—it's genius, it contains volumes. I guess that when you grow up as a writer, you're trying to break out of that.

CW: Do you think you wrote propaganda?

TBD: Well I was trying not to, but I wasn't grown-up enough to know who I really was. To me, my last two novels do feel a little bit as though a pane of glass has been inserted between me and the work. And I think that's because I didn't understand myself properly and my impulses and who I was. That only comes to you in your forties, I think.

CW: It's hard to say that knowing yourself is important for writing without making it sound that what you're writing is . . .

TBD: All about you, yeah.

CW: So what's the difference?

TBD: Look, I think writing forces you to be honest with yourself about who you are, about all the smallnesses of your soul. And, after a while, you stop going for the grand gesture because you realise life isn't made up of grand gestures, it's actually made up of small things. And you start to interrogate yourself properly.

I think the person who really taught me to do that was Alice Munro. I've never known anyone to interrogate shame and jealousy and greed, all those venal things, better than she does, and yet still make absolutely riveting fiction out of it. I started reading her in earnest probably about 2005, and I read her continuously for about ten years.

It's like I was saying before. You realise that darkness is not, 'oh my god, everybody dies'—not that that's not dark and difficult—but it's actually: everybody dies, but the way you try to steal an extra piece of cake at the funeral is the really interesting thing.

I don't know anything about suffering—real suffering—as I might if I lived in a country where there was a war happening or something. I don't know about real genuine trauma, but I do know about how every human exchange has some darkness in it.

CW: Another thing you and I have talked about occasionally is a tendency among readers and some writers for 'diagnosis'. In my case, for example, people said my war reporter character Mandy had 'post-traumatic stress disorder'. Or that my protagonist in another novel had 'commitment phobia' or whatever. Something in my writer self just rises up powerfully against that.

TBD: Yeah. Way back when *Bombora* was published, a couple of people said to me, in a worried sort of way, 'It's not very feminist, is it?' I was stunned. I mean, *I'm* a feminist but life is complicated, people don't always behave in a feminist way, or if they do, then that's another story of darkness and weirdness and all that kind of stuff.

If everything is reduced to post-traumatic stress disorder, then it doesn't live any more, does it? There's no fiction in that. I mean, Mandy is just a bitch who was a war correspondent! [*laughs*]

CW: Yes! Or, she probably does have it, but in itself that tells you nothing.

TBD: I've got this theory, that the advent of Freud really changed fiction. Fiction used to do what Freud does. I mean, you'd have to speak to a proper psychologist or psychoanalyst about this, but Freud had the idea that forming stories out of your experience starts to make sense of that experience. Now, fiction always did that before. And then Freud comes along, and fiction starts to get a bit more diagnostic after that. It starts to be influenced by the idea that everybody has a solvable problem.

CW: And that if you give it a name, it is the same solvable problem somebody else has.

TBD: Yes. That here you could group together all the people who have post-traumatic stress disorder and here are all the people who want to have sex with their mother, or whatever. But we're writing in an age when everybody in the West, their passion is to know themselves, when fiction is really about the *unknown*, so you have to work away from it, we've got to turn our backs on it.

CW: But we've just been saying you can't write unless you know yourself.

TBD: But it's a different thing, isn't it? Okay, so maybe we replace the idea of knowing yourself with *being* yourself. For me, what has happened in this later part of life is that—it's as though I've been camped outside myself my whole life. And finally I've started to move the furniture in, *at last*. You're allowed to live in yourself. You've just been watching yourself going around doing stuff and at this age, you start to go, 'You know what? This is what I'm like. And it's not wholly attractive. And I'm going to displease people sometimes, and I'm going to live with that. That's who I'm going to be now.' So maybe knowing yourself is just being yourself.

CW: Very interesting.

TBD: The last thing to say about that diagnostic thing is this. When we get excited in finding a new book like Joan London's *The Golden Age*, which we've both loved so much, that's about two twelve-year-olds falling in love in a polio hospital . . . in the hands of some other idiot that would be about post-traumatic stress disorder and something-affective disorder and illness and what it does to children, but in Joan's hands, it's about being a child becoming an adult, it's about finding a vocation, it's just about being alive.

It's so thrilling. You couldn't put a label on it.

CW: Let's go back to this wellspring of your new stories: adolescence. I have in my notes here that Franzen phrase, 'hot material'. This age, late adolescence and early adulthood, seems to me to be your hot material. I kind of marvel at the depth of this tap-root that you have into that experience—not just your own but new, quite fictional experiences of that age. You seem to be inventing more in the stories than you did in the novels, which came much more out of your own life. So the stories are more fictional and yet—

TBD: And yet more autobiographically energetic, which is so weird. It's like the more I make up, the more I can do. They're not massively removed from my own life, but this period of my writing has been about a really mystical, hard-to-explain thing about finding a voice. I've been looking for a voice for years and years and years. Suddenly, finally, this one turns up.

I don't know what Freud would say about this, but I think for me, a lot of the period of being, say, fourteen to twenty-six, those years were really vivid and exciting, but they were also years in which I was constantly pretending. Always trying to figure out what would be the best way to negotiate whatever social situation I was in. Really socially anxious, deeply uncertain about who I was.

I was taught to be nice and good, and I really was trying to be at that time. I mean, obviously there is value in being nice and good. But also, I had such an animal self inside me, and my whole job seemed to be to keep that animal self down. And now I am at ease with her, that animal self, now that I've moved into my own self, the wellspring just seems endless. Because I held it down, I had a fucking lid on it for so long, that when you take the lid off it just gives and gives and gives.

CW: Tell me about the animal self.

TBD: Okay, I suppose I mean the sort of coarser side of yourself. The shitting side of yourself, the side of yourself that has desires, that wants to *eat*, you know. All those sorts of things. I've never actually said this, so this is interesting—I grew up feeling obscurely ashamed of that self. Of that *hungry* self, I think that's the main thing. Like, I didn't have sex until relatively late, but I actually was just riddled with desire as a teenager. Just *riddled* with it. If only I could have figured out how to do it properly, how not to be so insanely self-conscious! Because to have sex successfully, you really need to have an animal self, don't you? You need to let her go.

I spent a lot of time turning away in shame from the terrifyingly stupid things I'd said, or ways I'd shown myself to be coarsely curious or arrogant or just *grubby*, you know? When you're a teenager, you're really physical and your body is changing and smelly and all that sort of stuff, and in my case, I couldn't cram it into various clothes. I spent a lot of time really trying not to know that self. And I know now that the reason I didn't have boyfriends all that time was I had too much shame. I couldn't expose myself.

So then, of course, I got into my twenties and started to drink a lot and have a lot of sex, but I was *always* ashamed.

CW: In *Six Bedrooms*, various psychodramas play out inside closed but shared territories, these high-stakes sort of arenas: the share house, the teenage party, the schoolyard, all this contested, jostling space. There are a whole lot of really interesting power plays going on all the time. I've come to think of this book as being in a way about a bunch of kids on a raft and they're desperately trying to push each other off in order to survive, to remain on the raft.

TBD: Absolutely. It's brutal, it's really brutal. I think when I was growing up I was on fire with desire and hunger and reading and all these sorts of things. And that person was really unacceptable in the kind of group I was in. I just felt like a misfit. Having said that, I know everybody feels like a misfit.

The other day my daughter had a situation where she was supposed to catch up with a bunch of friends and they were late to meet her. That happens all the time. But because they're just teenagers, they didn't ring her, they just left her sitting there, for ages and ages, and I was with her. By the time these kids reached her, I was so angry. I was *beside* myself. I was the angriest I've been in years, and working really hard not to spill it all over Alice because it had nothing to do with her, but it obviously tapped into that old thing. Alice had to react as though she didn't care that these guys were late. Because in the world of teenagehood, you don't show that kind of thing. It's not good. It rocks the boat, it makes you look awkward, it makes you look like somebody who *wants*. You're not allowed to appear as though you want anything—that you want people to turn up, you want people to be your friend, you want a boy to like you. At the same time that you are *consumed* with wanting, you are not allowed to seem to want at all.

And it was really interesting to me that here in Alice's teenagehood, I suddenly—internally and slightly externally— lost the fucking plot. So I think that repressed self is part of what has gone into the work.

CW: Which is extremely good for fiction because . . .

TBD: That's right. You just get your pen and you dip into that ink, don't you? And then you write.

CW: Another thing that's going on in these stories, is that the kids are all experiencing various yearnings and tyrannies—there are boys ordering girls to be their girlfriends and the girls obeying. Then we have girls ordering their friends around because someone has to exercise power. You have these quite ruthless control games among the young people, and at the same time you've got a parental level that is quite unstable. The only stable parents are jerks, and minor characters. For the rest, you have parents in multiple marriages, having affairs, being boozers or whatever, and yet all that is completely in the background. So it's a really interesting planet that these kids are on, where the only authority figures in their life are completely unstable, but not in a dramatised way; it's just normal. It makes for a lot of shifting ground beneath their feet.

TBD: Yeah. There's something about having your own kids that makes you realise a kid is infinitely adaptable and that, unless you tell them that there's something wrong with the way you're living, they don't notice it, they just live it. That's why it's so miserable when terrible things do happen to kids, because really they are just trying to adapt all the time.

And it comes from my childhood too, where my parents were very happy together and stable, but they didn't talk about anything. So you would know things were going wrong with other families but, because nobody ever discussed it, you just thought, oh well, that's what it's like, let's just get on with it. These days, parents are much more open with their kids, which is both good and bad, I think.

CW: So what does this weirdly unstable superstructure do for the stories, do you think?

TBD: It's a really interesting observation and I haven't thought about it. My mum once said to me about my kids that, 'Until they're ten, you're a god. After that, friends are gods.' As a parent you have no influence any more; it's what friends want that becomes what your child wants. And obviously I have seen that happen.

So parents really *are* in the background and all the terrible dramas that are playing out in the teenage life, parents really don't have any influence over or anything to do with. They can't do anything about it, it just happens anyway. I mean, I'm always talking to parents who are chugging up to the high school to intervene in some shit that's going on, but I want to say, 'You can't.' You can't. It's a whole world that you can have nothing to do with. And even if you do, it's going to go on without you, unless you hold their hand and walk next to them every single moment of their lives. You just have to let it unfold. But the instability thing about the parents in my stories is interesting, given that, really, our house was quite serene because Mum and Dad loved each other a lot and so it was happy. But at the same time, my mum in particular was such a vivid, alive, complicated, difficult person, as well as being an excellent person.

So I think that all those troubled parents might be somehow extensions, expansions, elaborations on a difficulty that I only ever sensed in Mum, that I couldn't name but I knew was there. Because she was really capricious. One minute she was thrashing you with an implement, you know, and the next minute, being in her company could be just so alive-making. And she was also really loving and really kind.

CW: Another powerful presence in the stories is other people's houses and bedrooms. Bedrooms of other girls from school, bedrooms of boyfriends, parents' bedrooms—there's an incredibly acute awareness of every bit of detail. I know you've called it *Six Bedrooms* because one of the stories is titled that, but the whole book resonates with really deep stuff about sex and private yearnings, and the strangeness of other people's yearnings in that space.

TBD: One of the things about my house was that goodness in a marriage was really valued. My parents were very faithful and loving and all that kind of stuff. So I became hyper-aware of 'badness' in other people's families. Like, back then divorce was much less common, although it was becoming more common.

I did know kids from families where there was *Playboy* kept on the table, for example. My parents would have *died of disgust* and shame to even have a *Playboy* in the house [*laughs*] let alone kept one on the table. But you saw things like that; you went around to people's houses and thought, 'Oh my god, that's how they live.' And my parents' sensitivity, I think, to other people's ill-behaviour made me hypersensitive to it. When you're a kid and you go to someone else's house— it's another country. You're just like, 'Whoa, you freaks, what are you all doing?!' And that can be caused by anything from different toilet paper to the *Playboy*.

So, the strangeness has carried over. Sometimes my kids have friends over and you know they're not so deeply rooted in their own family because of the way they suddenly inhabit your house as though it's theirs. Which can really give you the shits. I call them fridge openers. You know, kids who come in, they open the fridge, and they just roam around the house. Your house doesn't seem strange to them, whereas to me, when I went to someone else's house it was full of riches because it was so different, but also frightening and wrong.

CW: I want to know how you do something. You've always done this, it's not new—you take a tiny moment of observation, but the way you use it enlarges it so it says everything. For example, in the last, incredibly moving story, Tasha talks about the time after her baby's father leaves, and the baby's feet no longer have anything to brace against when she's feeding him. Nothing is made of it in the story, but it's a devastating line. So: how do you find a moment like this, how do you identify that it is the potent one, and then how do you just throw it away in the narrative like that? Because it's the throwing away that also does the work.

TBD: Well that, to me, is simply to do with being experienced. Your life is made up of these moments and as a writer you learn to identify them. Those moments are a bit like a pebble in your pocket, they're just there all the time and every time you put your hand in your pocket, there they are again. And the more experienced you become as a writer, the more you know how to situate those and how to use them as kind of . . . if we're going with the pebble thing, as kind of magic stones, touchstones for a work.

So, that line about the baby. When I used to breastfeed my son Paddy, he was so physical. Russell used to sit next to me in bed and Paddy used to press his feet against him, pushing at him like a kangaroo, doing these kicks into him. I've been carrying that around forever because I had to wean Paddy because I was going on a book tour, and I decided I would wean him when Russell was away because I knew it was going to upset me and for some fucking stupid reason, I thought, 'It'll be better to be upset with Russell away.'

So, Russell wasn't there. And I was feeding Paddy for the last time and his feet were doing this starfish sort of thing, he was about fourteen months old and his feet were kicking away and there was no Russell to kick against. And it broke my heart. So I'd been carrying that around, that pebble in my pocket, for ages.

CW: Did you know you were carrying it around?

TBD: I did. I always remembered it. It was one of those moments in your life that—again, it's like the oil well or whatever, you take the lid off it and it just gushes at you, you know? And it can be tiny.

CW: So, you never forgot it—but did you write it down?

TBD: I didn't write it down. That one's just been with me forever. But you've got pockets and pockets full of these pebbles, these things you don't have to write down, they never go away, they just stay with you.

CW: I think I forget them.

TBD: I think you don't, though.

CW: Maybe I don't.

TBD: I bet you don't. You learn to use them. But when you first start out writing and you've got a couple of moments like that, you head the whole book, like a train, towards them. It's like, 'Here we come, big emotional moment', and you write towards them. But you keep failing—you think, 'What am I doing? Why am I fucking up this great thing that I've been waiting to write for all these years?' And it's because of the way you approach it. You're approaching it wrongly. You're making a massive drama when, in fact, if you approach it quietly and sideways, it feeds its power silently into the narrative and, with any luck, the reader, a good reader, feels it. Reads it and goes, 'Whoa!' Because you haven't stuck a whole lot of signposts pointing at it going, 'Melodramatic moment coming, great grief, huge sadness, here it comes!'

CW: But also it appears while the story is moving rapidly towards something else.

TBD: Yes, there is movement; it is not stilled. I think one of the problems with my earlier fiction was I always put stillness around those things. But the thing is, even when the thing happened with Paddy, I didn't hang around feeling it; I had to put him to bed. I didn't hang around wailing about it.

So yeah, you learn to feed those things into your narrative and your instinct, with experience, grows and grows and grows. So now is the time I can use that instinct properly at last. The last thing to say about this is that what you've really got to do with a moment like that is not surround it with *other* moments like that. You've got to clear the way for it.

CW: But not too much, as you said before.

TBD: But not too much. Isn't it interesting? It's so great to talk about this properly because no one gives a shit about this kind of thing except other writers.

CW: Speaking of too much stillness, we've often joked about a kind of avoidance I used to do a lot in writing—the 'she said nothing and turned away' syndrome. It was a way of implying some sort of deeply held feeling or suppressed drama when actually there was just nothing there. And I didn't even know how to press the work to find out what I did have to say—it was just easier to 'say nothing and turn away'. And I used see this a lot in work that appeared to be influenced by Carver, that very pared-back prose. It implies that less is more, when a lot of the time—as I was doing it, and you occasionally did too—less was just less. But with your stories you've really left that evasion behind.

TBD: Yeah, yeah. For you and me both, we've got enough skill to just wander around the landscape and describe stuff—what people are doing, what they're thinking, what the trees look like, what the birds look like—and get away with it, as it were.

But with my short stories it felt like every single description came out of a quickening feeling. It was like it needed to be there, instead of me just standing around passively observing. And sometimes observing is enough for readers. But it's not enough for you as a writer, is it? There's very little, if anything, in any of these stories now that makes my brain go dead when I read it. Which is what some of *Safety* and some of *What Falls Away* were doing for me, where it was just like, 'I'm doing a decent job here but I'm not pressed, I'm not moving forward.'

And it's not to do with plot, is it? It's not to do with plot. It's to do with a kind of urgency of the material.

The new work is better because I'm older and it's less dreamy, less . . . something. I've always loved what Kingsley Amis said about Martin's work, that it was 'compulsively vivid'. And I think some of the stuff I do is compulsively vivid, although I don't use words as well as he does.

This new feeling of urgency for me came from a feeling of pure joyful invention, but it doesn't even feel like inventing, it feels like I'm really naturally *in* the work, experiencing the events I am writing. Whereas in the 'she said nothing and turned away' voice, we're really just cranking it out. Just filling up the page. You can't force this naturalness, though. It's not a moral thing, it's not like *I'm* better now because that's happening. I'm just lucky, you know.

CW: And yet you do have something that has jokingly come to be known as 'the betterment project'. What's the betterment project about?

TBD: Well you're absolutely right to bring it up right now, because I started the betterment project about three-quarters of the way through writing these stories.

It was about going back and finding all the 'she said nothing and turned away' moments, and saying *no*: those moments are not allowed in these stories. It has to be better. It's like making sure you love all of your children and not just four of them out of ten, you know? You have to be proud of and happy with *all* of these sentences. All of them. It won't do to just have seven out of ten that are okay.

CW: What is it that makes you proud of a sentence?

TBD: If I can find, discover, uncover that impulse. That quickening feeling. I remember one of the stories I really worked on bettering—it's called 'The Bridge'. That story originally began very slowly, with description, introducing you to what was going on. But I think I learned a bit from being edited in my reviews by James Ley at *Sydney Review of Books*, about moving paragraphs around; I just took a paragraph out of the centre and put it up front, and it *instantly* bettered it. So putting one of the more vivid, quickening sort of ideas right at the start then allowed me to go through and take out some of the deader things.

The whole book, to be boastful for a second, the whole book is full of these moments that just made me feel so happy and excited when I wrote them.

I was saying to my editor the other day that my favourite line in the whole book is in 'J'aime Rose', when Rose is climbing the stairs of the house that's got many storeys, which is by the river, and she passes a bedroom and sees a Ken Done painting in the distance. I was the happiest woman alive to have written that line, because it was so true to my experience of all those houses that I inhabited when I was a kid.

And in 'Firebugs', there was an excitement when the kids were making a little fire, and I wrote that the brother threw in a jacaranda flower, and it sizzled and 'fluffed out sweet smoke'. I thought the words 'fluffed' and 'sweet' there were just right. So the whole book is full of these things that made me kind of chuckle, made me interested. Instead of that thing when you're rereading your work and you groan with horror.

CW: There seem to be at least two things in what you're saying there. One is about finding the truth of the moment, and the other's about amusing yourself. A little while ago you sent me an email when you were proofing the Tasha stories, and you said after you'd fixed this or that you felt 'this lovely, almost silly energy'. You said: 'The Tasha and Judy and Mum stories have a laughter in them that I've spent years trying to find. This lovely feeling of being surprised at the sudden zigging or zagging of Tasha or her mum, and this huge pleasure.' Is the betterment project perhaps at its heart a search for surprise?

TBD: The *true* surprise, yes. I mean, it's not like I want a three-legged dog to turn up or something. It's simply that characters become like real people when they do something that both surprises you and confirms who you thought they were.

There's that brilliant thing in the Peter Carey interview in *Making Stories* where he says there is a moment, with a character, when there's a little feeling 'like an osteopath's click', and suddenly the character gets up and you think, they're alive! That's what those moments are like. You just feel the people are alive and they make you laugh, not because they're funny, but from pleasure. Because they're being themselves.

CW: Let's talk about the 'badness' you alluded to earlier—the idea that writing is enlivened by petty human feelings. Your teenagers are full of the kind of ruthless survival instinct that makes them live and the mothers and fathers are all fucking around, stuffing up and being completely self-absorbed. But they're not dramatically terrible parents, they're just bad in little ways that somehow make it come alive.

TBD: Yes. Look, once upon a time, to be a woman artist, you had to be somehow out of society. You had to be mad like Virginia Woolf, or childless, which was seen as a sort of full-on difference. You had to have somehow separated yourself from the world. That was the only way you could break free. But these days, there's much more space and it's possible and desirable to both be an artist and live a decent life. You and I are happily married and I've got kids and we've both got jobs and good friends and, you know, we're not cutting a swathe through society with our screaming, drunken fits, we don't have to do that sort of thing.

But at the same time, to be an artist is to access a kind of badness or madness in yourself. You have to, in order to do it really well. And everybody's got that—it's just that you have to find it. And I realised that, for me, it's most deeply present in that time of my life because that was the part of my life, as I said before, in which I was being least true to myself and at the same time, feeling most powerfully. So, that's had a kind of magical effect, a kind of alchemy of those two elements, I guess. And then you write those things down, indulge those feelings, to let characters live.

CW: I sometimes think they only come alive when they do something inconsistent or against their own interests.

TBD: When they fuck things up.

CW: Yes, then you've got some spark and movement, whereas when you read books that are full of good people behaving well but then having a tragedy or something, it's like there's no internal conflict.

TBD: And there is no tonal change, either, because the person is suffering at the beginning and suffering at the end and they never really have to do anything.

CW: I want to talk a little now about managing a writing life. I've become quite fond of that Flaubert advice, 'Be regular and orderly in your life like a bourgeois, so that you may be violent and original in your work.' You seem to have the most organised life of any writer I know in the way that you manage your time and where you put your attention. You're very stringent about holding the noisy, outside world at bay—no social media, no television, no obsessing about current affairs. You don't seem to lose energy by engaging with the world in the way I do, leaking energy and emotion all the time in pointless distressing about the world's chaos.

TBD: Yeah, but you've got more spare time than I do. I would probably be more similar to you if I didn't have the kids. And of course, on the inside it doesn't feel organised at all, it feels insane. But the reason that it works is because it is selfish.

It's not a saintly ordering of what I do, it's because I need the space. I get depressed when I'm not writing and I get depressed if I don't get enough time with the kids. Because to sit down and play with a kid properly is a bit like sitting down and writing properly—you procrastinate with just this bit of housework or that, and then finally you sit down with them and you get out the toy or the book or the game or whatever it is they want to do and suddenly you've got access to this incredibly alive world. But you've been avoiding it because it does mean giving your whole self over, and everybody's a bit resistant to that.

The reason we live up here in the mountains is partly financial but partly it's the same reason I don't do social media—it's because I just love being with people and am really non-resistant to the flattery of an invitation. I find it really hard to say no. But I know that I'll be better served if I do a good job of my work in life, which is to be in this family and to write. So, it's definitely about preserving the self. It's not that I'm bravely turning away from television and party invitations. I've just got a good internal barometer and I know when the pressure is too high.

And, in fact, I was really interested in that stuff that Sue Smith was talking about in your interview with her, about the body. For me, I know when it's gone too far because I get a migraine. I only get a migraine about twice a year and it's just classic. Every single time it's like, 'Well, there you go, you added one too many things into the mix.'

CW: Tell me about walking. What does that do for your writing?

TBD: Well, it unloops thought. You're thinking, 'I've got no idea, I've got no idea what to do here.' And so I go for a walk because I need to keep fit, because I feel tired and fat when I don't keep fit. I don't really always enjoy it that much but I try to do it every single day just to keep moving. But then, almost every time I go for a walk on my own, it brings me the solution I was looking for. Maybe it's because you're distracted enough—because you need to look around when you cross the road or whatever—you're distracted enough from yourself to let the creative play start to happen, and then your mind just goes, 'Here's the thing you were looking for.'

I've had times in walks where I've gone out with a problem and I've said a sentence over and over, or a question over and over to myself, and within a kilometre, the answer to the question comes up. I've also had really productive walks with Russell where we walk and we just talk over—not large problems, but we just talk over something that one of us is tinkering with and one of us will go, 'Aha! I've just figured it out.' It's interesting isn't it? Scratch a writer and you find a walker, I think.

CW: It does seem to be almost universal, that walking—or movement, anyway, for some people it might be running—brings creative solutions.

TBD: Yes. Or swimming, maybe. It must do that releasing endorphins thing as well, so that relaxation and pleasure in the brain must lead to something.

CW: Another recurring, consoling phrase for you comes from Annie Dillard's *The Writing Life*, where she talks about writing as 'sitting with the patient'.

TBD: Yeah, isn't it nice? I think the hardest thing for me to do, not just because of time constraints but just because of who I am, is to return to the work. It's so great when it's going well and yet I'll do almost anything not to do it. It's the most ridiculous conundrum. Annie Dillard uses all sorts of metaphors to describe this returning to the work. There's one which is the exact opposite, where the work is like a lion that you leave in a room and it becomes untamed if you don't attend to it. So different from the metaphor of the patient.

In this image she says something like, 'It's like attending to a sick patient, all you can do is sit up with it.' For me it hasn't got that despairing note, it's more an injunction just to keep turning up, keep turning up. That's all. Just do it.

CW: But there is a certain quality of waiting in it, rather than acting?

TBD: Yeah, being prepared. These days for me a writing session is about three-quarters waiting and a quarter writing what I actually want to write. But in the waiting I do write, I just write crap. I just write anything that comes into my head about the character until it stumbles across one of those moments and then it starts.

So I guess it's about being there, allowing time to play out. And trusting that something of value will come. It's just about being by the work's side, I suppose. That's what I'm allegedly trying to do with a new novel at the moment.

CW: If there are a few qualities essential in a writer's nature or personality, what might they be?

TBD: I think the main thing is just an unpreventable interest. You just can't stop. You cannot stop yourself reading; it's a compulsive interest in words and the way they work.

You also need confidence. I don't know where you get that from except by practising enough so that you get good at it, so that somebody says you're good at it, which gives you just enough to keep going until the next thing. For me, there was a huge and vital moment when I was seventeen and a writing tutor said to me, 'You are a writer.' Which seems so corny but it was really an astounding moment, it was a huge moment.

So: confidence, interest in the words—and you need to be smart. I actually didn't realise that for a long time, because you spend so much of your time as you write flailing around thinking, 'I'm so dumb.' And you're often a person of uncontrolled feelings, which can make you feel like a stupid person. But actually you need to be intelligent. You need to be intelligent enough to understand words and the way they work, to be able to read well, to be willing to change. You need to be really sort of flexible and open.

It has to be something that goes well beyond just wanting to be a writer and wanting to be published—which of course is what you want. It would be interesting to see what we did if writing wasn't available, what sort of people we'd be, or where that energy might go.

CW: I often wonder that about myself: if I couldn't publish, would I write? Would you?

TBD: I don't know what the answer to that is either. I think I'd be writing letters. But actually, one of the pleasures of writing is getting good at it, and succeeding. That's one of the reasons you keep doing it. Not because of the imagined material rewards, of which there are none, but it's an actual physical feeling of satisfaction.

I think writing is having a conversation with life. And you can't stop yourself speaking to life and hearing its feedback to you. It makes living so . . . *alive*. It's so funny that the image of the writer is somebody who's always indoors and everything, because I feel just so vital, you know. I feel so vital when I'm writing and when I'm reading. When I'm living in books.

JAMES BRADLEY, novelist and literary critic, grew up in Adelaide in the 1970s and 80s. He trained as a lawyer before moving to Sydney and turning to writing. His first book was a poetry collection, *Paper Nautilus*, published in 1994 when Bradley was just twenty-seven. This was followed by his first novel, *Wrack*, in 1997, which was shortlisted for the Miles Franklin Award, earned Bradley a selection as one of *The Sydney Morning Herald*'s Best Young Novelists of that year, and won the Kathleen Mitchell Award for a young writer. His second novel, *The Deep Field*, won the 1999 *Age* Fiction Book of the Year award, and a second listing as a *SMH* Best Young Novelist.

In 2006 he published the international bestseller *The Resurrectionist*, chosen for the massively successful Richard & Judy Book Club in Britain. Between this and his lauded climate change novel published in 2015, *Clade*, Bradley published *Beauty's Sister*—a retelling of the Rapunzel fairytale, in novella form—as well as short stories, reviews and essays in publications including *The Times Literary Supplement, The Guardian, The Washington Post, The Monthly, Locus, The New York Review of Science Fiction,* and most major Australian newspapers and literary magazines.

Throughout his career as a fiction writer Bradley has also worked as a respected literary critic, and in 2012 he won the prestigious Pascall Prize for critical writing. He has also edited two anthologies—*The Penguin Book of the Ocean,* and *Blur: Stories by Young Australian Writers.* Bradley and I don't know each other well, but have moved in the same circles for well over a decade.We have many mutual friends, and our 'careers' have moved at a roughly similar pace, though he is younger and began earlier than I. My first contact with him was in 1999, in an email to thank him for his insightful review—largely generous, but not without useful criticism—of my first novel. It is one of two reviews in fifteen years of publishing that I have found actually constructive, in the sense of showing me how to improve my work. Several times in recent years Bradley invited me to present a guest lecture to his Faber Academy novel-writing class in Sydney, where his skill as a teacher and the respect he engendered among his students was obvious.

Bradley is a penetrating thinker, and in 2009 turned to blogging at www.cityoftongues.com as an experiment, partly to overcome what he saw as the constraints of traditional newspaper and magazine publishing. He wrote for *Australian Author* that in blogging, 'I found myself genuinely enjoying the process of writing for the first time in a long while.'

Embracing the 'rush and rawness' of the online space gave Bradley freedom to write about anything he was drawn to, from music to comics to politics, and perhaps generated a freshness and openness in his approach to more traditional essays and the novel form too.

Some of his personal essays have been especially powerful, notably a perceptive and moving meditation on creativity and depression, published in *Griffith Review* in the same year he began his blog.

One of the deepest satisfactions of persevering in the writing life over a long period can be the way one's youthful anxieties about status gradually dissolve as one matures in company—and community—with one's fellow writers. Bradley speaks thoughtfully about this shift from the first to the second act of his creative life, and how he discovered a path back to his own particular, authentic—even joyful—experience of the writing process.

It was a privilege for me to talk with Bradley about his work. This interview took place at the terrace in

Sydney's inner west where he lives with his partner, the novelist Mardi McConnochie, and their young daughters, Annabelle and Lila.

CW: How well do you understand the genesis of your material? Do you know how the seed of a book comes to your mind?

JB: It depends. With stories, there tends to be a particular thing—usually a scenario or a concept, I guess—about which I think, 'That would be really interesting,' but it can also be something more fragmentary than that. I published a story last year called 'Skinsuit', which I really like—which began simply with the word. I was driving in the car and I thought, *skinsuit*. I just kept thinking, 'What could a skinsuit *be?*'

In the end I tried out a few different things—one more science fictional, another weirder—until I realised the idea connected with some other things I'd been trying to unravel about childhood and fantasy and the darkness some kids endure, and once that happened I knew I had the story.

With novels, I also sometimes begin with the title. With *The Resurrectionist*, for instance, I knew as soon as I started reading the historical material that became the book that it would be called *The Resurrectionist*, and would internalise that word with an act of literal resurrection. So the title came with the idea and then was woven back into the structure of the book.

Often, though, I begin with something more abstract, a feeling that there's something I want to write about. *Clade* was very much like this. I'd been thinking about climate change, thinking about the future, thinking about finding a device or a structure to help me get at it. But more often it's a feeling, a mood or a kind of affect I'm drawn to. The particular feeling of freedom and release an adolescent might feel riding on top of a train at night, say, or a kind of creepiness, or sensation of desire, and I probe at that until I can unravel something from it.

Then again, they do occasionally arrive almost fully formed. There's one novel in particular I've been working on for years, on and off, which came to me one night in bed, and I went out to the kitchen and wrote the first chapter of it in an hour or two, then mapped out a coherent outline in another hour.

Interestingly, though, despite the fact the first chapter is one of the best things I've ever written, I haven't ever managed to finish it. Mostly that is because I've never felt entirely comfortable that I have the authority to write the book, but it may also be because I already know too much about it as a whole, whereas I kind of need the process of writing to be a process of discovery.

CW: Do you usually write outlines at an early stage for your novels?

JB: [*laughs*] I wish! I'm actually a terribly disorganised writer. In a way that's weird because I'm also a bit of a structure nut, so I'm always very focused on the structural elements of a book. But when it comes to the process of writing I work in a very freeform way, without a lot of planning beyond a rough sense of what happens and what some of the signposts are along the way.

Indeed, when I begin a book, I frequently don't have anything, really. I'll have a couple of scenes, a feeling, and in those early stages I just write, waiting for characters and some kind of voice or sense of what the book *feels* like to emerge. Once I've got that I start looking for rhythm, for a sense of where the moments of movement and stillness are, and then, once that sense is in place, I start sticking it together and trying to move forward into a draft.

Then I tend to write fast, to leave problems to one side and just keep pushing on and looking for the emotional logic and narrative shape of the book.

There are advantages to doing it that way but it also means it can be a very messy process, especially since although you usually find ways to fix the problems you push through, you don't always.

In between *The Resurrectionist* and *Clade* I almost published another novel, but eventually didn't because I knew it didn't work, and although there were a lot of good things about it, the problems were just unsolvable. At least part of what went wrong was that I had a structural problem in the first draft that I'd decided to just write my way through and fix later, but I never did manage to fix it. In retrospect, I suspect that if I'd sorted the problems out at the beginning, it might've been okay, but because I didn't, the whole book failed.

Probably partly as a reaction against feeling like my process is a complete mess, I've actually spent the past few years trying be more disciplined and organised. I'm writing a series of young adult books which are very plotty, and that's been really fun—quite different from what I've done in the past. I don't know that I had a clear idea of what the story was, but I knew what the *shape* of the story was, and I knew where I had to get to. I knew that stuff has to *happen* every two thousand words. [*laughs*] I wrote the first one in the gap between finishing *Clade* and doing the editing on *Clade*—and it was such a different experience, after writing a book that has almost no story, to be writing one that's *all* story.

Having said that, even if my process is a mess, it's important to me that my books move fast, that they have a kind of urgency to them. Usually that's something to do with narrative but not always: people always think narrative is the only way to give books urgency, but it actually isn't, there's a series of things you can do.

With *The Resurrectionist*, for instance, I deliberately stripped out a lot of the plot and story elements, but the book has a real propulsion which is a function of its structure and the mood and language, all of which are designed to push it forward. So you can achieve urgency without relying solely on story, although I'd have to say it doesn't tend to make the process of writing it a lot of fun. [*laughs*]

CW: That's fascinating—can you say a bit more about this? Because nobody really talks about how narrative tension can come from things other than plot.

JB: It's much easier when it does come from plot. And obviously I don't really know if my books have the urgency I want them to have because I never read them as an outsider. But there are definitely ways of creating tension and movement without relying on plot. In a sense, you can strip stuff out so you're moving constantly from one moment to another.

The most obvious way is by stripping out the connective tissue, so the reader keeps moving from point to point without getting a chance to draw breath. I suspect it's a technique that wouldn't work if you applied it across an entire novel, but it's one you do tend to see when writers are trying to repair books.

I could easily be wrong about this, but I've always thought the first fifty or sixty pages of Tim Winton's *Dirt Music* read a bit like that. There are all these tiny chapters that you just skip through, one after another, until before you know it, you're through the bit that isn't working and into the good bit. The point is that it's structure providing the momentum, not plot, or at least structure and that incredible, jagged writing Winton is capable of. You can have a voice that's leading you, in a quite particular way.

But you still want to have stuff happening. Stuff happening is good. [*laughs*]

CW: Well, it is something to aim for [*laughs*]. Look, I too feel this way, I don't want my books to be slow—but why is that important?

JB: I don't know, because I don't actually mind reading slow books. I've just been reading Knausgaard, who is almost the definition of slow, but is brilliant precisely because of that slowness, and the way the books mine that tension between mimesis and the banality of detail.

But I'm always incredibly flattered if someone says, 'I couldn't put your book down,' or, 'I read it in two sittings,' because I want people to be pulled along. I want them to be involved. Although, now I say that, I find myself wondering whether that *is* genuinely what I want, because the truth is I actually don't think about readers much at all, either before I write or while I'm writing. What I want is for it to feel right to me.

But all the same, looking at it from the outside, I enjoy things that feel urgent, and I suppose I want my books to be the same. I want people to be involved, excited, interested. I get annoyed by all those glib generalisations about the problem with the literary end of the market being the fact the books don't have any story, but there's still an element of truth to it: a lot of literary novels don't have enough going on in them, not just at a story level but at the level of ideas.

As a reader, what I want to feel is that there's something at stake, that something *matters* in what I'm reading. That doesn't have to be about story, it can be about ideas or morality or a particular sense of newness or quality of observation.

Part of what I loved about Ben Lerner's *10:04* was the sense that, at the end of the day, what brings it alive is the electricity of the prose, the way it's so alive and aware, the way it both embodies and enacts that quality of *noticing* that you usually only come across in poetry. It can also be a process of speculation or some kind of intellectual argument: certainly with a lot of the science fiction I like, what excites me is the sense it's exploring ideas and possibilities in provocative ways.

CW: Let's move on to the use of place in fiction—how important is it, in your writing?

JB: Very. I tend to start with place pretty early. People talk about place as if it's one thing, but I don't know that it is. I think it's several. Place is always a psychological landscape as much as anything, so that's about effect, it's about mood, reinforcing the stuff that's going on elsewhere in the book, thematically or metaphorically.

There's another kind of place which is about attentiveness to an environment. It's not just in writing about natural places, but it is the kind of thing you see in writing about natural places: an awareness of what things feel like, the movement of the sun, the sounds, that kind of thing.

Then I think there's another sort of place, a world-building process you go through: constructing the world that the book's in. That's about knowing what the house they live in is like, all that stuff. This is always particularly clear when you're writing something historical, where it requires a much more rigorous imaginative process.

I tend to start with the mood end of it. I want it to be about a particular feeling, and places are always about feelings, I think, in my books. So in *Wrack* it's about the sand hills near where I grew up. In *The Deep Field*, it's about Sydney in the summer. In *The Resurrectionist*, it's about an imagined London and Australia, which is its opposite.

But by the same token I need that mood to give a kind of heft to the writing, to give it an imaginative energy or depth: one of the books I'm working on at the moment is set in Adelaide in the 1980s, and although one of the things that drew me to it in the first place was the fact I wanted to write about my own adolescence, I think I'm going to have to transpose it to Sydney if I'm going to get the distance from the material and the place to make what I'm writing *real*, to make it interesting.

The flipside to all this is that I don't like writing books—or reading them either, a lot of the time—where I feel the book is a kind of history lesson. Some books confuse the business of documentary with the business of fiction, and it seems to me that really you simply want a place to feel *alive*.

I have a real rule about writing historical fiction which is, I don't care what the street's called, I don't care what shops are on the street, all that stuff that you see where people say 'four doors down in Fishmonger's Lane there was a tobacconist, and next to the tobacconist . . .' I hate that stuff. Because it seems to me they're actually enacting an anxiety about their own authority over the material and, often, a deeper anxiety about the imaginative prerogative of fiction.

Density of information doesn't make fiction real, density and quality of *imagination* makes fiction real. I try to avoid explaining things in any more detail than I would if I was writing about the contemporary world.

Oddly enough, I've realised retrospectively that this is the same technique science fiction writers learned from Robert A. Heinlein: his decision to make his imagined futures feel real by disposing of all the explanatory stuff and just dropping his readers into them and assuming everyone understands the world. Here we are, we're on the moon, there's an airlock, over there's the talking computer, etc etc. It's possible it's a technique I picked up subliminally from all the science fiction I read as a kid, but I suspect it's one I came to on my own while writing historical fiction, and trying to find a way to renovate that sort of writing for myself, to make it feel real and contemporary.

CW: Do you consciously research? Some writers have a research phase and then a writing phase—what's your process in that regard?

JB: I have no process! My process is chaos. I always think it's funny that I end up being asked to do talks on research, because in fact I'm the shoddiest researcher on the face of the planet. I do a little bit—you tend to already know a bit about the stuff you're writing about—but then I work out what I need to know as I go along.

It's also all so much easier these days than it used to be. Back in the 90s researching novels was hard: you had to go to the library and look things up. Now you can just go straight to Wikipedia. But the odd thing is even in the internet age, the stuff you want to know is usually not online. You want to know what it smelt like, what it looked like, felt like, to give it the imaginative thickness it needs. And that's the sort of stuff you get out of diaries, out of novels and old photos and things. So I do tend to read around things I'm writing, to look for things that will give them the texture they need.

It's not that you borrow it from people, necessarily, it's just you—you can somehow absorb it. Does that make sense? There'll be surprising details . . . I was working on a book set in Japan after the war for a while, which I've not finished but I love, and I remember having a lot of trouble getting a handle on the feel of the place until I read a diary in which somebody talked about the smell of the hickory they burned for cooking, and it all fell into place. So it tends to be weird little things like that I'm after, things that make you suddenly go, 'Oh, okay.'

CW: And that can open up a whole lot of other stuff.

JB: Absolutely. By the same token there are things you can't avoid having to research. I had to understand medical education to write *The Resurrectionist*. And then I just changed it all. Because I don't think you should allow research to tie you down; you should make it up. And if something is complicated or confusing, change it! You can always stick a note at the back saying, look, it's not quite what happened. But what you are doing is creating a novel—you're not beholden to the past, you don't have to get it right.

CW: Yes, this anxiety is interesting—because if someone is reading a novel, in the main, they want to go with the world that you've made.

JB: That's right. And the writer is always trying to make sure you're not chucking the reader out of the world. That's why you want to get *most* stuff right. I suspect this anxiety has grown more pronounced over the past twenty years because people seem to have become more anxious about the idea of fiction generally. What is it? What's its status?

When you're promoting a book, everyone wants to know the story *behind* the book. They don't want to know about the book—what the book is saying, how it works, the logic of the language or the narrative, that's completely irrelevant. That's partly because it's just easier to market facts than ephemeral things like voice, but it's also because there's a deep anxiety about what it is that makes fiction matter, about what it bases its claims to legitimacy on. The critic in me thinks that's a function of consumer society, of the sort of alienation that reduces everything to a function of value. But whatever's behind it, it's definitely a real thing.

Another effect of that tendency, and of the increasingly information-laden environment we live in, is that we're all much more anxious about detail, all the time. The fact we're so surrounded by information can sometimes be quite disabling because it makes you feel, 'I can't do this, I need teams of researchers! What colour underwear did they wear? When was the tram invented? When did people start saying "hi" and "hello" instead of grunting or saying "good day"?'

I also think people often use research as an excuse not to write. The real work comes in the imagining, not the researching. But having said that, if you're going to write about China, then, you know, you should go to China. If you are going to write about the police, you should go and spend some time with police.

CW: Do you have what you would call a writing routine? How do you structure that aspect of your writing life?

JB: It's completely ruled by children. My day is very short because I have to drop the kids off in the morning and then pick them up in the afternoon. I know a lot of people who work in the evening but I'm always too tired. So I tend to get the kids off to school, which can be quite a dispiritingly slow process, and then I race home and stuff around for forty-five minutes doing email, reading Facebook, all that kind of stuff, and then I try and turn all that off and work until lunchtime, for three or four hours, in a pretty solid way. I try to write two thousand words a day, but I don't usually get that.

CW: That's a lot!

JB: Well, I aim at two thousand, but I also know I usually don't get past one thousand, so I treat that as a fallback. So, if it looks like I'm not going to get to two thousand, I'm allowed to write one thousand, but I have to write that much. I know the focus on word count sounds a bit instrumental but I have a real thing about it these days.

I had a very bad time writing for a lot of years and one day I decided to actually take the advice I give to students, which is, *just write.* Even if it's crap, write two thousand words and then write another two thousand words and then write another two thousand, and at some point, you'll work out what the problem is.

As it happens that's exactly where I am with the book I'm writing at the moment. It's not working and I know it's not working, but I'm forcing myself to keep going because I know if I do I'll work out the solution to my problem. That can be pretty dispiriting, because you spend a lot of time thinking, 'This is terrible, this is terrible, this is terrible, it's not working,' but eventually you have the moment I had yesterday where you suddenly think, 'Hang on, but if I moved that scene back to here, perhaps that would begin to fix the problem.'

Sometimes, if I'm trying to work really hard on something, I'll think, 'I need to write six thousand words a week'. And if I can get that done during the days, that's great, and if I can't, I try to do it on the weekend.

But, probably like you, I also have a lot of freelance work that I have to do and just . . . stuff! Because Mardi has been working full-time for the last year or two, a lot of the organisation, running the house and getting the kids' meals and all that descends on me, and every time they get sick I lose a day, there's a lot of stuff that intrudes. But you get good, I think, at going, 'I have to just get this done.'

CW: It's refreshing to hear a man talking about this domestic load, because mostly these questions are only asked of women. So: how has having kids changed your writing life?

JB: It's totally destroyed it! [*laughs*] Well, at one level it is the worst thing that can possibly happen because it is *so* consuming, organisationally. And emotionally, I find it incredibly draining. I love my kids to death but I find the level of emotional intensity around them very difficult.

Apart from that, it's harder just finding time to write, because your economic pressures are increased so exponentially by having kids; you *have* to make money. You can't just eke out a living anymore, you have to have money. Which, when you're a writer, is always a source of great anxiety.

On the flipside, it makes you a lot more disciplined. You don't have the luxury of spending four days fiddling with a scene, you just have to get it. And that discipline is quite important. You become much more efficient, I think.

I also think there are things you find out about yourself, a series of quite complex emotional things that you come into contact with through having kids, which expand the way you write, the way you think, the sorts of things you pay attention to. So, it's both good and bad. It adds complexity and depth to your life in a series of ways but it makes a lot of it much harder at the same time. So it's a pushmi-pullyu kind of thing.

Kids have probably also got something to do with me deciding I had to change the way I was writing and what I was writing over the past few years. I had a really terrible time writing *The Resurrectionist*, then published it, then I wrote the other book I mentioned earlier, which I hated every minute of writing, and didn't end up publishing. The funny thing was that deciding not to publish it was an incredibly liberating experience, because aside from the structural problem the book wasn't entirely unlike *The Resurrectionist* in its fascination with violence and psychological disorder, but even more than *The Resurrectionist* it was also all about mood and voice and a particular kind of abjection, and that meant the process of writing it was about trying to be in that space myself, to erase myself and try to exhume all this awful stuff from inside myself, and to piece the thing together without any of the pleasure of narrative to work with. Once I decided not to publish it I thought, 'I can't do this again. I need to write differently. I want to *like* writing.'

At the same time I thought to myself, 'I have twenty, thirty books I want to write, and I'm getting on for fifty,' so I decided to try to work differently, to stop being afraid of failing or not being perfect and just to write the things I wanted to.

I think that is partly about having kids; you can see mortality bearing down on you. And that's actually been very liberating, learning to say, 'I just want to write the book. I don't want to *worry* about writing the book, I just want to write the book.'

CW: I think almost every writer I know comes to a point where they just are completely disillusioned—with their own work, with Australian writing, with the hardship of being a writer—and then they find a solution, somehow, that changes things. But first, why is it miserable? What's the nature of it?

JB: I don't think there's a single answer to that question. Sometimes you're miserable because the thing you're writing isn't working, sometimes it's more complex than that. But

I also think there's a real phenomenon where you get into writing because you love it and you want—you need—to do it, but if you're good and you're lucky then at some point you start to become professionalised so you are doing it for money, and then you think, I *need* to make money from it in order to do it. And you end up writing what you think you should be writing. I was certainly doing that.

CW: You mean for some unspecified approval from . . . ?

JB: The really stupid thing is I don't know the answer to that. All I know is I was so miserable. I hated writing. And I remember thinking, 'I don't want to *live* like this. I don't want to spend the rest of my life doing something I hate. I don't want to be broke and have no stability and, all of that, *in order to be unhappy.*' Do you know what I mean? [*laughs*] If I'm happy, I'm prepared to do those things, but I'm not prepared to do them and be unhappy.

So, I made a conscious decision to try to develop a healthier relationship with writing. I already had a sort of model for that process that had come out of deciding to run a blog for a couple of years, which had also been the result of a quite conscious decision to try to uncouple what I was writing from a professional context, and to get back to just writing what I wanted to, instead of being constrained by what I thought I could sell. And so I started to write different things, things I felt like writing that I had no idea what other people would make of.

At the same time I began to become aware of two things: first, that I'd started reading science fiction again, and was finding it really challenging and interesting and enlivening. And second, that my friends who worked in genre fiction seemed to have a much healthier relationship with their work. Whereas most of the literary writers I know are miserable, all the time, about what they're doing, my friends in genre seemed to *like* their writing. That isn't to say they don't find it difficult, but they seemed to spend less time torturing themselves and obsessing about status and all the rest of it, and more time actually writing.

So I decided that instead of beating myself up, I'd do what I'd recommend if a student came to me with the sort of problems I had, which is to say, 'Don't write what you think you should be writing, write what you want to. And then pick a project, don't think about anybody else, and just write it. When it seems hard, write another bit and then write another bit and bit and another bit and when you get to the end, you'll have a book. Then you can make a decision about what you want to do with it.'

The silly thing is that taking my own advice was incredibly liberating. I don't know if it looked all that different from the outside, but I felt I was doing different work. And I think, also, the feelings that were going into the work were more positive, so I think rather than all my doubt and misery going into the work, I felt there was some engagement and fun going into it. And as I went along I also realised that by writing for myself again I'd become much less concerned with what other people thought, which was incredibly freeing.

CW: This leads nicely into what I want to ask you about sci-fi. Well, my clarity about terminology in that sort of genre is very cloudy. But let's say sci-fi. You've written somewhere that you developed an early taste for the fantastical and magical and then you tried to 'give it up'.

JB: All my teenage years I read nothing but science fiction and fantasy and comics. I really never read anything else. And then when I was about eighteen I read, back to back, a Thomas Hardy novel and *Waterland* by Graham Swift—and I had a road to Damascus moment where I realised there was a whole other world of books I hadn't realised existed, that were really exciting and interesting and didn't have aliens or spaceships or broadswords.

People in the science-fiction world talk about 'mainstream'. There's the mainstream and then there's all of them. So I started reading what they call mainstream fiction. For the next twenty years I really read almost nothing else—there were a few science-fiction authors I read and loved—Gibson, Le Guin, Neal Stephenson and so on—but mostly I read literary fiction and classics. And then, when I was about forty, I began to get bored, and eventually, almost by accident, I started reading SF again. Over the past few years I've worked to get a handle on the contemporary scene, but I've also spent quite a lot of time reading my way back through the books I loved as a teenager, in particular a lot of the New Wave SF, which has been a wonderful experience: some of it doesn't hold up but a lot of it is fantastically good.

Having said all that, I find the way people talk about genre really problematic. It seems to me that as soon as people start talking about genre, they're really talking about status, and what they're articulating is an anxiety in one direction or another. I become really frustrated when you read people going through these complex contortions in order to justify a particular snobbery or to justify a taste. And it's all predicated on the notion that there's some coherent thing which is fantasy or science fiction, or 'literary fiction', which seems to me to be the most meaningless term of all. It's always seemed to me that you're much better off thinking of these things as a whole series of traditions, tropes, devices, subgenres, things that overlap. They intersect, and people write into them and out of them.

CW: So the categories are meaningless?

JB: Well, they're not meaningless, but they're certainly not rigid or even particularly coherent. Certainly there's no one discrete, stable thing that is science fiction or fantasy any more than there is one discrete, stable thing that is literary fiction: instead they're amorphous umbrella terms used to describe a vast array of often very different works. And as soon as you accept that, a couple of things start happening.

You stop needing to worry so much about status, but also it becomes really clear that literary fiction, which people think of as being this special exalted thing, is itself a set of tropes and traditions; it tends to be about middle-class life, it tends to be about families, it tends to be contemporary or historical.

Once that is clear to you, you begin to see that you can be a really fantastic writer like Guy Gavriel Kay, writing fantasy novels, or you can be a really fantastic writer like Alice Munro, writing about middle-class life. I don't see why we have to set up boundaries that preclude one writing or another, and I think as writers you don't want to set that up either. I've just found, over twenty years, that whenever I *try* to do something, it won't work, so I just have to do the thing I need to do next. And it will be what it is.

CW: Well, whatever we call it, this sense of the speculative, the otherworldly, the magical—what appeals to you about it, both reading and writing it?

JB: Different things. There's a glib line about science fiction which is both true and not true, which is that 'it makes the metaphorical literal'. So, people 'burn with desire', for example. There's something about that process of bringing the strange into the world that reveals this world in other ways.

There are also certain ideas that are difficult to talk about with the tools of realist fiction. So, with *Clade*, I was trying to write about climate change. It's such a huge amorphous thing that the tools of conventional realist fiction just aren't adequate to the task of addressing it. But science fiction, which has always had an interest in immensity and wonder and vast spans of time and space, has evolved techniques that will let you get at it more effectively.

I also think we live in a world that is increasingly science fictional. The technology around us—computers and drones and networked information and all the rest of it—is obviously science fictional, but so are the gulfs between rich and poor, the increasing intersection of the real and the virtual, all those kinds of things. What is science fiction and what is real has become a very ambiguous question. So, I'm interested by that.

With fantasy—and to be fair, I have a pretty ambivalent relationship with fantasy fiction—the good stuff offers a fascinating way to re-enchant the world, and get us back to another kind of relationship with nature and each other. I'm also interested in the way it plays with archetypes, because a lot of that stuff seems to be very deep and to resonate in quite powerful ways.

There is a fascinating book called *Gossip from the Forest* by a woman called Sara Maitland from a few years ago—it's complete hokum at one level but really interesting and fertile at another—which argues that the fairytales of Europe are inextricably bound up in the forests that used to cover all of the continent, and that when we read them we remember our own connection to those forests. There's something really interesting to me about that idea, and the notion that part of what fairytales are doing is connecting us to a whole other way of being in the world.

CW: How interesting. Maybe they're about finding your way through some sort of darkness, the darkness of the forest. Going back to science fiction, you seem to me to be very interested in the merging of poetry and science.

JB: Science does have a poetry. I'm fascinated by science and I'm fascinated by the natural world; by the otherness of animals. There's something about seeing things that have not been seen before, understanding how it all fits together, which I find incredibly exciting because it underlines the fact that the world is infinitely strange and infinitely beautiful.

High physics is a weird kind of religious poetry; I think that trickles down through it. And I'm deeply fascinated by space, like the photos of Ceres at the moment, as they go towards Ceres. This thing we discovered two hundred years ago, it's been a blob in the asteroid field that no one could see—and now we can see it's a little planet and it's got markings and . . . I find all of that just astonishing. Like the idea that there is an ocean under Europa which is bigger than all the water on Earth, and this ocean may be salty and may have life in it. That's mind-boggling, and beautiful!

I do sometimes wonder why I find it all so wondrous. I'm not religious, but it's possible that my fascination with nature is an expression of the same desire for connection and transcendence that other people go looking for in God.

CW: You are interested in many different forms of writing—fiction, criticism, even comics. I loved your essay about writing a comic. I'm one of those people who has always been very prejudiced about adults reading comics, it seemed nonsensical and childish. And then I read the *New Yorker* cartoonist Roz Chast's illustrated memoir and I loved it. And it couldn't have been done without being a comic. Would you call that a comic or an illustrated book?

JB: I'm wary of saying anything too definitive about comics simply because although I'm a passionate consumer, I'm mostly interested in the commercial end of the market. I like superhero comics, I like science-fiction comics, I like stuff that is . . . I think some of it is very good but it is not the cerebral end of the market, let's say, and I'm not really an expert on anything except the stuff I like. There are people like Chris Ware who are doing amazing things with the form—his most recent comic, *Building Stories,* is the most extraordinary thing—and other people like Dylan Horrocks, who don't just write wonderful comics but are also historians of the form, or the Australian Pat Grant, whose work is so emotionally rich and painful. In terms of your question and the distinctions, they all have their own views about terminology. Some of them hate the term 'graphic novel' and they think they should just be called comics, others embrace the term. So I don't know what you'd call it.

What I do know is that I've always loved comics, both for themselves and as a form. As the Roz Chast book demonstrates so eloquently, there are things you can do with images and pictures that are very difficult to do in other ways.

One of the things I think is really fascinating about the superhero comics I'm interested in is that in the Marvel Universe and the DC Universe you actually have the single largest fictional creation that's ever been made. They are vast. There are hundreds of thousands of characters, spreading over fifty, sixty, seventy years. The *Mahabharata* is not that big!

I love the sense of narrative complexity and interconnectedness that arises out of that scale, so if you've been reading them for forty years like I have, you're always operating with a deep well of knowledge that enriches it all.

Peter Parker is still around—he was a fifteen-year-old character when I started reading them as a kid, but these days he's in his late twenties, and although he hasn't aged that much in some ways, I've seen him change and grow. And there's that sense of narrative exaltation that comes from the way suddenly, something will click into place. You'll go, 'Oh my god, that man, the villain here, it's the Molecule Man, I remember the Molecule Man from 1982. And he's back!'

If it's done well, it's like having a little jolt of that quality Cocteau describes when he says that everything that happens in a story should be absolutely surprising and completely inevitable.

CW: You seem to have a lovely playful sense of these comics.

JB: I suppose, although that's partly because it's a good time to be a reader of comics because changing technology is driving a real renaissance. It used to be that to read them you had to go to comic shops, which I once heard the comic writer Matt Fraction describe with horrible accuracy as 'dungeons of creepdom'. [*laughs*]

CW: A very boysy sort of space.

JB: Oh, a very boyish thing. But digital delivery has changed all that, and as a result more and more women have started reading and writing comics. And in its turn that's driven a strategy by the major publishers, and Marvel in particular, to create more comics *about* women.

CW: But have they done that?

JB: Absolutely. Although the creative teams are still over-whelmingly men, Marvel have a whole range of comics headlined by female characters. Some of these are comics like *Captain Marvel* and *She-Hulk*, which is an absolute joy, but Thor is now a woman, and there are all-female teams of X-Men and so on. And while they still tend to have double-D boobs and skin-tight outfits, even that's changed a bit. And Marvel particularly have allowed their writers to go back to what was the joy of comics in the first place. So they've been writing these comics that are just fun. They're incredibly sharply written and hip, they're colourful, they're beautiful, they're warm, they're crazy, they're great. They're like the comics were in the 60s again, and that's fantastic, but incredibly contemporary at the same time. They're not grim, they're not miserable, they're not gritty. They're just fun.

CW: I can see there's a real joy in having had that connection with them since you were a child, and they're still going with you.

JB: The underpinnings of comics, superhero comics particularly, are essentially fascistic. They're about uber-men who know better, and I suspect that at some level those fantasies are always at play when you're reading them. But there is also just a sense of freedom and joy that comes with them. I remember when *Superman: The Movie* came out in 1978, the tagline was 'You'll believe a man can fly.' And that sense of wonder really is a big part of what they're about, especially for me. But at the same time, one of the things that Marvel have done very cleverly with their movies is to retain a sense of distance and humour about the material. So there's almost always a character in it who is the audience, just going: *'Really?'* [*laughs*] There's a scene in the most recent *Thor* movie where he gets on a train and there's a place you have to put your bag and he hangs his hammer up there and walks over and sits down. That stuff is great. There's a goodness at the heart of some of them which I like: a sense that the world can be made better.

CW: A sense of possibility.

JB: Yes. I also think that when you're a teenager there's a lot of stuff about feeling like a freak, and different, and all that kind of thing, and I think they speak to that in interesting ways.

One of the best comics around at the moment is *Ms Marvel*, which is written by a novelist called G. Willow Wilson, an American who lives in Egypt and is a Muslim convert. It takes place in the Marvel Universe, and it's about a Muslim teenager in New Jersey who gets powers.

Like all Wilson's stuff it's very sweet and funny, but it's also interestingly subversive, because like *Spider-Man* was in 1963 or 64 it's not just about superheroics, it's about being a teenager in the burbs who discovers they've got superpowers, and about how you try to manage that and balance high school and your parents, who don't want you to go out and keep sending you to talk to the mullah because you've been hanging out with boys. And, perhaps most interestingly, it's not about *being a Muslim*, it's about the ordinariness of being a Muslim teenager. That's not exceptional, that's just who she is.

CW: I want to talk a little about your critical writing now. Does your criticism feed your own fiction, or not?

JB: I sometimes worry that the professional critical stuff feeds the critic on my shoulder a bit much, if that makes sense. You become even more keenly aware of why what you're doing looks like something else, why it isn't good enough, why it is not substantial. And that can make you very worried about the things that can go wrong when it goes out into the world.

I also sometimes worry that I end up intellectualising a process that shouldn't be intellectualised, that I end up overthinking the writing. Because I do actually believe that romantic notion that writing comes from within, and that trying to intellectualise the process too early is often bad for the work because it can kill that ineffable mystery all writing needs to have at its heart, that thing that makes it alive and irreducible.

Part of the problem is that they're such completely different processes. That's not to say writing critical stuff is not creative, because it is. But it's also fundamentally an intellectual process, and depends on making connections and unravelling things and being alive to distinctions and the contradictions in your own thinking, whereas writing a novel or a story, you need to get into that weird dreaming state, so it's a much more instinctive process. Of course, there's a whole lot of intellectual stuff at work as well, about crafting and shaping and working out why isn't this working and so on. But it's much more fluid and quite different.

I go through patches where I really love reviewing and I go through patches where I don't like it at all, where I'd like to give it up. Most of the time, I'm somewhere in the middle.

CW: What do you think are the most important skills or qualities of a good reviewer?

JB: Your obligation is to be interesting and insightful, not to police boundaries or anything like that. I have a problem with people who feel like that's what they're doing. I don't think of myself as a conservative reviewer. You need to read in a generous and hopefully thoughtful way. You need to be able to connect the thing you're writing about into a framework, so that you can see what it's connected to, what it's related to, what its historical background is, which is partly about breadth of reading but also about thinking about what's going on in the world more generally.

I also think you need to be honest, although that's not the same as being cruel or harsh. And you need to think about what the book's trying to do, because the review is not about you. The review is about the book.

Ultimately, though, you need to say some interesting things. If you can say two or three interesting things in eight hundred words, that will usually get you through.

CW: How do you go about managing the balance between a public engagement—in criticism, and social media and public speaking—and the quiet space of writing itself? Is this an easy transition for you, back and forth?

JB: When I started doing media for *Clade* I found it incredibly confronting because it's quite a long time since I've done any, and over the last five years I've got used to completely managing the terms of my engagement with the world through social media and blogging and reviewing, where you have a very high degree of control over what you say, how you say it, when you do it. And suddenly having people asking me questions that I had to answer in public just threw me for a massive loop.

I think that like a lot of people I have a complex relationship with the public stuff, though. Although part of me is a bit of a show-off, and I quite like doing panels and all that kind of thing, I also get very anxious about them, and I'm always frightened I've said something terrible. In a way, I'd like to have a lot less of it in my life and spend more time writing and reading and just being alone. I particularly don't like the way social media intrudes into my personal life. I don't like it when I catch myself checking Facebook when I'm sitting around with my family. And a lot of it makes me feel false and almost fraudulent.

But at the same time I accept that if you want to be a writer in the twenty-first century, you've got to do the public stuff. It's part of your job and there are parts of all of our jobs that we don't particularly like. I guess you could just choose never to do it, but I don't know that that's really an option unless you're Cormac McCarthy . . .

On the flipside, some of it is quite useful because I live a very solitary life. I have almost no adult company. Mardi goes to work in the morning, I look after the kids, I take them to school, I pick them up, I cook them dinner, she comes home at six o'clock, and I see her then. That is actually the extent of my engagement with other human beings. So being able to talk to people on social media, or even just read what they are saying, can be really valuable because it makes me feel much less isolated and like a crazy person. I think I'm like lots of people who write, though; I'm a weird mixture of quite gregarious but very solitary. I like people, but in quite contained bursts.

CW: You've written beautifully about depression and creativity. I don't like the romantic linking of suffering and art, and yet it's hard to deny that there often seems to be a relationship.

JB: There's clearly a link. To be an effective writer of fiction you need to be someone whose skin is a bit thin. You need to bruise easily and to have the awareness and the sense of empathy that comes with that.

I also think of that famous Keatsian notion of negative capability, of putting yourself into someone else's mind, because most people who suffer from depression will be familiar with the sense that there's an absence at the centre of yourself, that your identity is very unstable. So when you're depressed you become very good at dissembling, at pretending you're okay, which means you're constantly performing identity rather than being some solid self. And I do think that sense of unstable identity is one of the things that lets you operate as a writer—and I guess as an actor as well—because it allows you to inhabit other people's lives. You're used to this idea that you can be different people and you can think in different ways. So the idea that your identity might not be fixed is in fact a sort of strength.

There's also a focus and intensity that you need to work well a lot of the time, and that is often the flipside of all of this stuff. There's a very funny study they did a few years ago in which a number of writers were asked to describe their moments of peak creativity—and what's fascinating is that their descriptions sound exactly like descriptions of mania. [*laughs*] In their minds of course they're just working at peak efficiency, but then, when they were asked to describe what it was like when things aren't going well, they all went on about how terribly depressed they get. So I suspect that flipside, the ability to really lose yourself in the work, to get by on four hours of sleep a night, to ignore everybody else, is both a part of the process and, equally, a sign of slightly disordered psychological settings.

CW: Some writers seem to have a horror of the idea that writing might be therapeutic. I used to feel like that myself, but now I feel strongly that, for me, while it's not anything like therapy itself, it does have therapeutic effects. There is something restorative about the act of writing. What do you make of that?

JB: I'm not very good at being still. The thing I've learned over recent years is that I'm just much happier if I'm working and writing. So I'm not sure that I find the writing therapeutic, but I am a much happier person if I'm writing than if I'm not writing. I'm not sure it's quite the same thing, but there's something about feeling that I'm working and engaged and doing something which makes me calmer and happier than if I'm doing nothing.

In terms of it being actually therapeutic, I'm less certain. I've definitely written a few things I've found very cathartic, but for the most part the work is an end in itself, and what makes me happy is making it *work*, rather than feeling I've resolved some deep personal trauma.

What I do know is that while most things you write usually just vanish into the world, in the past few years I've written a couple of things that people seem to have really connected with and found affirming or helpful or liberating—and that was fantastic. Fantastic in a way that I'm not sure I would have anticipated, because you get so good at cutting yourself off from any notion that people might actually be reading it at the other end. [*laughs*]

CW: You sort of have to.

JB: You have to.

CW: You have to let go of expectation.

JB: You do. Oddly enough, I've written about a number of very personal things I find almost impossible to talk about in person, and been completely unfazed by the thought people were reading them out in the world or—and this is even weirder—by talking about them on panels or in front of audiences. It's like the public me and the writer me can do things the private me can't. But in terms of writing as therapy, I just don't think of it like that. Instead, it's more that I can't imagine who I'd be if I didn't do it. I think I write because I don't know how not to.

CW: Let's talk about *Clade*, particularly the use of time. I thought the timescape was brilliantly done. How did you conceptualise time in this novel, how you were going to show the effects of climate change in a narrative sense?

JB: There is a philosopher called Timothy Morton who has written about what he calls 'hyperobjects'. He says hyperobjects are things that are too big to be comprehended within our frame of reference. Things like climate change, that are just too big, too diffuse, too extended through time and space for us to actually get a handle on or talk about and conceptualise.

I have a few problems with Morton's arguments, but I also think they're interesting and quite useful, because climate change *is* very difficult to think about. We see it in our own behaviour. We all know we have to change our behaviour, that we need to consume less, drive less, live differently. Yet we don't seem to be able to enact that in our own lives. And that's not just greed or laziness, it's that the whole idea of connecting the abstract notion of climate change with the everyday world defeats us at some deep psychological level.

Quite early on in *Clade*, though, I realised I wasn't just writing about climate change, I was writing about kids and parents, the way we're all connected not just to the past but to the future by the people who came before us and the ones who come after us. So I wanted the book to try to capture that sense of constantly moving on into the future, of the way things change and keep changing, and that individual lives are really just part of a much larger process of change.

When you look at a lot of the material that is around at the moment, all these writers who want to write about climate change, about loss—they all end up really quickly talking about time. The David Mitchell book, *The Bone Clocks*, is clearly about deep time, that's what he's trying to write about. The silly *Interstellar* film, William Gibson's new novel *The Peripheral*, they're all about deep time.

And they're all trying to do something similar to what I was trying to do with *Clade*, which is to find a way of connecting the huge, abstract, geological process of climate change, and the substrate of grief and loss we all feel about it, to a more human scale, because that's the only way we can make it comprehensible to ourselves.

The structure of *Clade* is designed to capture this sense of falling away, of loss, but also the way the future opens out in front of us. There's a feeling of hastening it's designed to induce, a process that's amplified by the way the book begins to toy with very large timeframes towards the end.

CW: It's hard to manage though, because with those leaps of time, you can't stay with the same characters. If you're leaping a hundred years, or two hundred years forward, you can't maintain that emotional connection with one set of characters.

JB: You can't. One of the things I did quite deliberately was to try to reverse the polarity of the way a book like this would normally work, so that instead of having the disasters in the foreground, it becomes about the business of life that goes on even when the world is falling apart, and all of the big stuff happens in the background. So ten years will go between two sections and although something massive has clearly gone on in these characters' lives, the book doesn't attempt to explain what that is any more than it tries to show the disasters or explain the global situation. So you're forced to engage with the characters and the changes in their world as they experience them.

CW: One of the really chilling things about it for me was that all these things I realise I've vaguely pinned my hopes on for the future of humanity—like solar power, say—in the book those things have already failed. It created a sense of urgency and terror in me, because I realised I had had this vague, uneasy faith that someone will work out a way of fixing these things, and then you tell me that those remedies have failed, in a casual line, in a sort of easy dismissal: 'Oh, back when we had the solar farms before they all went bust.'

JB: But then something else comes along.

CW: Yes. At the launch you stressed that this was not an apocalyptic book, that apocalyptic books were a form of cop-out.

JB: There's always apocalyptic stuff around. Apocalyptic stories are one of the ways we process our anxieties, one of the things we use to engage with them in a manageable way. And because of that I think apocalyptic fiction and end-of-the-world scenarios are actually quite important in some ways. But I also think there's something not just consoling but absolving about them, a sense in which they relieve us of the responsibility of thinking about the real problems we face—by showing us worlds where the worst has already happened, so there's nothing to be done about it. And I don't think that's good enough with climate change. We need to be thinking about what it might actually be like, living in a radically altered world.

At the launch I talked about that amazing speech by Ursula Le Guin where she says people look around the world and say the power of capitalism looks inescapable, but then goes on to remind us that so did the divine right of kings. The possibility of imagining a different future is one of the things science fiction does really interestingly.

So one of the things I wanted the book to do was to suggest to people that perhaps the future isn't just one thing, and that in order to take possession of it, we have to do more than just wring our hands and say, 'It's all going to end.' We have to start asking how we think about it, because the world's not going to end but is clearly going to change, and it's going to keep on changing. History doesn't stop, history continues. In ten thousand years, history will be continuing. I do think that endless end-of-the-world scenarios, at one level, are about an inability to imagine the future. And we're in a late-stage capitalist society and it's almost impossible for people to imagine alternatives—but we *need* to imagine alternatives.

CW: This leads me to the importance of hope in fiction. At the launch of *Clade* you said something about coming to this material at the time in your life when you have small children. Would you have written the same book if you didn't have children? Would *Clade* have the same glimmer of hopefulness?

JB: I might have written a book about it, but I don't think I would have written the same book. But having said that,

I also think I am basically a hopeful person, and perhaps the book reflects that. That's partly because a world without hope would be horrible. But it's also because the human experience over the last hundred years, despite the horrific things that have happened, has been broadly positive. We live longer, billions of us have risen out of poverty, most of us live lives of material comfort that our ancestors couldn't have imagined. Not everyone, obviously; the gulf between rich and poor is widening, there are these negatives along the way. But still, in lots of ways, things have got better. People are freer, there's less oppression of people who aren't the same as everybody else, there's less violence.

But at the same time, we're borrowing against the future to fund those achievements, which means I look at my kids and think, 'You're going to live in a world of reducing opportunity, where there will be no birds, a place where the oceans are empty and anoxic, where water will be scarcer, and tigers will only be in zoos.' And that makes me incredibly sad. I suspect we'll turn some of that stuff around but we probably won't turn all of it round. So although I think *Clade* is trying to balance those two things, I suppose it is a hopeful book, in a weird way. But it would have been so bleak if it wasn't. It would be unbearable if it wasn't.

CW: Well—and this is a question for myself as well, to do with the novel I'm writing now—what's wrong with a bleak book?

JB: I don't know. Perhaps the shapes of fiction demand hope. After all, there's a level at which books are always about a movement of feeling, and although that proceeds in different ways to different kinds of resolutions, it does usually lead us to points of openness and possibility. And bleakness is about the absence of possibility. Or perhaps it's just that while fiction is essentially artifice, it's also trying to extract something real, something true, from our experience of life, and at the end of the day, the experience of life is about possibility and change.

Or it might be something about the novel in particular. Ursula Le Guin says somewhere that although Hollywood and writing workshops have lulled us all into believing fiction is necessarily about conflict and opposition, that's an extremely patriarchal way of thinking about it—and that it's equally possible to analyse stories in terms of moments of connection and disconnection.

I've always been fascinated by that idea, at least partly because it seems to me most novels end on moments of connection and possibility, but a lot of short stories end on moments of disconnection.

That might be simply because we're used to novels that do particular things, or because while we don't care if something that takes half an hour to read ends on a moment of disconnection, if we're going to spend an entire week reading something we don't like it to end on a grim note.

But it might also be because the novel, and fiction in general, works best when it's expansive, when it embraces possibility, because that's the nature of life, and in the end the real business of fiction is capturing lived experience; allowing us to experience other lives and other worlds.

'IT WOULD be difficult to think of another novelist quite as original or fearless as 55-year-old New Zealand author Lloyd Jones,' wrote novelist Delia Falconer in *The Monthly* in 2010.

The author of fifteen books, including novels, short stories, fiction for children and a memoir, Jones came to international prominence in 2006 with *Mister Pip*, his extraordinary riff on Dickens' *Great Expectations* set in war-torn Bougainville, narrated by a fourteen-year-old girl. The novel won him many new admirers, as well as the Commonwealth Writers' Prize, and was shortlisted for the Booker. It was also made into a feature film starring Hugh Laurie in the title role.

Jones was born in Lower Hutt in the Wellington region of New Zealand in 1955. After attending Hutt Valley High School and Victoria University, he left his homeland and took off on a road trip across America, a journey that became a defining experience for him as a blossoming fiction writer.

He describes himself as a sports-mad kid until struck by meningitis at the age of nineteen—a temporary plunge into physical frailty that was a factor in turning his attention towards literature.

As well as the Commonwealth Writers' Prize, his work has garnered many other accolades, including the Tasmania Prize for Fiction, New Zealand's Deutz Medal for Fiction, the Kiriyama Prize, several Montana awards as well as many international shortlistings, including the Booker.

My first 'meeting' with Jones was not a meeting at all, but online, in a classroom. I took part in a webinar master class Jones gave about voice in fiction, held in Queensland and hosted by *Griffith Review* and its editor, Julianne Schultz. I found the way Jones spoke about fiction so fresh and exhilarating that as soon as the class finished I wrote asking for an interview.

Our conversation took place in Adelaide, at the townhouse Jones was renting while working at Adelaide University, where he had been invited as the first writer in residence for the university's J.M. Coetzee Centre for Creative Practice.

Jones describes himself as having a 'contrarian' nature, and certainly his fiction speaks of an impatience with rules and an urge to combat or challenge convention. The vastly different settings and material of his novels—his subject matter includes the civil war in Bougainville, painting, the birth of the All Blacks' rugby team in 1905, the Argentinian tango in World War II New Zealand, African refugees in contemporary Germany, political intrigue in Albania—makes categorisation of his work impossible. He told me this striking change in each book's material is usually a reaction against the previous work, and he spoke often of the quest to discover 'a new way' of storytelling, or even of reading.

In conversation Jones is thoughtful and quiet, speaking of his own work with an unassuming thoroughness of self-examination. For a man of his achievements I also found him unusually modest.

While speaking carefully, he gives off an air of restless physical energy. When I arrived for the interview he shot out of the apartment to get a sandwich, then to unpeg some laundry, and then an unforeseen urgent request for a faxed document saw us break up the conversation with a brisk walk to the university, continuing to talk on the way. I was left with the sense of someone keen to keep moving—physically, intellectually and creatively—and it seems to me this restive, searching spirit may be the lifeblood of Jones' work.

CW: You're in the middle of another book now, I understand; how far off do you think it is?

LJ: Oh God, that's a good question. I'm wrestling with two projects right now, but the one that's further down the track is problematic. Often my writing projects are. I mean, I call them 'writing projects'. I don't say 'I'm writing a novel', because it predetermines too much.

Often I get a bit caught up in trying to reject the conventions of narrative, which pushes me out into an area where it doesn't work, and then that kind of redirects me back to where I probably should have been all the way along. But temperamentally I'm not suited to doing this in a sensible way. [*laughs*]

I think too, with every project, that as much as you're trying to figure out how to write in a new way, you're also trying to show how something can be read in a new way. Inevitably for me it's always about finding the language; that's the key. The language will unlock everything. I'm not at all concerned about plot or anything like that. That will take care of itself if the language is there from the outset.

CW: It's interesting you talk of going to a place that doesn't work and coming back. I've heard you speak about the centrepiece of *Mister Pip* as the 'fresco' of words and phrases written on a baby's bedroom walls—which has nothing to do with Bougainville or Dickens.

LJ: That's right.

CW: Was that a starting point?

LJ: It was, and it's a very good example of what I'm talking about. I had this notion that you could open a book up at random and just dip into it and get something out of it, without the usual sort of causality and narrative. But of course, it lacked some kind of connective tissue. Why is this being written? What's its reason to exist? If you can't answer that question, something vital is missing—and it was. I mean, it was an imaginative risk, but without the underpinning of some vital need to be told. But that is a good illustration of how I was sent back to a much more conventional mode of narrative—not that it's all that conventional in the end, I don't think. But I think it must be a personality trait, you know—I'm just contrarian.

CW: But it's brilliant, because it must push you somewhere very original each time.

LJ: That's the hope. The hope is—and it's always a vain one, of course—that you are going to uncover something new and vital, and find a new way of telling. I think that's what it's all about. I think every project really ought to begin with the question: why am I writing what I'm writing?

CW: But can you answer that question at the start?

LJ: Well, I sort of do . . . it may be a made-up proposition, and it's just a starting point, that's all. But I'm writing to find out the answer, to some extent. I'm writing to unlock something I don't know exists. It's in me somewhere, and I'm in search of it. I'm trying to find this thing. It's exciting when you surprise yourself. Then you've tapped into something—if you are excited, then it will be exciting on the page.

CW: And the energy comes from the discovery?

LJ: I think so. When you are on song you just find connection everywhere. The world just suddenly connects. And you can't believe nobody else has seen this, and you're a bit worried that somebody *might* have, because it's so obvious. That's when you're on song, when you have unlocked that thing. It's all there in the subconscious somewhere, waiting to be dragged up and connected and pieced together in an interesting way.

So I suppose the starting point is often artificial, and that's probably where dissatisfaction sits, and pushes you into a territory where you have to take more imaginative risks.

I'm really straining here to actually make sense of it, and in a way I don't want to because it's such a mysterious process, in every writing project. Like this thing I'm writing now; I mean, it's not working! Why isn't it working? You would think I would know by now, but I don't.

It's almost like every time I set out on a writing project I'm learning how to write all over again. But I've done it often enough now that I know the frustrations are all part of it.

CW: Do you know at the start whether it's fiction or non-fiction, or is even that quite mysterious?

LJ: Well, if you want something new and surprising then I don't think you should acknowledge that, because it will just get steered into known territory. You'll feel like you are just pouring cement into a mould.

I often do, of course. Somebody will say, 'What are you working on?' and I'll say, 'I'm writing a novel.' But even when I say it I am inwardly wincing because . . . there are so many artificial demarcations around these categories, novels and so forth. I prefer just to think of it in terms of prose—and what happens, happens. Then at the end you look at it and say, 'Well, what's that?'

The only time I haven't really gone in for that, when I was aware that I was writing a particular genre, was the memoir, because I don't think you can fool around with the facts. I think you are rightly constrained by those. So I had no problems telling myself, 'I'm writing a memoir.'

As for the other stuff, I just suddenly feel encumbered somehow if I say, 'Yes, this is a novel.' Sure as hell it will look like a novel, it will obey the conventions of one, and so I will be walking in the hallways of tradition rather than the imagination.

CW: What would happen if you did try and 'write a novel'? Does it just go dead for you?

LJ: Well, where it would go dead for me would be if I plotted something out. If I said, 'Right, this is going to be twenty-five chapters,' and I had notes for each chapter and all that sort of thing. I can't imagine why I would write that thing; it's already known. It doesn't need to be written. It would be like doing a jigsaw—no, not that interesting. It would be like painting by numbers or something.

It's very hard to explain this because the entry point into writing and literature is story. That's the thing that excites us when we are eight years old and twelve and twenty. That's where we enter into this game. But we try and run away from it as fast as we can once we realise more important things are at stake. And story takes care of itself anyway, don't you think?

CW: Maybe. Eventually . . .

LJ: Yeah, eventually. Things happen. Things just happen in the most mundane ways: 'Oh, it's raining. I have been caught without an umbrella.' That's an event. What will I do now?

CW: And yet your narratives are still very compelling. With *Hand Me Down World*, for example, the narrative urgency is very strong from the beginning, with that question, is she going to get the baby back? At what point do you find this necessity, this question?

LJ: It's a curious mix, I think. You are absolutely right to describe it as an urgency because that's when things take off for me. It's an emotional state I get into, really, and it has to do with language—the excitement over the voice that I have uncovered, the voice will take me places. In *Hand Me Down World*, all those different voices, all those interior lives, that's interesting. As soon as I realised that would be the mode of delivering this particular narrative I was excited by it, because you find yourself coming up with endless possibilities of perspective on this person who is passing through the world. Nameless, faceless—well, not faceless, but without any identity other than that which is imposed on her by all these other people. That excited me.

Say with *Mister Pip*—I had that section about that bedroom, but it was moribund. I had just finished reading a part of that section out to a friend of mine on the phone. As I'm reading it out I'm realising, 'This is dead, this is dead'—you know, you can tell by the quality of the listening at the other end of the phone. It's—well, you'll know this, I'm sure—it's terribly, terribly deflating and disappointing. But it's also liberating, and I move quite quickly from one state to the other.

Anyway, so I'm on the phone to this person and I've been given tickets to the ballet and she is a former dancer and she says something like, 'I don't know what to wear tonight.' I said, 'Why don't you wear your roller skates?' and laughed. That was the end of that. I put the phone down—and immediately I wrote a sentence about a white man towing a black woman behind him in a cart. Now, where did that come from? Roller skates perhaps, possibly? Who knows, but it was the most interesting sentence I had written for a long time. Then somebody has to see this event, of the white man towing this black woman behind him. At that very moment, the voice of Matilda comes to me at the *same* moment Bougainville is flushed up from the depths. And so, suddenly, the civil war provides a kind of a tension to everything else that's being described. Also, that naive voice is playful, fun. It was liberating, after the constipated word drawings I was doing in the previous drafts.

CW: That is fascinating, and to me it seems completely natural. I can easily understand how all of that happened— and yet it's so mysterious, it's almost inexplicable, isn't it?

LJ: In a way you don't really want to know, do you?

CW: No, and it doesn't matter, I suppose. You end up sort of making up a story about how you wrote the book afterwards, don't you? Can I go back to your earlier writing life—you began writing in your twenties, I think. Do you remember what that first impulse was?

LJ: The first time I actually entertained the idea of becoming a writer? Well, there are a lot of ways of describing that and none of them, on their own, get to the nub of it. So I'll put a whole lot of things forward here. First of all, books weren't mysterious things in the household I grew up in. My mother knew where the gold was. She knew it was in the library, and we were all led to the doors of this magnificent library from an early age. That's the first thing—books were in my life.

CW: But you weren't an especially bookish kid?

LJ: No, it was all sport for me. But still, compared to all my mates, I read and they didn't have books. But when I was nineteen—this is just one element of this whole thing—I got meningitis rather badly. Three people in New Zealand got it that year. The other two died.

CW: Wow.

LJ: And in two weeks I went from being incredibly fit—very, very fit—to walking around on a cane and having to rest after fifty metres.

CW: How terrifying.

LJ: Yeah, it is. You see how quickly life can just drain out of you. It's amazing really. I really do think that changed me in some way. Not in a very obvious way but . . . I became more interested, I suppose, in more ethereal things, like poetry. I really, really liked poetry. I didn't understand it, although I thought I should. I remember reading e.e. cummings around that time, and not being able to make head nor tail of it, but I liked the idea that I was reading it.

Then I started a postgraduate degree in politics. I was studying seventeenth-century English, the civil war . . .

there were an awful lot of political treatises that you had to decipher. It was another language, you know. I was living in Auckland, and one moment I'm reading this stuff and the next moment I'm writing a poem. It was the very first thing I ever wrote, and it was about Rangitoto, the island. That was pretty exciting, really. Terrible poem of course, rubbish. I wrote other poems, you know—the sea dashing up the rocks, endless things about the sea. [*laughs*] I read a lot of Pablo Neruda around that time.

So that was just suddenly finding language as a toy, as a plaything. Making a mark on a sheet of paper the way a toddler in a highchair establishes his presence in the world by dragging a jammy finger down the wall. It was an act of self-assertion. Entertaining the idea of becoming a writer happens a bit later. But around that time I give up the postgraduate degree because I think, 'Well, this is more interesting.' So I go back to Wellington, get a job unloading aeroplanes. Most of the time I read novels, which used to really piss the other guys off, or one old boy in particular, who would sit behind his desk, grey jacket on, stack of pens in his pocket, looking out the window at the rain falling. And I would be reading a book, which annoyed him because it belittled his job in a funny sort of a way.

I read and read and read, and then I saved up for a fare to America.

From Los Angeles I got a month-long ticket on the Greyhound and I just journeyed.

You've got to imagine what New Zealand was like in the 1970s. There were no black people, for example; I had never seen a black person. And suddenly to arrive in this country that was so big and loud and noisy and extroverted . . . and in the newspapers they had these wonderful cultural pages—in those days the book culture there was second to none in the English language. Not now.

So, all that was exciting. Sitting on that bus looking out of the window at a landscape cinematically changing by the minute, and the person sitting next to me . . . you know, Americans talk. So there is a kind of a narration going on on my left-hand side, and a cinematic thing happening on the right. There are a lot of things happening, and you've got an option: you can write a letter, as you did in those days, or you can just start writing things down, as I did. And so, at that point, one finds one is living as a writer.

I end up in Schenectady in upstate New York, staying in this old derelict hotel—the State Hotel—filled with old people waiting to die, and Vietnam vets. Crazed, mad. And I'm on the top floor, writing my novel.

The novel was called *Eckstein* and it was about a photographer who can only look but can't really interact. And in a funny sort of way Eckstein is me, on that bus. It's kind of mapping out the emotional distance that this guy has in relation to things seen and heard. This was exciting: writing freehand, filling the wastepaper basket. At night, the Vietnam vets prowled the hallways. Often you would have to push one away in order to open the door.

I remember this woman who worked at the hotel, I thought she was a bit of an old bag—she was probably younger than me now—and she used to clear the paper basket. She looked at me one day and she said, 'Lloyd, honey, if you ever want to write a letter to somebody, you can write to me.' [*laughs*]

CW: She thought you were writing letters and throwing them away?

LJ: She assumed I was writing letters, because what else would those words be? But in a way I should have followed her advice. I probably would have learned more about writing if I'd thought about what she said, thought about writing her a letter that she never saw, about what I was thinking and doing and seeing and hearing.

Anyway, at that point I'm telling myself—but not the world—'I'm a writer.' I'm twenty-four. And then I thought, well how does one become a writer? There were no writing schools I was aware of and it probably wouldn't have suited me if there were. Temperamentally, I wouldn't have been right for it because I'm not a good student. I have to learn in my own way.

But at the start of that bus trip, quite randomly, I pick up a book in San Diego. It's called *Young Hemingway*, about his years up until the age of twenty. I could really relate, because here is somebody who has already lived the life that I'm living right now. I sort of read it like an instruction manual. He got a job as a newspaper man, on the *Toronto Star* or whatever it was. I thought, 'Ah, that's what I've got to do. I've got to get a job as a newspaper man.' So when I got back to New Zealand I became a reporter, which was a very, very good thing to do. And I wrote in the hours before I went to work.

CW: In an interview you mentioned a Saul Bellow novel that changed what you were working on. What was it?

LJ: Oh yes, in Schenectady. Quite near the hotel was a very good bookshop. There is a great serendipity involved in just picking up the books that are right for you at that time. I wandered across there—this was when I was still convinced by my genius—and I just happened to pull out this book and I opened it up at random. It was *Humboldt's Gift*. And everything that was wrong about my book was right about this. It just had the smell of life on the page, and it had voice. People were bursting out of the pages. It had music. I wouldn't say it was deflating, it was exciting. On that same day I bought Susan Sontag's *On Photography*. And—I'm sure it's the case with you, that the big leaps you make are from the books you happen to pick up. It all seems like it was meant to be, in a curious sort of a way.

CW: Yes! And you wonder what would have happened if you hadn't picked it up! It does seem so crucial, every time, that it was *that* book, doesn't it? I had a young writer contact me yesterday, he's nearing the end of his first novel and having a hard time, and he asked me what I thought he should read to help him finish it. It's an impossible question. What one needs is so personal, I could never advise him.

LJ: Yeah, that's where there's more mystery. He has to go into the library and wander around and have something catch his eye for some reason, and speak to him at that moment in time.

CW: Yes, speak to him about *his* book, connect for him in a way that I would never be able to detect. So, the idea of voice seems to be crucial for you. You've talked a lot about voice being the key to writing.

LJ: I think so. It comes down to how you view language, and making a distinction between words as mere conveyers of information, and words as musical notes. It's a big, big difference.

With voice, language is particular to every individual. We all speak in a slightly different way and we use our words in a slightly different way. Those words lock us into the world in a particular way. That particular way is what contributes to literature. We don't all have the same experiences. We've got to find the voice that speaks of that unique experience. Inevitably then, if you take that view, voice is central—and it comes right back to that vitality you alluded to. That energy, that reason to tell. It all comes back to satisfying the question of voice.

CW: It's very difficult to explain the concept of voice, isn't it? I think a lot of people see it in terms of the character's voice, not the voice of the book. How does one explain it?

LJ: Well, it's not the voice we speak with, it's the voice we think with. It's the interior life brought to the surface. Obviously the story has to be done through language, but it's not the voice we might whisper. It comes back to the advice of that woman in the hotel: 'Why don't you write to me?' Pico Iyer once said writing should have the intimacy of a letter. I think he is right. You should feel, as a reader, that you are being singularly addressed, you know, quietly.

CW: Are you always writing to someone?

LJ: I should be. That's another way of getting that vitality into it, I think, the idea of a piece of writing being addressed. Otherwise, why else is it being told? Even if the reader is a phantom in your own mind, perhaps you have to adopt the position that you are telling someone.

After all, language is an act of persuasion. Who are we trying to persuade? The phantom reader. How can I make you see this hill the way I see it? I will use language to create the picture so you can only see it the way I see it—an act of persuasion.

CW: Do you need a lot of confidence for that persuasion?

LJ: I guess so. That's an interesting point, because when my writing is at its crappiest—which no one ever sees—there is a degree of passivity sitting behind it. It's like there's no determination to make it believable, there's no inner belief in it. It may be that in those instances, if I did think in terms of addressing it to somebody, it would suddenly have that little raft of air under it.

CW: In your master class you said something intriguing: that 'the writer's fidelity must not be to the eye'. The fidelity is not to what is seen.

LJ: Did I say that?

CW: I thought it was very interesting, because it runs counter to so much of what one is taught—and I've taught it myself— which is to 'see it in your head, like a film'.

LJ: Yeah. Well, one of the discoveries I have made was that . . . initially I used to write fairly cinematically. So my sentences were loaded with detail, a lot of visual detail. I thought that's what was important: providing word pictures. It wasn't until I read people like Carver in the eighties, a lot of those guys—Tobias Wolff, Richard Ford, people like that—that I understood voice is the thing.

At that point I began to close my eyes, and write with a pen. Writing then became a kind of an aural thing, rather than a visual thing. Even now, like a lot of writers I suppose, I tend to write the first few pages in freehand. Because if I write straight onto a screen, I'm looking at what I'm writing, I'm not hearing it. It comes back to the voice thing. I've got to be . . . I'll be seduced by the sentence magically appearing on the screen and some other critical factor comes into play: Oh, is it any good? Oh no, I should go back and take that brick out and put a new one in here. That's not a way to proceed, no. So yeah, the fidelity, the fidelity has to be all the time to the voice.

CW: What about the creation of character?

LJ: What about it? [*laughs*]

CW: That comes to you through voice as well?

LJ: Yeah, it does, but character reveals itself in interaction. Character reveals itself in what that person sees, what they think, how they respond to the situation at hand. I mean, I don't think you need to fully kit out a character in the first page, say what they look like and give their back story and history. None of that is interesting.

It's more interesting, I think, that every character starts off as a mystery and slowly reveals themselves. That's why we read. Why are we sitting in this café with this person who is miserable or has no money? What's going to happen to them next? We'll leave the café with them and see what happens. As you go on, it's through events, really, that character reveals itself. But I must say, I never really think about that.

It's a curious thing, because as a reader I actually quite like reading a bit of nineteenth-century description about what they're wearing, descriptions of faces—probably because

I can't do that. If I could, I suspect I would. But I don't think it's terribly important. I think the situation, and how they respond, is important. The reader decides what they look like. The reader needs more credit for bringing completion to a story. Leave a bit of space around it.

That was the great lesson from Carver, who learned it from Hemingway, of course. The reader does an enormous amount of work, enjoyably, in those stories. That's why we find them such powerful experiences. Without having that work to do, if all the work is done on our behalf, all we can do is sit as we would in the cinema with imagery sort of washing over us. There is nothing left to be done. It becomes a sensory experience. It doesn't become a creative act—reading is a creative act, when you are given the opportunity.

CW: Let's go back to *Mister Pip* for a bit. You referred to Matilda's voice as playful, and you've spoken before about the need for playfulness on the writer's part. But given the very sad subject matter you are dealing with, this can be a difficult concept to understand. Can you tell me about the role of playfulness for you?

LJ: I probably don't mean it in quite the sense you have taken it. I'm thinking about in terms of a readiness by the writer. A combination of playfulness and intense concentration—two impossible things to hold at the same time. It's a lightness in oneself, a sense that anything can go, anything can happen here. Don't predetermine anything. Be prepared to be surprised by what just sails out of you onto that page and go with it. That's what I mean by playfulness.

CW: A kind of experimentalism?

LJ: That's what play is, isn't it? Just playing around, seeing what will happen, trying something out. I think that's when you flush something out that you couldn't otherwise arrive at. I couldn't possibly have sat down and said, 'Right, I'm going to write from the perspective of a Bougainvillean girl from the age of twelve to thirty-something. Now, who else will be in this? Oh yes, a charismatic white teacher.' No, it would never have happened. So, playfulness kind of takes you there.

CW: It must have been exciting when you realised you had this young girl's life to write from. Were you daunted by that?

LJ: I remember one day going to a publisher's party in Wellington. I was driving down with a poet friend and he said, 'What are you working on?' I said, 'I'm writing this thing from the perspective of a twelve-year-old black girl.' Then I burst out laughing—because it just seemed so improbable. Yeah, it was exciting, and it hasn't happened that often. There have been a few moments where it just seems to happen magically.

Halfway through writing that book I had to go down to Central Otago to work on a documentary film. I was on the brink of saying no, I couldn't do it, because I couldn't give up this thing, it was happening in such an extraordinary way. Then I thought, 'Oh, I need the money.' So I went, and I found myself getting up very early in the mornings.

It was winter, six o'clock or something like that. I would be walking around, and the air down there is very dry and incredibly cold, very cold. And the book was just pulling me. It was like being spoken to. It was almost like I was just channelling this thing, you know? I somehow got into a zone, a very special place. I'm resisting saying things like, 'I was given the story', or 'It was a gift,' or any bullshit like that, because I also worked hard for it. But nonetheless, in this final form, it was a kind of a magical transaction.

CW: Amazing. Have you ever had that again?

LJ: I've had moments. I haven't had it for the whole duration of a book. Most of the time, when a writing project is going well, as I said earlier, things will connect in ways that were just meant to be. You find yourself utterly amazed at how this thing is writing itself. You are just a kind of co-pilot. It's a curious thing.

CW: Do you always recognise when things are connected? With the fresco of words in the bedroom, for example, and then the twelve-year-old Bougainvillean girl—did you think, 'Yes, these are part of the same thing'? Or did you think, 'Now I'm going to work on this girl and leave that bedroom thing aside'?

LJ: I was quite prepared to leave the room, because it hadn't worked. But then at a certain point in the writing, when Mr Watts is talking about his wife Grace being pregnant, it suddenly just became clear. 'Ah, of course. They will create the room for the unborn child.'

In a funny sort of a way, maybe at a subconscious level, perhaps the narrative was always driving towards such a point. Who can say, really? That's why, when we discard stuff, whole drafts of stuff, it's not a waste. We've uncovered material that will find its way into something at some later point.

CW: Have you ever thrown a whole book away?

LJ: Oh God, yeah. Yeah. I mean, most of what I write is absolute crap.

CW: You must write quickly, then. You've published a lot of books—do you mean you throw stuff away as you go, or you've written a whole book and then thought, 'No, that's no good'?

LJ: I have done that. I usually don't . . . you know, I wouldn't call it 'a book'. I would think, I've written hundreds of pages of something that has been forced onto the page. It's been hard labour. You always know, actually, when you wake up in the morning. I always write first thing in the morning, and if I lie there for a minute longer than I need to, I always know, 'This is a sign things aren't going too well are they, Lloyd? You'd better own up to that fact.' [*laughs*]

CW: But I feel like that all the time! Do you push through that feeling, or is it a real signal that you've got to chuck stuff out?

LJ: Well, you just keep banging your head against the wall and you find out what's wrong one way or another. I do think sticking with it is terribly important. I don't think when the going gets tough that you can just walk away from it for a couple of weeks and think taking a leave of absence is somehow going to cure the problem. I really do think you've just got to keep at it, keep picking away at it. And at some point you will get some clarity.

It may come from a moment of acknowledging, 'No, this is all wrong. This is completely wrong,' and just pushing it aside. And like I said earlier, often there is a little moment of discovery too—when you know exactly what's wrong with it. And then suddenly you are off on a different course.

CW: Can we talk about your ease writing from the point of view of female characters? You seem to do it very naturally, which isn't always the case for other writers.

LJ: Well, I wouldn't describe it as an ease. But, first of all, I just make no distinction. Why should one? Literature deals with the particularities of an individual, and that individual is only known to us, the writer, and will only reveal him or herself as everything progresses in the writing.

This notion that men cannot, should not, write women characters is completely anti-literature. It's absurd. Anyone who believes that just doesn't understand literature. The whole ability to imagine the other goes right to the core of writing, really, and the value of literature.

I think we get caught up in the generalities. The media is very good at appealing to and dealing in generalities. That's what it does. But literature pulls us back from those group positions, tribal positions, to the perspective of the individual, which should be the most representative of humanity. Not groups and affiliations, and particularly not those who want to put fences around themselves and say, 'Do not come in here. You don't understand this.' What absolute horseshit!

Who actually ever understands another person, anyway?

In the case of *Mister Pip*, for example, someone will say, 'Oh, how did you manage to get into the skin of a fourteen-year-old black girl?' And I say, 'I didn't.' I got into the skin of a person who happened to be called Matilda and who happens to be a Bougainvillean girl. Does she exist? No, she doesn't. She only exists on the page. And her existence, whether you believe it or not, depends on my ability to be persuasive, which comes back to my use of language.

It's not like I'm trying to depict someone who already exists out there. She doesn't. And I don't think people who advocate this discussion around who you can write about, white people writing about black people, men writing about women—I really, honestly don't think they actually understand what it's all about. I really don't. As you can tell from the tone of my voice, I find it intensely irritating.

CW: I agree with you completely. Writers should be allowed to write from any perspective—but there are many who can't, who do it very badly. They can't fully imagine the other.

LJ: Well, in that case they suddenly think, 'Oh, I'm writing about a woman . . . I've gone from cats to dogs' or something like that, right? But that's a false boundary. It's completely artificial.

Why is it thought perfectly normal for a man to be able to get into the skin of an axe murderer, but not the skin of a woman? What makes us have some affinity with axe murderers that we don't with women?

The point is that identity lives on the page. That's where it all lives. It's not trying to draw down from life. The playground is on the page, in language. It makes things exist or it doesn't, and that's where it works. And this person called Sally, Helen or Angela, she's . . . the sum of her is just the detail that's provided on the page. It's not some imperfect facsimile of somebody called Angela or Sally, who already exists out here, that we are drawing some comparison between the two.

CW: You've several times quoted a remark Samuel Beckett made about James Joyce, that is very important to you. But I'm not sure I fully understand it. Beckett said, Joyce's writing 'is not about something, it is that something itself'. Can you talk about this a little more?

LJ: Yes. He's not writing about something—'about' suggests an object. In other words, it thrusts you into the task of describing something that's already there. But the *something* is emerging from the actual writing. So it's not starting with any objective in mind, but an objective actually results from the act of writing. It's a subtle distinction.

CW: Is it partly also about being inside the work rather than outside it, approaching it from a distance?

LJ: Yes, I think that's a good way of describing it. If you're writing about something, you can see it all clearly in your mind, but that's the antithesis of what we were talking about earlier. You can't see it clearly in your mind, but something is emerging. And as you're putting words down, more clarity is achieved. So you're writing something that's going to deliver you somewhere, rather than writing about something. You get it.

CW: I think I get it. But it's an interesting thing. You could spend a long time pondering it, I think. Which makes it more interesting.

LJ: I found that anecdote enormously liberating, actually. It's something I did instinctively, but when I read that, I felt, 'That's it! That's exactly my own modus operandi.'

CW: How do you know when your work in progress isn't just decorative—that it has the necessary urgency you spoke of earlier, that need to be told?

LJ: Well, I think the act of writing begins as an act of engagement with something, not necessarily something you can see, but with ideas. For example, my work is all about engagement with identity. If I look back at everything I've written that is of any use—it's always been a grappling with or an engagement with identity. That's always been the starting point. So, if that is what you're really grappling with, however decorative the surface might be, it's going to have some fairly rich underpinnings. Identity slides around. It's not fixed.

How do we know if something is more than simply decorative? Well, it's like a reef. You'll see it, just sticking out now and then. There's some undertow there. There is something on the surface that's kind of in communication with something else you can't see very clearly, but you feel. So it has a kind of richness.

And I think it offers a texture too, when you are really trying to work an idea out, you're not actually putting it on the page, but the language is dancing along on the surface, while it's also hinting at some other layer. I think that's when you've got something going. There is some dynamic there that's not one-dimensional, it's not just one layer of decorative stuff.

CW: When did you figure out that identity was what all your work had been about?

LJ: When I wrote the memoir.

CW: Oh, that recently? Do you think that having discovered that, it will now disappear from your work?

LJ: It already has. It is very strange actually, to have this kind of ball of irritability rolling around inside of you, and it's all about identity.

CW: Do you work every day, and at the same time?

LJ: Mornings belong to me, as a rule. It's always been like that. And sometimes very early in the morning. I like what Toni Morrison had to say about the twilight hour and the twilight state of four in the morning, that she's neither asleep nor is she fully awake. It just seems like the door is open. The door to the subconscious is just a little bit more open than it would be at any other time of the day. You can hear more clearly, which is important if you subscribe to the notion of voice. I work not for very long, really. It depends where a project is at. In the writing of a first draft, I don't think you need long. An hour, two hours. But once you have it, once you've got that mound of clay, it's hard to drag yourself away from it. Then you can just play around for hours on end, eight hours, nine hours. That's a different stage.

CW: How has the writing life fitted with making enough money to live on?

LJ: Well, that pattern of working was forced on me, in a way, because of the working day. I had to write around the margins, plus the children and family life and all that kind of thing. I've worked as a freelance writer for a long time. And *Mister Pip* obviously made a big difference.

Now, to be honest, I don't really care. I remember a guy I knew at Hutt Valley High School. He went to university and got a law degree, then he ended up on Wall Street and made a bit of money, and then lost a bit of money. Then he ended up in Israel as a Lubavitch Hasid, living in a very religious town in the north of Israel. He's married to a really gorgeous Yemeni woman, and has an army of kids, I think about six kids. I said to him, 'Tony, how the hell do you make your living?' He said, 'I don't know.' He said, 'God provides.'

And I thought, 'Fuck, that's terrific! I'm going to adopt that approach.' And so I pretty much have. Something always happens. Something rolls around, a project comes up, some money comes in, you write something that makes more money than you expected. It just happens. And so I tend to make sure I have a decent amount of time for the writing, because that's the thing.

And God provides. [*laughs*]

Photo: Patrick Cummins

ASK MALCOLM Knox how many books he's written and he has to think carefully, looking to the ceiling as he whisperingly tallies them up. At the time of this interview at his home in Sydney's Queenscliff, the count had reached twenty-seven: five novels (one published pseudonymously), twelve books of non-fiction, eight ghost-written autobiographies and 'another two corporate books'. He published his first books—the novel *Summerland* and the cricket book *Taylor and Beyond*—at the age of thirty-three. When we spoke in 2014, he was forty-seven.

His work across all forms has received consistently high praise, garnering prestige and prizes for both fiction and non-fiction. Patrick Ness, writing in *The Guardian*, called Knox 'shrewd and whip-smart'. Comparing his *Jamaica* to Tim Winton's *Breath*, published the same year, Ness captured Knox's gaze with this summary: 'If Winton is an aria, Knox is early Rolling Stones.'

Brought up on Sydney's affluent, conservative North Shore, Knox excelled academically and on the sporting field in the private-school world of his youth, and seemed destined for a conventional, alpha-male professional life until he stepped sideways from the law into literature and journalism in his early twenties.

He speaks of this time as a strikingly formative one, and it appears to have given rise to much of his fiction, which has often dealt with the murky underside of male privilege and friendship.

The probing intelligence he brings to bear in examining male behaviour in his fiction—at school, in sport and later in the water in surf culture—is also evident in his journalism. In book form it has ranged across subjects as diverse as the jury system, the mining boom and the illicit drug trade. As a cricket columnist he is widely respected not just for his knowledge but a poetic sensibility to the history, subtlety and nuances of the game that resonate far beyond the field.

He is also an accomplished feature writer and investigative journalist, evidenced by his two Walkley Awards—one for his exposé of the fraudulent author, Norma Khouri, and a second for an account of the ugly circumstances surrounding the cruise ship death of Dianne Brimble.

Knox has ghostwritten a number of bestselling sporting biographies—for cricketer Adam Gilchrist, footballer

Ben Cousins and horse trainer Bart Cummings among others—and has written and spoken eloquently on the complex ethical and artistic task of the ghostwriter. In this interview he speaks intriguingly of the way the ghosted voice must both capture and invent the 'real' voice of the subject, and how his thinking on this has bled into his fiction over time.

His novels include *Summerland*, *A Private Man*, *Jamaica* and *The Life*. Published in 2011, *The Life* was an adventurous stylistic departure from his previous fiction, creating a vibrantly colloquial, erratic voice for the washed-up surfer Dennis Keith, inspired in part by the surfer Michael Peterson. Since this interview he has published another novel, *The Wonder Lover*.

Though he has contributed substantial time and energy to writers' organisations (as a Copyright Agency board member, for example, or on various judging and grant assessment panels), he shows little interest in the approbation of anyone but his readers—he is scathing, for example, about the 'sheep-like' devotion to literary prize lists as arbiters of what to read, or of quality.

I have crossed paths professionally with Knox often over the past decade—we share a publisher and our novels have often been released at around the same time—but have only got to know him a little better over the past couple of years.

In conversation he is intelligent and thoughtful, speaking slowly and quietly with an even-toned, almost deadpan delivery that at first can come across as guardedness. But this impression is soon undercut, first by his quick, wry sense of humour and second by his openness, indeed his *un*guardedness, in answering questions on which other writers might be more evasive, such as the issue of competitiveness, or the closeness of his writing to real life.

I have interviewed Knox twice before, and each time have been struck by the quite forensic way he will parse a question as he answers, considering all angles and often challenging, then defending, his own position as he articulates it. One can see, in this methodical style, a trace of the legal mind that might at one stage have led him to the bar—and in both his journalism and his fiction, to uncovering material that others might prefer stayed buried.

CW: You've published twenty-seven books in the space of a couple of decades. What's the relationship between the different kinds of writing you do?

MK: Well, I don't feel there's much relationship between the fiction and the non-fiction, say. Certainly my methods of working are quite different, and the times at which I'm working on them are quite different. There's a different impulse behind doing it—obviously the impulse for some non-fiction books is purely financial, which is definitely not the case with writing fiction. I think there are probably relationships between the two that I'm not quite aware of. One example that I only thought about later was the overlap between ghostwriting Ben Cousins' autobiography and writing *The Life*.

I had ghosted about three books before I wrote *The Life*, and I'd started developing an idea about voice in those ghosted books. The research for ghostwriting is an oral process, and there's a version you do in which the moment the words are uttered, and then written, it becomes, in a way, the 'official untrue'. It's a performance.

It's not just about stuff the person will give up versus their secrets—it's a way of talking that they perform, which is different from their internal voice and their internal life. Ben Cousins is a very honest person, and was wanting to tell people the story of his drug addiction, but he didn't have the words for it really, and I could only give him the words up to a point, because I could only try to approximate his words.

So all this opened up a space for a character like DK in *The Life*. It wasn't cause and effect, because I'd started writing *The Life* before I met Ben Cousins, and DK's very different from Ben Cousins. But it was more that in the overlap of that period, I thought, 'Oh, there are some commonalities here'. And there were times I was telling myself, 'I'm writing the truth here, even though it's a made-up person and it's fiction, this is the truth that somebody like Ben can't get out.'

CW: It's interesting you say that. You're so good at replicating ordinary speech in all your novels, but especially in the voice of *The Life*. One interview I read did make a link between your talent for rendering speech and all that listening you've done in your ghostwriting work. The suggestion was that the ghostwriting has developed your ear for a certain vernacular and idiom.

MK: I don't think I had heard a voice like DK's; that was a composite of voices I'd heard in the water, surfing, and in everyday life, more than a voice I was working with professionally. But that said, doing those ghostwritten books you do think a lot about idiom, you think a lot about a person's way of speaking. And you work extremely hard, not just on the vocab, but the entire package of rhythm and syntax and usage that everybody has which is different. The freedom of fiction that I tried to exploit in *The Life* was the freedom to write a voice in its raw form.

When you're ghosting, it's not just a matter of capturing the person's voice, it's a matter of capturing their written voice, such as it is. So you're halfway—you know, a very poorly ghostwritten book is one that will read as if it's been written by Julian Barnes, because the person speaking, the 'author' of the book, will never speak that way. But at the same time it's not a verbatim representation because that would be incoherent. So in making someone up such as Dennis in *The Life*, I could go in that verbatim direction because the beautiful conventions—or non-conventions—of fiction permit you to. Readers may not always permit it, but the art form permits it.

CW: Given your enormous output, you clearly write very quickly. What are the effects of writing fast—good or bad?

MK: Well the good effects . . . I go back to when I had a number of attempts at writing novel-length fiction before my first novel was published. A common failing of those was that they took a long time to write, and during the time I wrote them all sorts of influences and new ideas came to bear on me, and so they were inconsistent in tone and voice, even in genre, whereas *Summerland* I wrote very, very quickly. I wrote the first draft in about six weeks. That and *The Life* were both voice novels, and when you're doing a voice novel, I think it is really beneficial to write quickly.

Summerland, in the fictional sense, is all spoken over the course of one night. And the six weeks it took me to do the first draft, in writer's time that's about one night. I do remember in that six-week period just having that voice in my head the whole time. *The Life* took about ten weeks to do the first draft, and I remember then, too, just having this one voice in my head.

It must be what having a mental illness is like, having another voice talking to you all the time, and if not talking to you, interpreting your own thoughts into its speech. I don't think I started *speaking* like Dennis, but in order to speak I had to reconvert what was in my head to me again.

But the downside of writing quickly is—I think it probably works against you if you're wanting to write, say, a book like Richard Flanagan's *The Narrow Road to the Deep North*. Let's just pick it as an example because I've read it recently. You can't write a book like that quickly; your heart rate has to be slowed right down and you have to maintain concentration over a very long period. You have to inhabit that book, and have that book inhabiting you, over a very long stretch of time. And maybe just because this is the way I am, or maybe it's because of the amount of work I do, I can't imagine having the power to write a book like that over seven years.

CW: You once told me that to write a novel, 'I have to stay in that dreamlike state, and stay in the voice'. It sounds like that still holds? You can't step in and out of it while you're doing other stuff?

MK: Yeah, I think it does still hold. In the redrafting I can go in and out, but not in the first draft. And, you know, I'll have—in the last twenty-five years I've had numerous false starts to novels. I don't know if this is the cause of it, but the manifestation of that is getting into that flow for ten, fifteen, eighteen or thirty thousand words, then letting it drop, going away—and then coming back and finding the fire has completely gone out.

CW: Back to the books you wrote before *Summerland*, did you just put them away? It seems quite a rare capacity, for a young writer to understand that they're not ready yet.

MK: I don't think it was a sign of maturity or self-knowledge. I think it was, first of all, having a deep conviction that they weren't any good, and secondly just being overtaken by a new idea. There's no real difference between the book where I got to the end of a hundred-thousand-word first draft and left it behind because I was swept up by something new, and something I'd written fifteen thousand words of and dropped. In both cases I never went back to them, I lost interest in them; just because one is nominally finished and the other isn't, it doesn't make any difference. I saw them all as being a long, long, *long* way from being finished, and ultimately not worth the bother.

There have also been plenty of those books since I've been published, as well. Even since *The Life* there have been a couple of forays that I've got to the end of and just put them aside.

CW: You obviously have no qualms about putting books away. To me it would be a devastating decision, to give away even a half-written novel, because I'm so slow.

MK: Yeah, well, maybe that's a good thing *or* a bad thing about writing very fast—you don't become so bonded to the thing that you feel you have to keep on doing it.

CW: I love the idea of that looseness. You must have a very solid trust that something else will come along?

MK: No. I don't have any trust at all! But maybe I'm loose because if I can't write a decent novel again, I don't feel that's the end of the world. If what I've done is the end of my published fiction, then that's a lot more than I thought I'd be capable of, and—I would be disappointed, but it wouldn't be the end of the world.

CW: You've written a great deal about group behaviour, across all your work—as a sports writer, in your jury room book, and in the novels. What interests you about group behaviour? What does it offer you, especially as a novelist?

MK: As a reader, I'm always more interested in the relationships between people on the page than descriptive or atmospheric writing. As a point of contrast, look at somebody like Gail Jones. I read her work and I admire it because of her artistry, I admire it in the way you admire things that you know you couldn't do. But she's at the opposite pole from me, in that her interests are kind of hermetic, her people don't depend on their relationships with other people in the way that my characters do. And as you say, my characters tend to depend totally on, and exist through, their relationship to each other. Why that is, I don't really know—I don't necessarily live that way, I live a lot of my days without talking to anybody, and I'm not a particularly social creature. I think it's just that as a reader, that's always what I want to know: what's happening between these people.

CW: You're often looking at a pack mentality among men, sometimes deeply misogynistic men—and again, not just in the fiction. I was heartbroken by the very perceptive feature you wrote on the perpetrators in the Dianne Brimble case.

MK: Yeah . . . and recently, I've been really fascinated—to an out-of-proportion degree—by that Simon Gittany murder case. I've been totally gripped by that.

CW: What are you trying to get to the bottom of in looking at these sorts of men?

MK: Well, I don't know. In a sense you're asking me to do the impossible, which is to analyse myself. It certainly comes from experience, things I've witnessed. *Jamaica*'s probably the most extreme example of what you're talking about. That is not written in a true-to-life way, it's a slightly cartoonish representation of the real women-hating stuff that goes on, for particular artistic purposes in that book.

Why am I drawn to exploring that? I don't really know. Other than that, I suppose, you're always drawn back to things that have caused you shock or trauma in your own life, and definitely, when I saw that kind of stuff in my university years

I was shocked, and I remain shocked. That this kind of stuff exists in a strata of society where, for a start, they should know better, but secondly these are people of influence and some importance.

So I suppose there is a sense of social outrage, or crusade . . . in the same way that you would want to uncover financial corruption, well you might want to uncover so-called moral corruption as well.

CW: It's interesting you say it is cartoonish or not true to life in *Jamaica*. I found *Jamaica* very difficult to read, and was shocked. But my husband said, 'I know those guys.' He recognised the way of talking, the things they said. He was appalled by it, but not shocked, as I was.

MK: I think it was cartoonish in that as I was creating a lot of stuff that those guys were saying, I wasn't thinking about what I had heard, I was thinking, 'What's the worst stuff I can make these people say? What's the most shocking stuff I can make them say?' That's why I feel it's cartoonish rather than naturalistic. It was me stylising these characters rather than—even in a fictional way—trying to remember in a naturalistic way. I was not even magnifying, I was inventing.

CW: Why was it important to invent that, rather than replicate reality?

MK: That's just what that book demanded. The people who've liked *Jamaica* most have been those who understood what it was—a comedy. Very black and highly stylised, but a comedy all the same. I saw *The Wolf of Wall Street* recently. There's a scene where Belfort is so fucked-up on Quaaludes that he spends several minutes working out how to roll himself down a flight of steps to get to his car, which he'll then crash. Half the audience was cringing and thinking how terrible this was. The other half (including me) was roaring with laughter. I'd say *Jamaica* provoked the same polarisation in response.

If you thought certain things in that book were plainly mimetic, you'd probably be covering your face and reading through your fingers, if at all. On the other hand, if you know that they're heightened for comic effect, but the kind of comedy that makes you slightly uncomfortable at the same time because it's not too far removed from reality, then you'll probably read it in the spirit that drove me to write it.

Returning to your question about groups, it's certainly been my experience, since a very young age, that people—let's say males, because that was mainly my experience—act differently under the influence of group chemistry. People are capable of much worse in a group than they would be as individuals, and they are capable of much better. So that interests me.

Am I conscious of it while I'm writing? No I'm not, but I do find it an ongoing fascination—the chemical change in a person when he becomes part of a group.

I just reread *Lord of the Flies* this week, which I hadn't read since school. I think I probably read it about three times in early high school. So that's nearly thirty-five years ago—and when I read it this week I thought, 'Wow, that book influenced me a lot more than I remember.' For these things we're talking about; groups of boys who you can imagine all being good kids on their own, being overtaken by the madness of the group. And that affects me in that book more than the madness of the external environment—it's not a return-to-nature book for me, it's a return to tribal behaviour.

CW: How much darkness can you get away with in a novel before a reader will turn away? I'm wrestling with this myself in my current work. Are you conscious of calibrating how much of this dark stuff you can do before a reader just puts the book down?

MK: No, I'm not conscious of it at all. You only find out later. [*laughs*] A friend of mine, who's read all my novels, said recently, 'Oh yeah, and then with *Jamaica*'—she didn't say, 'You lost me,' but she said something like, 'You just went so far out there, that weirded me out.' I can't remember her words but she told me this about five years after the reading of it. And I thought, 'Wow, really? Is that what I did?'

But then I know other people who say *Jamaica* is their favourite book of mine, and I have no doubt it's their favourite because of those extreme flashes. So you know, it takes all types.

CW: I find that quite comforting. Maybe I should just forget about those concerns and not censor it . . .

MK: I find that whenever I start thinking about what 'works', especially commercially . . . I have a friend who is the Australian Reading Public. She is a very dear friend, she's about sixty-five, reads a lot of fiction and her tastes match perfectly with what you might call the literary bestseller. You know, the Barbara Kingsolvers, or Anna Funder, could be Kate Grenville . . . that kind of literary bestseller. Her tastes are spot on. Publishers or agents should employ her as the lab rat of what works.

And I've had times when I've thought, 'Bugger it; now I'm going to write something that she'd like.' And you know, everything just shuts down. Because that's not the way it works. The books I've published have never been written with her in mind, and she has generally liked my work—but not as much as she would like those others, the kind that she's one of a hundred thousand people who tell each other about them, and fall in love with them.

One of the factors, to unpack it a bit further, is the whole likeability and identification-with-characters issue. The sense of entering a book hoping to find a friend, or an unforgettable person who you're just going to feel really happy to have spent time with. Seeking company in a book. But not only is that not how I can write, it's never been the way I've *read*.

CW: Do you think this likeability thing is a recent phenomenon? It drives me up the wall.

MK: I don't think it's recent at all, but it has certainly become almost a cult. A reading cult, that this is a basis on which to judge a book's quality. And of course it's oppressive to anybody who writes seriously, because if they write seriously they probably read seriously, and they know how many horrible characters there are in the great books.

But it's not as if the conventional likeable character is the only character that can sell a book. Look at *The Slap*.

CW: But it was a big talking point for that book, it became a kind of national contest, to vote for who you liked or who you didn't. Rather than looking at all the layers of that book, about stuff like the education system and class and all that stuff.

MK: I felt kind of insulted by all that discussion. I thought, 'Well, I read *The Slap* and it never crossed my mind whether these characters were likeable or unlikeable.' It just didn't pop up.

CW: Another idea that recurs across your writing is competition—the physical contest.

MK: Yeah. Well to me it's just a facet of what you were talking about earlier—you've got people in a group, seeing how they're relating to each other, and which situations will bring out some revelation or development in their character. I'll throw them into some kind of physical contest to see what that does.

It's obvious that this comes out of my experience as a person and professionally—I was a sports writer for about four years, and I played a lot of sport, and now in my journalistic work I've been focusing on sport again for the last two to three years.

CW: You write about it so vividly, the body and the intellect are really powerfully merged. What is it about the physicality that interests you?

MK: I don't see pursuits of the body as being not intellectual, not spiritual. I would find it a bizarrely naïve outlook if anybody in this day and age, since about the 1950s, were to characterise athletic pursuits as not involving the mind. People have no hesitation in writing about sex in a way that involves the spirit and the mind and the intellect, it just goes without saying. Well, snowboarding is the same. Or swimming, or cricket or anything—*walking*, you know.

And the physical contest can be a useful narrative device. It also interests me because for various cultural reasons, it's not a very heavily tilled field in literature, and I feel I might have a hope of bringing something that is slightly original to readers from it.

CW: Do you think you are a competitive person?

MK: Yes and no. You ask anybody that question, and there are people who just shy away from competition, who have almost a physical allergy to competition, and the reason, when you dig down, is that when that person gets in a competitive situation they want to *kill* everybody. They're *so* competitive that they're afraid of what it brings out in themselves.

I'm not like that. I enjoy a ritualised competition. So when I played a lot of sport, I was known as someone who was completely placid and non-competitive off the field but then would have what you call white-line fever, was highly competitive on the field. I am probably still like that, not competitive in general life, but put me in some kind of clearly defined contest and I'll be very competitive.

CW: I wonder if men have a healthier relationship with competition than women. Among women writers, for example, there seems to me a deep, deep shame about any possibility of competitive feelings.

MK: Well, I've just bifurcated life into competitive things and non-competitive things but of course it's not really like that. Literary competition is a great example of that grey area, where—what is it? Writing is not competitive, it's the *opposite* of competition, and yet there is competition for sales, competition for prizes, for recognition.

And when it comes to that, I'm in a sort of constant tussle between instinct and commonsense. Commonsense is always telling me that a) this is not a competitive pursuit, and b) I've been on prize judging committees and funding allocation committees, and once you've been on them you know that this is not something to be taken seriously at all. And yet, I am one of those white-line fever people who, once you put me in a ring or on a court, I'll want to win like anything. So, when people say your book is 'in contention' or on a shortlist, all of a sudden somebody *has* put a ring around you, and you want to win.

I play tennis nowadays about once every two years; I've got nothing invested in it at all, and I was never any good at tennis. And yet if you put me on a tennis court, unless I'm up against somebody really good, I'll be trying everything to win. That's *tennis*, where I've got nothing invested! But it's because when I'm on the court, I can do something about it. When you're in a literary competition you're just a bystander in the hands of a process that you don't respect, and very often people you don't respect.

CW: The thing about tennis is that the point of it is to win, whereas with writing . . .

MK: Yes—winning is not the point. It's a bastardisation of the point of literature, so it's inherently corrupt. That's all the commonsense side of it. But you know, the old hoof starts to beat up and down, and you snort and scratch, and you realise suddenly that you've been tricked into thinking you're in a competitive sphere.

I do find the procedure that attaches to prizes very frustrating, and I get frustrated by the unquestioning and sheep-like attitude towards the prestige of a prize. It's an authority-loving instinct, to say, 'Oh, that's the Booker prize, I'll rush out and read that book now.'

I was in a bookshop in London last year and heard these people talking with the owner about a book, and they were all agreeing that the book—I'd never heard of the author—was, 'Oh well, it's very good, it's the best book by far, but *she's not really ready for a Booker yet.*' [*laughs*]

You know, you want to have a wash after hearing that. And I'm sure people who win them can feel the same way. I know people who've won prizes and they're obviously happy to have won, but they still feel like they want to have a wash.

CW: Let's talk about the schism between the private and the public, which is another interest of yours, both in fiction and non-fiction. It loomed especially large in the Norma Khouri story. What's so interesting to you about that hidden self?

MK: Well to me that's what fiction *is*—the private lives of ordinary people. That's why we call a certain type of novel an autobiographical novel rather than a memoir, even though every word of it may be literally true, because it's interior, it's secret, it's unverifiable, it wouldn't stand up in court. So that's a fundamental starting point, that the private and the secret is the essence of it.

And I think, from growing up in a very staid, rule-bound conservative world, you're obviously going to be drawn to the idea of façade, and what's behind the façade.

Your moments of becoming wise to the world are very often moments of—'Wow, that's the headmaster of our school, and I know he's a secret alcoholic.' Or, 'That's my friend's mother, and I've found out that she's having an affair.' When you're in that world, where being the headmaster, being the parent are very important status-filled positions, and the codes of behaviour are given high prestige, there are going to be moments of enormous excitement for you as a kid in the pulling down of that.

So I'm always interested in stories of double lives, and Norma Khouri was a great case of someone who led a double life in a very extreme way. And you know, I'm aware of it in myself. With Norma, my attitude was, 'Don't try to bullshit a bullshitter.' I felt a kind of kinship with her. You know, you're always going back into yourself and asking questions, and I think that doubleness has been there at different stages of my life, so it's fertile ground . . .

CW: What kind of doubleness do you find in yourself?

MK: Well, when I was a kid, I was captain of my prep school and senior school, but I was also quite a naughty kid, secretly naughty, and I had official roles but I knew who I really was.

And that could be traumatic at times, trying to reconcile the two—it led to getting into trouble, and big sort of personal crises, of just getting caught and exposed, and then the question is, 'What do you do now, do you 'fess up to who you really are, or do you try to hold the line?'

I certainly felt that I was on a certain path, but by the age of about twenty or twenty-one, I thought, 'I'm not going to be able to follow this path. I can do as I've been doing, but I'm always going to be repeating this drama of maintaining a pose.'

CW: Was there a fear that your real self was always threatening to burst through?

MK: Yes, and that I was going to get caught, again and again.

CW: What was this path set out before you?

MK: Well, if it was scripted it would have been studying law and going to the bar and going into politics or whatever—it gets a little bit vague beyond that point—but that was a pathway that was there. There were a few reasons I rejected that. One was, going back to your earlier question, a fear of competition, a bit of a fear of failure.

But the other was a fear of *success*—of getting to that point and knowing, 'I'm a bit of a fraud, I'm not who people think I am, who people want me to be, and eventually I'll be stripped and exposed.' I'd be like one of those politicians we read about all the time who's fallen from grace.

CW: Is writing a way of playing out those different parts of yourself?

MK: Yes it is. It is. Certainly in various books I've gone out on that path—*Summerland* was probably the book where I've done that the most, imagined someone like the me I could have been if I'd continued on that path. It's a sort of imagining of how everything could have turned out.

CW: I want to ask you about the powerful mothers in your fiction. It doesn't get remarked upon much, but in, say,

A *Private Man*, the mother is a very central, powerful figure. And Mo, DK's mother in *The Life*, is an incredible operatic invention. Where do they come from, these women?

MK: Well, they're not like my mum at all. But both of my grandmothers were very strong characters, and we had a family matriarch on my dad's side who was principal of Pymble Ladies' College for thirty-three years. She was one of these pre-feminist feminists, a very high-achieving woman, a very strong and dominating woman who didn't encourage the same in the girls under her care. A kind of Margaret Thatcher type, who wasn't married.

In my family there's been a strong streak of women of stronger moral fibre than the men, women of greater steadiness and leadership capacity and, you know, goodness. And men who were extremely passionate and tempestuous and really up and down. Throughout the family there has been this contest between male passion and emotionality, and female steadiness and strength, while still playing out against the underlay of traditional gender roles.

CW: That's fascinating.

MK: But the gender roles are taken very seriously, you know; father's the breadwinner, but father's the emotionally up-and-down one, and riven with weaknesses. I've never really gone into it in writing—maybe it's one of the things I won't feel allowed to do while my parents are alive.

CW: But maybe it leaks through anyway?

MK: Yeah, it leaks through.

CW: You've had to deal with a fair bit of negative response to the fact that you write very close to life—like the reaction from the Michael Peterson fans who felt *The Life*'s DK was too closely based on him. You once said that writing from real life is more original than making something up, because the latter would necessarily be drawing on a common imagination. Most people would see it in the opposite way, that making things up is more original.

MK: Well, as a reader I'm drawn towards non-generic fiction which is very often based closely on life, and following the happenstance of life. I'm drawn much more towards that than to, say, science fiction and fantasy.

Some people will say, 'Look at the amazing imaginative reach of J.K. Rowling', or Tolkien or whoever. I don't see great imaginative reach in that kind of fiction. I see a substitution of one world for another, which—because it's got to communicate with its audience—relies on a deep level of familiarity.

The symbols of the created world must correspond with what's familiar, otherwise it can't work at all. So if the symbols have to correspond, then this is telling us what we already know, and the plot conventions must feed what we already know.

So yeah, I do think greater leaps of the imagination are required to find something in the real, rather than to sit down and be George R.R. Martin and invent a world.

CW: Given that, can you identify the process or the point at which the work separates from life, and becomes art?

MK: It's hard to talk about in a general sense, but I can talk about particular cases. They're pretty different.

The thing with *The Life* and the Michael Peterson stuff, that was just really annoying, like a blowfly. It was annoying that I was being criticised for basing a book on Michael Peterson and not being upfront about it, when I *was* totally upfront about it. The only constraint on my writing 'this is a book based on Michael Peterson', which is what I wanted to do, was that the story departs completely from Michael Peterson's life and a murder is committed which never happened, and characters come in who never existed.

So I end up creating a character that is a lot like Michael Peterson, except for the bits where it's not like him at all. And if you care, you can figure it out. The best response was from Michael's mother herself, who said she was having great fun spotting who was real, who wasn't real, what happened, what didn't happen.

Michael Peterson has since died, but he was still alive at the time, and a lot of people felt—not an ownership of him, but an ownership of the myths around him. There was a bit of a feeling that their territory was being encroached upon by somebody who didn't have pure motives.

So that's fairly easily explained. What's less easily explained is the other books where I've based characters on real people and then made them do things that never happened. And that goes back to *Summerland*, where the two main characters were based on real people, probably recognisably real to others who knew them, and yet everything they did in the book was made up.

So again, you have the situation where the people upon whom those characters were based said, 'That was kind of fun reading that, I could see it was based on me but I know I didn't do any of those things', but then they're confronted by others who say, 'Oh my God, is that what you really did? How can you bear this person exposing your secrets in this way?'

They just get tired of saying nothing's been exposed, and they end up, unfortunately, feeling: 'Everybody thinks this is me.'

I've always thought there have been three rings around this stuff—two harmless and one harmful. The harmless are the inner ring, who know who's who and what's what—and that may be a very small number of people. And then there is the outer ring, to whom you are complete strangers.

CW: And that outer ring doesn't know or care who's who and what's what.

MK: Exactly. But in the ambiguous middle ring are those who think they know you, and think they're getting to know you better through what they're reading in this book, and who can then affect you in some way. And they're the people who cause the problems.

I never knew if this happened, but I was very fearful of that middle ring with *A Private Man*, that people who vaguely knew my dad would think that I'd written about my father having a secret pornography obsession! I mean, I've never heard of anybody coming up to Dad and saying anything like that. It may have happened, he just wouldn't have told me.

CW: Do you have any sense of an audience or a kind of reader as you're working?

MK: You know, I used to. I used to have a pretty strong idea, just of someone who was very like me. Male or female, but about my age. Not a real person, but someone with a deep love of a certain kind of literary art; someone like me. And I suppose that's been weakened over time with the cruel realisation that the world is made up of people who are *not* like me. [*laughs*]

But I think my publisher Jane [Palfreyman] comes closest to embodying that person. She's somebody who's always got my work very well, and when she and I talk about other books, I really feel I'm talking to a kindred spirit. So she would probably be the nearest thing and has remained so. And you know, while it would be more commercially beneficial if the person I was on that level with was that other friend of mine I talked about before, if I'm just writing for Jane, and giving her pleasure or whatever it is she gets out of reading my work, then that'll do. And if her type are shrinking in numbers or reading less, then what can I do?

CW: This reminds me of something you said once: 'Writers write from faith, and sometimes put themselves through hell in the name of faith.' What is the nature of this faith?

MK: Sounds like I'd just come out of church! I can't remember saying that. Look, obviously writing is a leap of faith because you spend so much time thinking: 'Why the hell would anybody want to read this?' [*laughs*].

That's the first kind of faith, and then there are all those today's-marketplace leaps of faith, the bread-and-butter leap of faith, which is, 'How can I justify spending this many days or months or years on this when I'm probably working for a pay rate of less than a dollar an hour?'

I don't know if that was what I was referring to, but we know people who have put themselves through very hard times in terms of supporting themselves and their families because they're powered by the faith that it's going to be worthwhile in some way. None of it sounds very interesting.

CW: Why do you write, then? What are the rewards of writing a novel as opposed to a more surefire kind of book?

MK: It's so hard to answer that question, because it implies that you think I know the answer. I'm tormented by that question all the time. All I know is that when you're really on that roll, you can't get off it. The question dissolves in the solvent of whatever it is that's driving you. So, I don't like the question. I ask it only when I'm not writing. When I am writing, it's kind of like matter and anti-matter. That question, itself, is the threat.

CW: Okay, how about this question: When you've had a good day's writing, what has happened on the page, or in you, to make it good?

MK: Just that I've done it, first of all. Nearly every day when I've done it, it feels like it was a good day. It'll then be a really good day if I go back and read what I've done that day and think, 'Oh, that worked.' That's a really good day.

The initial really good day is just knowing you've been immersing yourself in, swimming in this river. It's the river that was flowing past you, the river that all those great books belonged to, even bad books that you liked belong to it, and from when you jumped in, that felt good.

When I come out of that room and I've been writing for five hours and haven't noticed the time passing and all of a sudden its three o'clock in the afternoon and I haven't had any lunch and I'm not even hungry—that's just great. It is like being in your element. It's an even better feeling on the days you go back and read it and you think, 'That bit worked.'

CW: What about when it's been a bad day, what are the symptoms?

MK: Well, first of all, a bad day is when you sit down and you're really fired up and something happens after fifteen minutes that means you have to get in the car and drive across town to attend to something, or you get a call from an editor who needs you to do something straightaway that you can't say no to. So a bad day is when you can't do it.

In the initial drafting phase, if it's not really coming to me, I just stop. I don't let myself have a bad day. I go and do something else—or I just keep going and sort of push through it until it becomes good again.

But a bad day, a *really* bad day, is when you go back and you read something and you think, 'Ah, what tripe.'

CW: Oh yes. What's the nature of this? There's something so defeating about it. It's not about wasted time . . .

MK: No, no, it's not wasted time, you'd be happy to waste the time. Well, it's coming up against your own inadequacies, and how far removed what you've done is from what you thought you were doing. It's showing you how dismally you failed. Because I'm a fast writer in first draft, I do many revisions and I find the revision process really enlivening because it's like getting back into that river again, and writing again. I revise pretty heavily.

CW: I love that sense of yours of being in the same river that other books you've loved have been part of. Do you feel, when it's going well, that there's a sense of connection? That there's a line . . .

MK: Oh yeah, from Tolstoy to me! [*laughs*] Well—insofar as a minnow might be swimming in the same ocean as the blue whale . . . but yeah, because you're doing the same thing. When I've occasionally taught classes, I always say to the students, 'You don't have to aspire to being a writer. You're either a writer or you're not. If you're going home tonight and working on your novel, you're more of a writer than the world-famous person who hasn't written anything for a year—you're a writer if you write.'

So for myself, I feel the same way: if I'm working in that language, I'm somewhere in that same element with the books I've read, because they are books that have fed into me.

CW: Do you have a sense of what unifies your work? Any sense of your 'project' as a writer?

MK: No, I don't. And when somebody finds unifying strains in my work, as you've done, I'm always a little bit confronted because I've never thought about it. I've never thought I was on a unified project, but of course readers will find that you are, quicker than you find that out yourself.

147

CW: In a nice review of one of your books, Owen Richardson wrote, 'People are brought up by books as well as by their parents', which I thought was lovely. I know Proust has been very important to you—what are the other books that brought you up?

MK: Well I first read Proust when I was about twenty. And now as you've made me think about it, I realise that was a big year, a big time for me.

But before that? My parents will say I was always reading, always had my nose in a book, and I guess that's right if that's what they remember, but I don't remember reading anything that made an enormous impact on me until I was about eighteen or nineteen.

Certainly the book that broke through was *The Red and The Black*. I thought, 'Wow, I've read a real book at last.'

I can see the same with my daughter Lilian—Lilian reads a lot, she's a prodigious reader, she often has her nose in a book. But she's often rereading for the fifth time something that's about two years below her reading level, just because she loves it. And I think I was like that, I was not really challenging myself, but just loving reading.

I remember being into those *Swallows and Amazons* Arthur Ransome books for a while, and before that I was into all those Hardy Boys and *Alfred Hitchcock* and the *Three Investigators* books. The books that were prescribed for school I didn't generally like. *Lord of the Flies* was an exception—I loved that.

Having this sheltered suburban life, I remember a book I read when I was about ten, called *The Silver Sword*. It was a Holocaust book, and wow, it blew my mind. And another book I read at about the same age was called *The Cross and the Switchblade*—I'm *pretty* sure it was a Christian book, because the cross was a priest in the book, and the switchblade was about gangs and drugs and all of that, and the cross eventually triumphs . . . but what I took from it was all this stuff about people knifing each other and shooting up.

CW: [*laughs*] Oh, you've just reminded me of *Go Ask Alice!* The supposed diary of the good girl who turns to drugs and dies of an overdose . . . I must have read it when I was about eleven. I loved it, I'm only just remembering this now. It was very thrilling for a little suburban country girl like me.

MK: I do remember reading *The World According to Garp* and thinking, 'Whoa, that's a real entry into a forbidden adult life.' Real racy stuff. I remember *The Godfather* having a similar effect—I did like racy potboiler fiction, and I liked the kind of espionage stuff, the Frederick Forsyth sort of stuff.

CW: So when you got to Stendhal, to *The Red and the Black*, what did it do that woke you up?

MK: It was the miracle of temporal transcendence. It's written in 1830 or something like that, and I remember thinking, 'What a miracle.' That this Frenchman in 1830, writing about a young, poor French boy about ten or fifteen years before that, has just tapped into all of my fears and worries. And the story was great as well. So it was somebody speaking across time, to me. It wasn't about me, but it was *to* me. I didn't see myself as that character, but I saw that the things he was facing were in some way the same things I was facing.

So by the time you get to the modernist era—and Proust was the one who made the biggest impression on me—you've got that same thing, but taken so deeply into the interior that not only is he addressing the same things that I'm addressing, it's like he's thinking the things I don't even know I'm thinking, but I am.

So that felt miraculous. And it felt worth doing. In all those earlier years, much as I loved reading and was addicted to reading, I never wanted to be a writer. I'd never thought about it. It was only at that later stage I thought, 'I really, really want to do this.'

I hope I've just got through my first apprenticeship novels, and I'm still fired up by the idea that I've only just scratched the surface, and can get a lot better, and write books that can do to readers what the best books have done to me.

MARGO LANAGAN is the internationally renowned author of disturbingly beautiful literary fantasies.

She grew up in the town of Raymond Terrace, just north of Newcastle in NSW, and in Melbourne. She began writing and publishing poetry in her teens. Excluding the teen romances written under various pseudonyms, at the time of this interview in 2013, Lanagan had published fourteen books—nine novels and five short-story collections, moving between genres and reader age groups with apparent ease. She comfortably occupies a respected place in several literary worlds, claimed by the literary fiction, young adult literature, fantasy and science fiction genres alike.

'Crossing over', indeed, is a recurring theme in both her career and the books themselves, which are alive with dreamlike morphings between different physical forms and planes of existence.

Her novel, *Sea Hearts*—an exploration of the Celtic selkie myths in which seals are heartbreakingly transformed into alluring women, and back again—was published to wide acclaim in 2012. At the time of this interview it had won three awards and appeared on five international and Australian shortlists. Since this interview, she has been co-writing the *Zeroes* young adult superhero series.

The first Lanagan work I read was the astonishing story 'Singing My Sister Down' in her breakout 2005 collection *Black Juice*, and I have been drawn to her unnerving, lyrical blend of mythology, fairytale and pure Lanagan strangeness ever since.

In person, her warmth and practicality and humour are a surprising contrast with the shadowy tones of Lanagan's writing. On Twitter she is a lively and mischievous correspondent to several thousand avid followers, an energetic online presence that's also in evidence in speculative fiction blogs and forums as well as her own blog on the writing life, Among Amid While.

In the Sydney literary community Lanagan is a popular and collegiate writer, organising writers' social events and active in what Thomas Keneally called 'manning the parish pump', having worked in the largely voluntary roles of co-judge of *The Australian*/Vogel's Literary Award for an unpublished novel and served on the Australia Council's Literature Board for three years.

My conversation with Lanagan took place on a sunny autumn morning, in the first-floor studio flat she had rented as a work space for the previous seven years. It was a short walk from her home, where she lives with graphic designer Steven Dunbar and the transient presence of their two adult sons.

One of six apartments in a large converted terrace in the inner west Sydney suburb of Lewisham, the studio was an enviable writing space—private, quiet and spacious, with a tiny kitchenette and two windows with leafy views. A large op-shop painting of a curled cat in icy whites and blues hung above the mantelpiece; the cat gazed coolly down over the author as she worked. At one point in the interview Lanagan reached to a shelf behind her and extracted several scrapbooks to show me the moody, evocative images she collects as part of her creative process. As she leafed through them, I felt I was being allowed a privileged glimpse into her visual imagination.

Lanagan's writing room, suspended between upper and lower floors, seemed a fitting place to discuss her attraction to the transformative shifts between different realms, and other compelling ambiguities emerging from her fiction.

CW: Can you tell me about this writing room, and how you use it?

ML: I first started working here in about 2006. We'd got to the point where our boys were teenagers and had to be parted. We couldn't make them share a room any more, so Steven and I gave Jack the study the two of us had been using. I managed just on the kitchen table for a while, and then I got a two-year fellowship from the Australia Council and decided, 'Okay, it's time to be professional about this'—after fifteen years of publication. [*laughs*] It was time to claim some space that was solely for writing.

The building is about two blocks from my house, so if I leave anything here or at home it's not a big drama to go and fetch it. There are six studio flats in the building—I share a bathroom with the two other flats on this level. This flat's nice because it's up high and you look out on trees.

CW: I am pleased to see you have a couch . . .

ML: Yes, a terrible trap. It's a very comfortable couch. But you do need an alternative to sitting at the table; you need to be able to go and read something in a slightly different position when you're stuck. And I have the odd nap as well . . .

CW: What does your ideal working week look like?

ML: If I'm writing a draft, I'll work at home first thing in the morning, because there I can work only two rooms away, rather than two blocks away, and in my pyjamas. I usually wake up earlier than everybody, and if I can get a couple of hours in before breakfast, that sets up a good day. I'm talking about four or five o'clock. And then I go for a walk with a friend at quarter past six. This sounds very methodical when it's actually a very scrambled and unreliable system. But the ideal working week would be if I woke up at least four mornings really early, got those two hours done, went out for my walk and then came up here, because the early-morning writing sort of opens the sluices, so when I sit down it's all there, flowing, ready to be brought out.

CW: The walk with your friend doesn't interrupt your writing brain?

ML: No, not really. If I've done some solid work in the morning, it's not a problem to socialise. And it's probably a good thing to do, to just get a bit of distance between you and your words. Between what you think is marvellous and . . . what it is! [laughs]

That's probably about the extent of any settling-in rituals. Other than that it's, you know: clean your teeth, make a resolution not to snack for another two hours, and get on with it. Usually on the walk up here I'm thinking about what I will begin on, so that when I come in I can sit down and begin rather than sit down and faff and have crises of confidence.

CW: How connected are you to the outside world while you're here?

ML: I'm not. I've got the phone but this is an internet-free zone for me. It's very essential. If I really need to stay in touch with things then I'll just work at the kitchen table at home. But that's not nearly as good because there are people coming and going, and other things that can be done—domestic things, and emails that can be answered, which usually leads to a lot of tweeting and Facebooking. Steven works from home too, and he's a bit chatty, likes a bit of radio, that kind of nonsense! [*laughs*]

CW: When did you first start writing?

ML: I started with poetry when I was a teenager, as a lot of us do. I had a bit of that published, and then I applied to go to the Nancy Keesing studio in Paris for six months when I was twenty-seven. While I was there, or maybe before I went, I'd decided I wanted to write something that was a bit more widely read. And I just wanted to feel more generous about it: I wanted to write *big* things, to *pour* stuff out rather than doing these tiny, perfectly formed things that nobody could understand.

So I wrote some really, really bad short stories over there. And I started on a *really* bad novel, which I entered for the Vogel Award—I am praying they only spent five minutes reading it and then put it aside before sending me a rejection letter. And then I realised that I needed to learn about narrative drive, and about writing stories that people wanted to read.

I became a freelance book editor when I got back, but not of fiction—mostly books about fishing or gardening, cookbooks and history books. Then a friend who was in publishing said, 'Well, we don't have anything for you to edit but would you like to have a go at writing one of these?' These were Bantam Wildflowers teenage romances. Here's one I wrote: *The Cappuccino Kid* by Melanie Carter. They were putting out a whole bunch of these, but they didn't have many authors, so as well as Melanie Carter I became four or five different people. I ended up writing a couple of *Dolly* Fiction romances as well. You could make okay money. I was very determined to be professional about it. They just gave you a flat fee, so I decided that for this amount of money, I would work on these for no longer than two weeks each.

I planned it all out with a chapter plan I stuck to religiously, and I wrote a chapter a day for ten days. And then if my plan exploded in my face one day, I had to rewrite the plan so it would work. I had to not undo anything in the previous chapters, and I had to finish that day's chapter. So it was good practice in plotting. These were very simple stories, and fairly straightforward to plot. Each one is about 30,000 words. I figured they had to be research free, they had to be stories I could write off the top of my head, and they had to be written fast. I did it for a couple of years—there was one six-month period where I wrote six books!—and then all that time I was cooking up this other junior fiction book I had in mind, *WildGame*, which came out under my own name in 1991.

I knew the romances were practice books, apprenticeship books. They were not coming from my heart—and *WildGame* wasn't either, particularly. I don't think it was till I was quite a way in that I felt that I was doing any kind of particular—it sounds terrible to say 'work on myself'—but doing anything that particularly *involved* me. Not until the gritty realist young adult books *The Best Thing* and *Touching Earth Lightly*.

The Best Thing is about a girl who falls pregnant to a boxer in Newtown, and the second one is about a sex-mad teenager who's—it's a terrible anti-feminist parable where the girl who likes having sex has to die in the end. [*laughs*] But it's about grief, really, it's about her friend coping with her having gone.

CW: Was it a conscious decision, then, to move into writing fantasy?

ML: It was pretty conscious. By then I had five or six books and they'd had good reviews, premier's award shortlistings and CBCA Notable Book listings, but they weren't making any money and they weren't selling overseas. I wanted to think that one day, writing could be a good alternative income. I thought, 'How can I work this so that might happen?' So I chose a genre with a guaranteed worldwide audience.

CW: That sounds very strategic.

ML: It was strategic. I didn't think I would ever write science fiction because I didn't know enough science, although you don't necessarily have to know an awful lot of science to write a science fiction story. But fantasy seemed like the way to go, seemed like the most fun.

So I embarked on the huge Fantasy Brick. I won't get that one out, it weighs a tonne. But it's an exercise in over-world-building. [*laughs*] I built this incredible series of cultures and histories and wars and communities and landscapes, and it just got to the point where I couldn't move a story through it. I just couldn't keep track of it. I worked on that for about three years, toiling away, going past my deadline year after year.

I had a contract for two books at that time, I think. I didn't deliver on either of them for a very long time.

With the Fantasy Brick I just—in the end I threw up my hands and ran away to Clarion West, a six-week short-story workshop for science fiction and fantasy writers in America. I just wanted to pick other people's brains—to ask, 'How do you cope with these enormous creations?'

I wasn't very genre savvy. I'm not very genre savvy now, but I didn't really know what I was getting into, I guess, and I wanted a better idea. And I just wanted a break. I wanted to do *one* thing. I was doing editorial work and I was being a mum and I was trying to get this book out, and I just wanted to have a single focus for a little while. So I went over there and wrote some short stories, which turned into *White Time*, the first story collection.

White Time didn't do very well at all. And that's when I decided, 'This is never going to happen. I am obviously not ever going to make a living as a writer, so just stop thinking of it like that. Just write the stories that are *demanding* to be written, rather than thinking of an idea and then thinking: *audience*, okay how do I pitch this to them?'

I decided to just write the stuff that needed to be coughed up, vomited up.

I went back to full-time work, as a tech writer out at Marayong, which meant I had a forty-minute train ride against the main commuter flow, so I was in empty-ish trains both ways. And I decided those forty minutes were going to be entirely my time; I was going to write some of those stories.

Every couple of days I would take something out of my ideas folder and I would chew on that, for forty minutes either way. That was how the stories in *Black Juice* mainly got written—and they were the ones that really started working for people, because I was putting more of myself into them.

CW: Did you think as you were writing that these were better stories?

ML: Well, they were more fun to write because they were just purely for me. There was no anxiety about audience, or about where they were going. It almost didn't matter if they didn't get published, although I was pretty sure they would.

But considering how poorly *White Time* did, I was really quite arrogant to think that Allen & Unwin would take on another book of short stories from me! But fortunately these were so different, they had moved on so much, that they decided to take another punt. And *Black Juice* did super well. That was where it all started happening.

CW: What do you mean when you say you were putting more of yourself into them?

ML: A story is only self-exploration after the fact, when it's set down and you look at it and think, 'Where did that come from?' But in the process of writing, I just mean I was getting out of my own way. Not being self-conscious; getting so absorbed in the story that I wasn't considering audience at all, I was just watching to see what's going to happen, trying various things, trying to feel in my gut what was the truest and best and most interesting and most fun way to proceed.

CW: Can you tell me about your interest in fairytales, and about the Peter Pan book you had as a child? These seem to tap into something primal that has real heat in it for you.

ML: Fairytales were among the many stories Mum read to us when I was very young. They just sort of go into your bones. I think it's probably the terrible warnings they have about the world, and these superstitious ways that you can act to save yourself.

It is just enormously appealing for children—it gives you a kind of hope, you know, that courage will come to you in the form of The Jewel, or the form of The Ring, or the form of The Fairy Godmother, to deal with things. It's very heartening. Fairytales look at things you're frightened of, but you're sitting there safe beside your mother so it's okay, it's a safe place to look at horrible things from. And they offer you improbable ways out, but ways that might be translatable into real-life actions you could take.

The book was *Peter Pan in Kensington Gardens*, with the Arthur Rackham illustrations. It's a beautiful book, an enormous thick thing—my great-uncle had given it to my mother when she was little. The illustrations were very dark. Lots of prickly trees, and this tiny baby wandering around alone in Kensington Gardens, being plucked at by horrible fairies or leaned over by trees, or helped by voles. [*laughs*] And you know, it's London! It's freezing! These winter winds, and moons, and fairies being blown along with lamps. It was totally creepy, but totally fascinating as well.

For me it held those really old fears.

I had the usual night terrors of children. I remember lying there, my heart thudding because I was so scared, and the sound of my pulse in the pillow becoming footsteps in the hall, becoming whatever scary thing I last read about—the doll Dido in Ruth M. Arthur's *A Candle in Her Room*, or the god Tash in C.S. Lewis's *The Last Battle*, or whoever— walking up and down the hall out there, which might at any minute pause at my bedroom door and put its head around and look at me. The worst terror.

We lived in a country town, and there were fields out the back, and cats would wander in those fields at night and make those horrible noises that cats do. I was terrified by that sound. My mother would say, 'It's just cats, you don't have to worry about it.' And I knew she was lying to me, that this was actually a small boy and a small girl out there, lost, calling for their parents. There was always a part of me that just knew those cats were kids.

CW: I want to ask about the worlds you create. I am always amazed by how they are completely unfamiliar but at the same time feel absolutely known to us. The tar pit in 'Singing My Sister Down', for example, or the gathering of 'sea hearts' in the novel—these feel like perfectly ordinary, familiar things even though I can't possibly know these places and things because you've just invented them. How did you come to this technique?

ML: If I were Farah Mendlesohn—she's written a fabulous book called *Rhetorics of Fantasy*—I would be able to explain exactly how it's done. But basically it's a way of hooking the reader in, of including them immediately in that world, giving them lots of assumed knowledge but also sneakily handing them knowledge. So you don't say, 'As you know, Bob, we all gather sea hearts this way and have since time immemorial.' [*laughs*] It doesn't much matter what a sea heart is, you just know that it's some edible thing from the sea, something the mothers get all weepy and nostalgic over. It just holds all the symbolic longing for their home, so that at the end, when the boy and his father sit down to sea hearts together, it hits you with extra force.

But also you tie it to the real world by making it a very concrete thing. So you say, 'You have to get the curd exactly right', or you have to cook it this way particularly. You surround it with a little convincing fog of interesting detail that you just make up out of nothing!

CW: But it's also about the voice, isn't it? The very ordinariness of the voice?

ML: Yeah. Because people don't go around constantly explaining their world to themselves. They get to a certain age where they know how things work, and then the only things that strike them when they walk into a situation are the things that are different from usual. It's something that I do almost so automatically now that it's a bit hard to describe. It's also not wanting to be bothered myself with explaining how it all works. I don't want to take the reader through all the stuff that I just went through. I just ask, okay what's the most interesting bit, the most juicy bit here?

I generally jump straight in. I have become more practised at choosing the right moment to jump in. I rarely have to cut more than a couple of paragraphs from a story beginning these days.

CW: When I read your work I'm reminded of Patricia Piccinini's disturbing sculptures—those strange, almost hyperreal forms that are so familiarly human, until you look closer and see they are also part animal, part alien, unfamiliar and unnerving. But also extremely tender.

ML: Yes, I can see that. There's another sculptor whose work I look at—Linde Ivimey. She does sculptures made from bones and hair and things. I've got a picture of one of her sculptures here. [*hunts for it*]

These are scrapbooks that I do for my work; this is the one for the next novel. I have been through a very intense period of scrapbooking in the last couple of years. I don't have one for each book, I'm not that methodical. But for this new novel I've actually got five scrapbooks, I've been procrastinating about it for so long.

CW: Wow, these are beautiful. I love this idea, I'm so going to nick it!

ML: Yes, well, do! I got it from the workshops of Jan Cornall—I just leapt on it as a way of writing without writing, of working on a book without actually having to produce any words! [*laughs*]

This is for the next novel, which is about an Irish convict who brings a goddess to Australia. So there are three sections to the novel—the Irish part, and the sea voyage, and then there's the arrival and the colonial Australian bit, and the scrapbooks jump between these three parts from spread to spread. They're only for images. I've got separate notebooks for words.

CW: It's very strong isn't it—because they're only images there's something very appealing about it at a non-verbal, gut level.

ML: Yeah. They're particularly good for when you get called away from the project and you lose contact with it. If you want to get back into the *feeling* of it, something like this is much quicker and stronger than reading through the draft that you did and the notes that you've made.

CW: I want to go home and do this right now.

ML: I know. It's very addictive! And it's really nice to have them to keep, as well. And useful, too, for showing people your process.

With the *Sea Hearts* scrapbooks I got Steven to photograph them, and then at the book launch had the slideshow going on a screen in the background. And I put them up online too.

They're so evocative; you put the colour and imagery in your writing up to a point, and you find more in your research, but there's something about actually having the saturated colour and the images that bypasses all that fiddling about trying to get the words right. Just communicates it straight.

CW: Do you think about colour much as you write?

ML: I do look at things. I visualise things fairly strongly and then examine that picture. A bit like you do with dreams—you know how, in a dream, an object or surface doesn't really have any detail until you apply your attention to it? And then it turns into a wolf's fur, right next to a wolf's eye, which the dream lets you look through and see into the wolf's mind, or whatever—it's a bit like that with visualising a story. Asking, 'What *is* that? I know the outside of a sea heart is all ugly and warty, but what's inside? What does it hold?'

CW: You seem very interested in transformations—physical slippage between human and animal, between forms, between different worlds, and between childhood and adulthood. What interests you about that?

ML: In the old stories these transformations are never dealt with in any detail; they're very matter of fact. They say, 'I shall now turn into a beautiful horse, Father, and you must take me along and sell me at the market.' And bam, there's the horse and off it goes. But I want to know what that *feels* like, I want to know what it looks like, and I want to feel the disorientation of anybody who's watching this transformation take place. I want to feel how uncomfortable that would be, and what it would be like to be in a new body.

It's the same with stepping from world to world. My favourite parts of the Narnia books were always those moments when the children fell out of boarding school into Narnia, or got sucked into the painting of the *Dawn Treader.* I want to tell moments like that very specifically, to imagine exactly the sensations and to know exactly how the fantasy world encroaches on and replaces the real one.

CW: Why do you think you want to know these things?

ML: I think it's just a desire to explore what *can't* happen. It's a bit like watching a really good nature documentary, you know—these *peculiar* creatures of the most astounding shapes doing all this stuff that we can't really properly translate or make sense of. You can sort of get the gist of it, you know it's about mating, but you can't ever actually *be* a cuttlefish! So I think it's just sort of poking at the edges of what you can apprehend, refreshing your brain by *trying* to go beyond what your own biology renders you capable of imagining.

CW: Do you think that's what writing is—the desire to be a cuttlefish?

ML: I think that's what a lot of fantasy writing is about, yeah. It's a longing to understand, pretending that you can understand, states of being you will never get to experience.

With the animal transformations, I always want to make sure that the animals stay really strange, that the animal-ness is *not* understandable, that they're not actually people dressed in bearskins. I want them to be foreign, as the seals in *Sea Hearts* are foreign. That's why in the end it didn't really work to have the selkies themselves speaking, or to go much further than the boy did when he told his father that the experience of being a seal was just not explicable in human terms.

CW: That was really a beautiful scene, I must say.

ML: That was the key to the difference between the two species. That you can't tell this man what it's like to be a seal, in the sea, thinking about him on the land, because as a seal, you *didn't* really think—your brain was wired differently. And the link between husband and wife doesn't *matter* in the sea, the way it matters out here. Seals just deal with the world in different ways, and there's no point in being distressed about it.

CW: Do you feel you are moving into another realm when you are writing?

ML: When you write, you concentrate really hard, and everything is pretty much absorbed in what you're doing. And even the part of you that usually watches yourself is absorbed. I know that when I was working full-time and I only had weekends to write, if I came up here and spent a day writing I felt as if I'd missed out on the weekend, because I hadn't actually noticed the time passing.

I hadn't appreciated the weekend time that I was having because the time-keeping part of me just disappeared into the concentration on what I was doing. So it is another realm—you are inhabiting the story as closely as you can. But it's not—I mean, I don't forget to eat. I don't forget to go to the bathroom.

CW: When your work is going well, what does that feel like?

ML: It's very exciting, in a quiet kind of way. You're carrying around this thing, and all the time when you're not actually writing you're still picking up things and weighing them in your hand, and seeing whether you can use them. And all sorts of things come at you as well, they connect themselves to the work you're making. You become this very super-aware *receiver* of messages. You know, you'll sit down with the Saturday paper and you'll find five things that you write down in your notebook because they all set off little chimes about what you're looking for in this book, or new possibilities. And—I can't remember who said this, but when it's going well you think, 'This book is the one where I'm going to be able to fit the whole universe in!'

So you kind of have this wonderful delusion for a while that you're going to cram all the things that you haven't managed to say before into *this* one. And then you have to pare that back and be sensible, and realise the actual size of the project. But not cut it back so far that you get bored. It's all so interesting, the balancing act you do, the ways you let yourself out into fresh fields and then draw yourself back in to keep the story coherent.

CW: You seem awfully prolific. Do you have the sense that you'll never have enough time to get all your ideas out?

ML: In a way. That's what short stories are good for. You can just pick one up and play with it for a while. Or perhaps two, because sometimes you need a second little idea to produce an interesting juxtaposition that suggests a story. You pick up those few things and play with them for a while, and then you can put that aside. You've prodded that and got a bit of juice out of it and a story has resulted. With novels it's a different process—you have to accumulate so much more around the initial idea, and you have to hold the whole thing in your head for so much longer. And you have to work out different paths through it, and make them logical, or at least make them ring true . . .

CW: Do stories come more naturally to you? The faces you make when you talk about novels are quite different from the face you make when you talk about short stories!

ML: [*laughs*] Well, no. Stories just let you off the leash earlier. They're easier because they're done quicker, they're a simpler exercise.

CW: We've had this argument before! People like me find short stories exceptionally difficult—and I've heard the writer Toni Jordan say this, that the problem is one has to create a whole new world for each story. It's so difficult, and takes so long!

ML: But you *don't* create them, you just imply them. You've got a rough idea of them, from—you know how you meet a person and you hear them say a few things and you immediately conceive, rightly or wrongly, of the kind of background they come from or the area they live in. You jump to conclusions.

Well, with a short story you just throw small things—at yourself at first, but eventually at the reader—that make them jump to the kinds of conclusions that will build the right sort of world (or close enough) in their mind. Manners, verbal tics, possessions, issues characters are having with the hierarchy they're in, items of clothing, ways they express or control their rage. Everything a character does or says—or *refrains* from saying—will tell you, and ultimately your reader, about that character but also about the world as they see it—which will be partly very true, and partly their own mistaken impression of things. And as your story progresses towards its denouement, all these little things, each of which feels more or less well placed, will be giving you different bits of world to try on for size, and one or two will hit exactly the note you want, so you'll build the rest of the world up using them as the key, then go back and haul everything else into line to match.

CW: What about the bad days—what does it feel like when the work is going badly?

ML: Things fragment. Things feel *stupid*. Characters just feel very shallow and—they don't resonate, they're not doing anything that you can sense any symbolic weight behind, they're just kind of playing in the scenery. And there's a lot of trying to go back to the last point where things felt good. Trying to find another trajectory, so you write out along that possibility. And then *that* collapses as well, so you go back again. Often it's the fact that I haven't got a voice right yet.

I haven't really established what I want the main character to be and do, and how best to shape them to achieve that.

CW: Do you know at the start what you have to say, or are you discovering that as you go?

ML: Thematically speaking I proceed very cluelessly. I don't really have any intentions in that sense, although I usually have an idea of what is going to happen. I usually have an idea of the interesting premise and the end point to which it might be taken. So I'll have the tar pit, say, and I'll have some kind of misdemeanour and I'll have the family standing around, and I will know from the beginning that the person in the tar pit is going to die.

With *Sea Hearts* I had written the end, the selkies going back to the sea and the boys being responsible and going with them, as a novella. So that section was always a given; the novel was really an exploration back from that point, working out how the witch had become the creature she was on the beach there in that first scene, all bitter and angry and frightening, and with such power over the boys and the town.

I usually write pretty chronologically. I usually write the first scene first, and I'll have an idea of where the last is going to be—just an idea, just a sketchy thing. And if I'm puzzled about how I'm going to get there I will jump about a bit and try to find scenes that interest me, and some of those will survive till the end and some won't. At some point I have to sit back and work out how they're all going to knit together. Sometimes they grow together naturally and other times they need to be rethought and remade. So some stories I will sit down and write from beginning to end in a single hit; others are made up of a kind of mosaic of scenes that takes a bit more work and thought.

CW: How do you respond to people who say your work is too dark or violent for young adults? I find it strange to hear the 'violence' in your work discussed as if it is realism, when I read it as a much more dreamlike, metaphorical kind of darkness.

ML: I'm not really bothered by that. I know it's dark, but you know, there's a lot of dark stuff out there. It's not as if I'm manufacturing darkness that doesn't exist somewhere in the world, and possibly a lot closer in the world than we would like to admit.

Also, there's this assumption that young adults are a clean slate, which gets sullied or spoiled when it meets darkness in a book. There's plenty of darkness and violence in young people's lives already, even if they're lucky enough to only view it on screen. I don't think we serve them very well if we give them a literature that only maintains the illusion of a cheerful, pain-free universe. It can't *all* be comfort reading. How does that prepare them for life?

CW: What attracts you to the dark? And how do you know if you might be crossing a line into using it for effect?

ML: I just think it's more interesting when people mess up than when they don't. What's the point of writing a story if there isn't something to be conquered or to be faced or to be worked out?

There's always been a bit of a mix of light and dark in my work. It's Piccinini again, that uncomfortable frisson you get when the icky or the abject or the just plain evil is jammed right up tight against a person or a relationship that everyone can recognise as tender, or loving, or kind. That energy—*these two things* so *don't go together, but yes, here they are*—is often what I'm trying to get a story to give off.

How do you know when you're faking it? I think probably I know that more at a story-planning stage than when I'm actually writing the scene.

I know it was very clear where the line was when I was writing *Tender Morsels,* where giving more detail would become inauthentic to that story. Where if I got any more graphic, if I described that actual rape rather than just leading up to it and jump-cutting to afterwards, it was going to become a novel *about* rape, which I did not want it to be. And it was also going to do things to my readers that were not part of the project. *Tender Morsels* wasn't about saying what a horrible thing rape is—everybody knows this is a horrible thing. It was a matter of respecting readers—or respecting the ones who were worldly enough to know what was going on, and protecting the ones who were not.

It was not a hard decision to make.

But a lot of reaction clusters around the fact of a book being for young adults. It's like there are these nodes of sensitivity and outrage, and sex is one and swearing is another, and if those elements come anywhere close to YA then everyone who might get sued or abused by parents, their alarm bells go off. And voices start speaking out and warning people—you know, 'Don't pass this to your more vulnerable clients'—in terms of students or library patrons or whatever.

A lot of people just get completely fixated on the danger, but, you know, children are pretty resilient. In terms of books, they work out what they're comfortable with and what they're not. And you're not going to make them read a book they hate—unless you *force* them to by having an exam on it. But if we present young people with a literature that's completely danger-free and anodyne, why would they be attracted to that, with so many other edgy media experiences out there for the taking, with so much edgy *life*?

CW: One question I've always had about fantasy is how you create enough narrative constraint that you can't solve every logical problem by just whacking in some magic. How do you decide the rules of your world?

ML: It has to be fairly limited. You leave the rules fairly open and squishy for a while, and see if they lead to interesting places. And then, if you find a *useful* bit of magic, then you tend to use that useful bit and constrain it in other ways. For example, in the early drafts of *Sea Hearts*, Misskaella had all sorts of powers—she could change the weather and she could bring up fish from the sea. She did an awful lot of fishing work! And there was this whole complex of other things around her, everybody knew she was a witch and so on.

But then to make the story controllable I decided that okay, she was able to see the natural forces flowing up from the ground, but the only way she could actually *do* any magic was in relation to the seals. That was the single expression of her powers. It's just a matter of practicality, because if she was too powerful, nothing that happens can be very interesting—

CW: She could just magic her way out of any difficulty.

ML: Yes. You know, she could just *fly away* to a place where people would accept her, or anything. So she had to have a little bit of power but still people couldn't give her proper respect, or treat her well enough to prevent her avenging herself by using that power. So pulling it in like that actually gives you the bones of the story, in the end. It's the constraints that make the story possible. You sort of feel around until a useful constraint shows itself.

CW: You seem to take much pleasure in naming people and places—you have many names in your stories, and they are so unusual. Is naming a way of getting into your characters?

ML: It is, definitely. Some names arrive with the character, and with some you try out a couple before you settle on one. I should show you the sheet my editor sent me for the first draft of *Sea Hearts*. She said, 'Now look, these are all the people here, I think you're going to have to pare this back.' And I read them—there must have been fifty or sixty of them—and thought, 'But those are *fantastic* names, I *love* them!' But I didn't realise that I'd let them proliferate so much.

I wanted the names in *Sea Hearts* to be nuggety and farmy and oceany lumps of things. I want them to have a kind of a rhythm to them, and for people to call each other by their first *and* last names, to have a strong sense of the families that everyone belonged to.

CW: You also have these wonderful names for foods and places, with this rich, rhythmic thing going on. How important is rhythm to you?

ML: A lot of the names come out of the rhythm of the sentences. You know you need a two-syllable town name, with the emphasis on the first syllable, in that sentence when it first comes up, and if you change it again you still must have that same rhythmical pattern even if they're two *different* syllables. And the same for people's names. I wanted all those *Sea Hearts* names to sort of lump in the mouth as you said them.

CW: Do you revise sentences much to get the rhythm right? Does it come naturally or do you work at it?

ML: Both, now. I sort of throw it forth to begin with—I try things out. And then I go back and fix the places where it falters or it starts getting clunky and I can see myself struggling. I try to find that point where I was confidently launching myself into a paragraph. It's thinking about larger patterns, really. When you're writing the sentences you're also thinking about the paragraph, and beyond that to the entire scene, or the entire story. And then you feel the rhythm faltering—so you put square brackets around the blundery bit and you keep going so you don't lose that sense of the rhythm. Then you come back and find the right word or phrase to fill the gap. Sometimes you've got the sense of it but you don't have the perfect word. You know there is one—it's on the tip of your tongue, but it's not there. But you know it means roughly *this*, so you put down that meaning in square brackets and go on, and you come back and find your way to the perfect word when you're fresher.

CW: In a normal day's work on a first draft, do you revise much as you go?

ML: Nup. I sit down and I write ten pages in a day. And then I stop and I try to leave it at an interesting place—I try not to leave it at the end of a scene, so I don't have to grind myself into gear the following morning to start on something new. For a short story, for example, I'll write right up to just before the climactic thing. I'll know exactly what's going to happen, and I'll be itching to *make* it happen but I know I haven't got the puff to do it today. So I'll stop, and leave myself the treat of finishing tomorrow, knowing that I'll do a better job of it first thing in the morning.

CW: Is that about avoiding the fear of starting again? Do you feel fearful when you're working?

ML: No, not any more. I'm not fearful. I think I got over a lot of that, actually, writing those romances. Because there were some days it was really easy, and I just sat down and worked and my ten pages would all be done by eleven o'clock. And then there were other days where I spent the whole day getting them. Right on five-thirty I would get the final words out, and I would feel that every single one of them had been crap. But I didn't let myself stop there and go back and fix them up; I'd go on. I'd just have this loose, messy chapter here that I knew would embarrass me later.

When I got to the end of my draft, that was the only time I would let myself go back and reread. And then, rereading the whole thing, I couldn't spot the days that had been so bad, I couldn't tell.

So I realised my feelings are completely unreliable when it comes to judging my own work at that level, from the middle of it. I just forge on, and then come back later and see the thing as a whole.

I don't really even bother now, thinking 'I wrote terrible stuff, I wrote shit'. I just don't beat myself up about it any more. Because it's not necessarily true—I can't tell, or I can't tell *now* from this point. Sometimes you see in retrospect that it's a weak scene, but you just needed to write it to work out how the rest of the plot was going to go. And that weak scene is as likely to get written on a 'good' day as on a 'bad' day.

You still have days where it's dragging, but it's not such a distressing thing. It's just a fact of life and tomorrow is just as likely to be an excellent day. Or, sometimes you have the darkness just before the dawn—you have those crappy days because you need to go out and stride around and reach a certain epiphany, reveal something to yourself through this battle.

Through asking, 'Why does it all feel so wrong? Why is it so hard?' you discover there's a reason—it's because I'm striving for something inauthentic. Or I'm trying to force something into this story which doesn't quite belong, or I'm trying to make something obvious that should be just suggested. Or, I'm trying to be too oblique and mysterious and I just need to say, 'She could control the weather'.

CW: Do you throw out very much?

ML: Yeah, yeah. And particularly in recent years, I've grown very happy to throw out large chunks of stuff and to redo things from scratch. With short stories that's fine because you can redo that reasonably quickly.

With novels it's harder but it feels very good to not be wedded to the way things were. I do the throwing out at redrafting stage. With both *Tender Morsels* and *Sea Hearts* I've got it as good as I could imagine getting it, at a certain point, and sent it off to the publishers. And then—when I get the editorial remarks from all the different editors (Australian, UK and US)—at that point the whole thing is open to being taken almost completely apart. Almost completely.

CW: Really, at that point!

ML: Yep. There are things that survive—for example in *Tender Morsels*, the very first scene I wrote was the scene where Liga's father uses the smoke to bring on the miscarriage and she tries to get out of the house, and she's banging on the door saying, 'Let me out, let me out or I will shit on the floor of your house!' That's the first scene after the Prologue, and it stayed there all the way through. But the rest of it came and went. I undo *vast* amounts—it's kind of freeing in a way, because I have written myself into various corners, but it's also very stomach-churning because I have to undo so much, I have to admit that I was so wrong!

CW: It can be kind of exhilarating to throw big chunks of a book away.

ML: It is, yes. But you have to be quite sure that you're not just running away from the thing. That you're actually running *towards* something, a new vision that works better than the previous one.

CW: In your work as a Vogel judge and as a grants assessor for the Australia Council you have seen a lot of work in progress.

Do you see common problems, or the same mistakes being made, especially by new writers?

ML: There are a number of phases that most writers go through. There's that first phase where they're just in love with words and they overuse 'literary' words, or words they enjoy reading, but that don't quite belong in their own story. So they tend to write these very ornate, writerly stories in which not very much happens.

Then, once they become aware of that, they tend to do the opposite and *under*write terrifically, and produce these very cryptic, very pared-back things in which, still, nothing much happens, because they still have a very narrow idea of what material constitutes story material. They're trying too hard to Be a Writer, to be *writerly*. Or trying too hard to be the writer they most admire—but that's also a useful way of getting to the core of how that admired person writes the way they do, and testing out how much of that method works for you.

And then they can wander in that wilderness for quite a while trying various things, before they get that 'Aha!' moment where they suddenly realise that they have permission to write about something that really vitally interests them. They realise that they can bring the desire to write together with this thing that they really *care* about, that they're allowed—indeed, it's the whole *point*—to insert that much of themselves into their writing. And that's when the good stuff happens; when they forget all about the reader and go flying off on this all-consuming journey, with the story bucking and dodging underneath them and surprising them at every turn. Their control sometimes slips, but *mostly* they're practised enough now to hold its head.

As a reader, you can tell when a writer has one eye on you. You know when they've laid out a story nicely, or commercially, with conventional readers in mind. It's different from when they've themselves been dragged along by the power of the thing. I'm all for that second kind of story, where the writer gives you the honour of accompanying them on a journey involving their whole self, with all their expertise in the service of negotiating that new, risky territory.

Because I'm a bit of a genre-head, I tend to find that a lot of literary writing doesn't really have enough happening for me—it's a lot about playing with the language and doing admirable things with it. Sometimes that's perfectly satisfying as a reading experience, but sometimes it just feels indulgent to me. It feels very separate from a lived life, and I want the writer to just go out into the world and get some more experience under the belt. Go and do some living and bring some of that life back into your prose.

CW: Do you know what drives you to write?

ML: When I got to around thirty I realised that no great passionate ambition was going to pick me up and move me along. There wasn't any occupation telling me that I was the person cut out to do it, except for writing. Writing was something I had proven to be competent at, and if I worked at it hard enough, I thought perhaps I could do something worthwhile.

But also I think it was the ambition I picked up from reading, from having other people's work do things to me that made me want to see whether I had the same power. It made me want to try different stories and see if I could replicate some of the effects I felt, on other readers, and if I could try for new effects that reading had never yet given me.

And at a kind of a small, very closely worked level, it's just a fascinating thing to be doing—to be working on a sentence that will, by its resonance and by the particular words you insert, evoke exactly the reaction that you want. There's something about that craft that will absorb you for days on end, and as you're moving through a novel full of that, you're not only evoking stuff at a sentence level but cumulatively working to evoke the big things, and ask the big questions. To fit the whole universe in!

But mainly I do it because it feels like the rightest work that I know how to do. It feels like the thing I was meant to do, when it's going well. It's like, *Okay, this is it.* This is the thing, the real deal. This is where I do my most wholehearted living.

AMANDA LOHREY grew up on the Hobart waterfront in the 1950s and '60s, in a family of staunch trade unionists and dock workers. Educated at Catholic schools, she went on to study at the University of Tasmania, followed by a scholarship to Cambridge University in the United Kingdom.

Her first novel, *The Morality of Gentlemen*, was published in 1984 to great acclaim. This was followed by five more works of fiction as well as *Secrets*, a collection co-authored with Drusilla Modjeska and Robert Dessaix, and two Quarterly Essays on politics. At the time of this interview in 2013 her most recent book was the short fiction collection *Reading Madame Bovary*. The novel in progress she discusses during this conversation was published in 2015: *A Short History of Richard Kline*.

Lohrey is a tall, imposing woman with a direct, mischievous gaze and an earthy warmth. Her approach to her work seems to blend healthy pragmatism with a serious creative self-determination—public praise or criticism, one senses, are of equal yet only passing interest to this naturally independent thinker.

She is refreshingly candid about topics writers often strive to avoid—failure, for example—and forthright in her opinions. The word 'bolshie' might almost have been invented to describe Lohrey, except it doesn't capture the sensitivity and interest in mystery that also flourish within her sharply critical mind.

She laughs easily, and often uses 'you' to mean 'I' or 'one', which has the effect of rapidly establishing a generous intimacy in conversation. It made me think she must be a good writing teacher, and indeed she spoke fondly of her experience of postgraduate teaching at various universities throughout Australia.

I spoke with Lohrey over a long rainy afternoon at my home. She was visiting Sydney from Tasmania, where she now lives, to accept the Patrick White Award the day before our interview. White himself established this award to acknowledge the body of work by a writer who has made a significant contribution to Australian literature. It is one of many prizes Lohrey has won during her career.

She sees writing as a calling, and her own vocation as being to 'chronicle the times'.

CW: Congratulations on the Patrick White Award. How do you feel about prizes in general? Do you care more or less about them now than you did earlier in your career?

AL: All writers I know have mixed feelings about prizes, for obvious reasons. When I started out writing there were hardly any prizes, so you never thought about winning one. Now there are so many. I don't want to sound mercenary, but the big thing is the money because it enables you to go on writing with less anxiety about income. Having said that, the Patrick White Award created a wonderful sense of connection with the old man and his generosity in investing his Nobel Prize money in a legacy for other Australian writers.

I think perhaps people can get too fraught about prizes, about who wins and who doesn't. Oh, sometimes you feel slightly wounded that you've been overlooked. But there have been times when I've looked at a judging panel and thought, 'Oh yeah, well they wouldn't have liked it anyway.'

CW: Do you think writers tend to believe their current work is their best work?

AL: Oh, absolutely. Always. The one you are working on now is always the one. That's the vision splendid, because you've got some great idea in your head and it's all going to be terrific. Then you finish it, and it's never as good as you hoped. But then there's that peculiar thing where you go back ten years later—you have to read at a writers' festival, say—and you think: 'Oh, that wasn't too bad, that was actually not too bad!' But always you're looking ahead.

It's always the one I'm doing now, and then the one I'm thinking about doing next. There are whole passages in my published novels, and characters, that I can't even remember.

CW: Do you have ideas for novels lined up behind each other in your head like that?

AL: I usually find the next novel suggests itself about two thirds of the way through the one I'm working on. Almost uncannily, it arises at a certain point. And that's how I know I'm about to finish the book I'm working on now; I start thinking about some other project. So I think, 'Okay, I'm nearly at the end.'

But you only know that from experience. It's so much harder when you're young, because you don't have any experience. You're panicking at every moment: I'll never write another book, I'll never finish this one, and so on. And when you 'teach' writing—ridiculous term—I think your main function is just to tell younger writers this and help them hold their nerve.

CW: Do you enjoy teaching?

AL: Yes! I love teaching. As you get older you like the contact with younger people—it keeps you in touch. There's also the endless surprises in what other people come up with, listening to the stories of their lives . . . I mean it sounds

Pollyanna-ish, but in my experience writers of all kinds are a fairly decent group. People who say writers are shockingly bitchy and egotistical I think have led sheltered lives. They haven't, for example, known many lawyers.

Most writers are good people to be around. You share the love of what you're doing, and you have common preoccupations. And this relates back to the subject of teaching. You know that if you can help someone even a little bit, then this is a valuable thing for them. It makes you feel useful. I especially enjoy postgraduate writing seminars, where you have ten or fifteen talented people of all ages and backgrounds—how could you not enjoy it?

CW: Do you have a solid working routine?

AL: No. I usually start work about eleven in the morning, my inner switch seems to come on at eleven. Even if for some reason I get up very early in the morning I seem not to be able to work until eleven. I don't know why this is; some metabolic thing. I work every day, but not to a strict routine. I never have a plan, I've given up making plans because they never work. So I just get up in the morning and go where the energy is—which sounds frightfully New Age, but it's the only way that works for me. Because as sure as I say 'tomorrow I'll do X', I won't feel like it.

I never make any social arrangements during the week unless I am heavily obligated. I remember Mary McCarthy saying, 'Writers should never lunch.' Given how sociable she was, and what a good cook, this must have been a sacrifice for her. But I don't make arrangements because sure enough, if I arrange something for one day, that'll be the day I'm really firing. It's uncanny. So that tends to make you a hermit.

CW: Do you do dinner during the week?

AL: I live in a remote place now, so there's not a lot of people to have dinner with. But no, I don't like doing dinner because usually I'm the one who's cooking, so then I've got to think: have I bought, have I defrosted, have I marinaded? And late in life I've begun to think I might have a bit of ADHD—the term, and recognition of the syndrome, wasn't around when I was young—because I haven't got the greatest concentration. So when I begin work I need to have nothing else I have to think about. Nothing.

I remember when I was young I heard Elizabeth Jolley give a talk where she said, 'You young feminists probably won't understand this, but if there's the slightest difficulty happening in the family I just can't work.' But we did understand. I think women are very porous; they are all the time taking in what's around them. Perhaps even more than men they need to shut off and have that ruthless focus that, traditionally, they've not been permitted.

CW: Did you have that focus when you were caring for a young child?

AL: I was very lucky. When my daughter was two, my mother saw that I was struggling with not being able to write. And she doted on her only grandchild, so she looked after my daughter for four mornings a week. And at the age of three Cleo went into childcare. Then, as she was growing up, in order to avoid the guilts, the minute she came home from school I stopped work.

I remember reading about Nadine Gordimer, how she would pause when the children came home, and have the servants bring in afternoon tea, and have a brief tea with the children and then go back to work. [*laughs*]

If I'd had more than one child it would have been really interesting, I don't know . . . I suppose I would've had the same routine: school hours. What else would you do?

CW: So you could focus thoroughly once she was out the door?

AL: No, still the eleven o'clock switch. It's always been around eleven o'clock, then I work through lunch. Eleven to two is the best time but if that's not possible then two until five. I have a bad back and can't sit at a keyboard for any longer than that, and even then I have to take regular breaks and walk around a bit. It won't be long before I have to work standing up.

CW: Are you only ever working on one book at a time?

AL: Usually I'm only working on one novel, but I might be doing non-fiction for the money because it pays better.

CW: What about stories?

AL: Most of my short stories are novels that didn't develop. Always I think I might be about to write a novel. One story in *Reading Madame Bovary*—'Letter to the Romans'—I was sure was a novel. I wrote about forty-five thousand words, and I had other characters, and this and that was happening, but as I went on I thought, this is getting worse, not better.

The energy is dissipating. The tone is going flat, it's getting full of naturalistic detail that is blurring the focus of the narrative, not intensifying it. I thought, 'No, it needs to contract and intensify into a small space. What happens in that enclosed space is really what it's about.' And I just cut out all the other stuff. The original plan was wonderful but it didn't work.

The best plans never work, do they? I sometimes got impatient with postgrad writing students who wanted to talk for too long about The Plan. I'd say: 'Try it and let's see what works on the page.'

CW: Is there any chronology in the way you write novels? Do you write them from beginning to end?

AL: No. I tend to work in what I think of as mosaic form. Or, to use another analogy, it's like putting together the pieces of a jigsaw when you don't have the top of the box to show you the completed picture.

At the end of the working day I leave myself a note about where I'm at and where I might pick up the following day, but often the next day I won't feel like following my own directions and will work on some other piece of the puzzle. So you might be working on this piece and then that piece, and you have to have faith that it'll all come together. And sometimes it does, and sometimes it doesn't. But the main thing is that you're enjoying it at the time. The first reader you have to keep interested is yourself.

CW: Do you enjoy it?

AL: Most of the time I'm getting something out of it or I wouldn't do it. There's certainly not much money in the kind of fiction I write and very little glamour. But you enjoy it in the way you enjoy a puzzle. And the great thing about fiction is you don't know where you're going. That's the fun. That's why I've never written a full-length non-fiction book, though I've had some good offers from publishers.

But with non-fiction you do the plan, you can see where you're going, you can see what's in every chapter, you know how you're going to finish up, you know what the introduction is—you're bored before you even start! The fact that other people might enjoy it is not enough. Writing is a very selfish undertaking.

But when you're writing a novel, there are lots of surprises along the way. For example, when I started my novella, *Vertigo*, I thought I was writing a short story about a bushfire.

And then suddenly this boy appears. Well, how much fun is that?

CW: Has the critical response to your novels changed over time?

AL: There are some male critics who think I started off promisingly by writing political fiction and I've gone downhill because I've 'narrowed' more and more into the domestic, which they see as a terrible falling-off of a once-promising career. I mean, they actually say this. Well I don't see it that way, obviously! [*laughs*]

People often ask me why I don't write political novels any more, and there are two answers to this. One is that I'm not interested in repeating myself and the second is that very few people are interested in reading them. After my first two (political) novels, which experimented with modes of realism, I realised I was publishing into a literary culture that wasn't interested in this. I began to feel like I was just having a conversation with myself. And it ceased to be enough. Talking to yourself is not enough.

CW: Isn't that a risk we're always taking, that this might be what we're doing?

AL: Well, it's a risk that any artist takes, painters, musicians, whatever. Writing, especially, is another way of having a conversation, a genuine desire to share something with the reader, to say: 'Look, isn't this interesting, the way we live now?'

CW: Back to your eleven o'clock switch—is there anything you do to make it happen, or do you just wait?

AL: I have to be sure there is no urgent domestic thing, some unpaid bill or whatever. I have to not have anything nagging at the back of my mind, so I'll quite often pre-cook dinner, pay a few bills, do an urgent email. I've got to have that out of the way. I think that might be a female thing, I'm not sure, but without being obsessive about it I do have a love of order. I can't, for example, work in an untidy room. Then I have to make a cup of coffee, but since I developed late-middle-age heartburn I now have decaf. When a masseur suggested decaf to me I laughed scornfully and she replied by saying you can trick the body and it's true. It turns out the caffeine is not the essential ingredient, it's the ritual that matters.

CW : You don't sound very distractible.

AL: I'm terribly distractible! John Tranter once said he could happily spend all day in a hardware store, and I love to potter around the house. And when I'm in the city I like to window-shop, to look at objects, to handle them, to get out of my head. One way I minimise distraction is to live in a remote area—there are not many people around me—and I never answer the phone and I never answer the door. I'm a big emailer but I can do that in the evening.

CW: You don't compulsively check email all day, like I do.

AL: I compulsively check it in the morning, but I don't compulsively answer it, unless it's urgent. I love email. I hate the phone, but email is a writer's medium, isn't it? No, I could spend all day on email. I often write long emails; you know, you write people long emails, and you get three lines back! [*laughs*]

CW: So between eleven and two is the best time for you, the juiciest time—

AL: There's no juicy time for me. I'm never inspired. You hear writers on panels saying, 'Oh, the character just took me over and it just flowed through me,' and I think, I have never, ever had that experience. Ever. Not for five minutes. Now, it might be because I've got a critical brain and have had a rigorous intellectual training. Maybe I'm overcritical, maybe I think too much, maybe I self-edit to a counter-productive degree—but, whatever, this 'taking over' process has never happened to me. Surprise developments, yes, but that's different.

It's like listening to other meditators who have had big experiences—white lights, visions, all that. I never have them.

CW: I love the story about meditation in *Reading Madame Bovary*.

AL: Well, that's my meditation. Thinking: 'Did I put the washing on?', 'Oh, I've forgotten to defrost the chook.' Other people have Experiences. I never have Experiences. It's the same with writing. I never have Inspiration.

The only rule I have is that I must have a free day—and that rule is *because* I have no other rules. I think this is deeply ingrained. My husband is a routine person: he must have breakfast at the same time, lunch at the same time, dinner at the same time and he must watch the seven o'clock news. But I hate routine. I've tried for years to have one and it never works. All I can do is clear the day, not answer the phone or the door, not make any arrangements and hope for the best.

And it might mean I get half an hour's good work done, or I might get four hours' good work done, who knows?

Sometimes I might have to read for two hours in order to write a hundred words. Not necessarily read on the subject I'm writing on, but something that gets me into the zone. By the way, I think all work-in-progress is mostly loose, uneven and sometimes downright bad until you're about twenty per cent away from being finished. This is probably the most useful piece of advice I can give to writing students; you must realise that more often than not you pull the thing together towards the end. So if you're reading a draft and you think it's no good, it very possibly *is* no good, but that doesn't mean it is not eventually going to be good.

The truth is that something happens along the way and you have to have faith in the process. Towards the end you finally see what needs to go and what needs to stay, but the stuff that's not very good—that's sketchy and unpolished—is a necessary scaffolding and, to mix metaphors, the fuel that keeps you going.

CW: Do you have definite phases of a novel's development, or is it more blurry than that?

AL: Sometimes I write the first third over and over and over twenty times because it's all so dreadful. In doing this I'm trying to get the voice or the tone right. David Malouf once said that you need to find your 'tuning fork'. It might be one paragraph, and you think, that's it.

For me it's about tone and rhythm. In books on writing there is too much emphasis on plot and characterisation and not enough on the more intangible elements. The most important thing is to find the voice, find the tone, establish the inner rhythm, the momentum that carries the thing along. E.M. Forster is good on this and *Aspects of the Novel* is still the best thing written on fiction as far as I'm concerned. All those dry and boring books on narratology they sometimes prescribe on university writing courses are a waste of time.

I especially recommend to young writers Forster's two chapters 'Prophecy' and 'Pattern and Rhythm'. You know, you're in a bookshop and you pick up a book and straightaway you know if you're going to be able to read this writer. You don't care what it's about, it's just coming at you and drawing you in. It can be hard to define why, but I think it's tone and rhythm. And that's what can be frustrating about some editors, they'll cut a word out of a sentence, saying 'You don't need that word.' They have a tin ear. In a literal sense you don't need the word but you need it for the rhythm of the sentence. There are some editors who can't hear that rhythm, or the structural rhythm of a paragraph. Who was it who said that all art aspires to the quality of music?

The other thing I aim for is a style that breathes. One reviewer called me a 'plain writer', by which he meant that I don't go in much for figurative speech and what's often described as 'poetic' prose. But I aim for a clarity and lucidity that creates a space between the words, a style that gives the reader space to enter into the text and have a conversation with it. Too much 'poetic' writing is congested and obfuscating. And the same applies to writers who give you too much detail, too much lengthy description or too much back story. It can be suffocating.

CW: Do you keep a notebook? How do you use it?

AL: I don't keep a single-purpose notebook but I always carry a small notepad and write scrappy notes in it. For one thing, I don't have a good memory. For example, right now I'm writing a series of dialogues between two characters in a park. So on my way here I went over to Enmore Park and I took a few notes, because I'm not very observant when it comes to nature. I never know the names of trees or plants. There's very little nature in my work, so I need to write things down, and sometimes break off a twig and take it to someone and say, 'What's that tree?' [*laughs*]

Or sometimes a line will flash into your brain—and if you don't get that down straightaway, the approximation doesn't work. It's uncanny. One of my favourite short stories is by Norman Mailer in an old collection called *Advertisements for Myself.* It's a story about a writer in New York who's having an argument in the street with his girlfriend and some of the lines that are coming out are fantastic, and he's thinking, 'If I just duck behind the telephone booth will she notice if I get my notebook out? Because I'll only remember an approximate version of this argument and I won't get the exact right phrasing.' It's a delightful story. I used to prescribe it sometimes on courses, just as a little joke amongst writers.

Because the writer part of you is always on, isn't it? There's this awful, ruthless, churning machine and it doesn't matter where you are, you're thinking, 'What's here that I can use?' I don't know about you, but that's how I am. Or if you are somewhere and you're bored, you think, 'Oh this is a waste of an evening, now what can I retrieve from it in the way of material?'

CW: In Norman Mailer's book on writing he says, 'You gotta rotate your crops.' My book in progress is always some kind of reaction against the previous one, but some writers' books might grow out of the previous one. What about you?

AL: I'm not sure I can relate to this. My main stimulus is what's going on around me right now and in my own mind it doesn't have much to do with what I've written before. Sometimes I think that if I were young now I might make documentaries. I've always thought of myself as a documentary writer, a chronicler of the times. I think all my novels are all about a portrait of a particular decade. *The Morality of Gentlemen* is about the culture I grew up in in the '50s and early '60s; *The Reading Group* is about a political culture I was heavily involved in in the '70s; *Camille's Bread* is about what was happening in Sydney in the '80s; *The Philosopher's Doll* is about yuppies in the '90s and the ways in which medicalised fertility presents new dilemmas in the fate versus free-will debate.

The one I'm writing now is about what is currently being described as the postsecular era, which includes in part the mainstreaming of what we once called New Age spirituality. The mainstream media tends to write as if this was still the domain of hippies when in fact it has penetrated almost every sphere of mainstream life in one way or another. This latest novel is about a man who prides himself on being a rationalist but who has a mid-life crisis and undergoes a religious conversion which completely throws him. He has to rethink who he is. As for my non-fiction, it's never been about generalised subjects like boats or gardening or bushwalking, but always about the politics of the moment.

CW: How much do you think a writer should be in the world and how much separate from it?

AL: That's a big question, isn't it? It's a problem that every writer has to solve in her or his own way. Because you have to be out of the world to write—but if you're out of the world too much for too long, you begin to dry, to become self-referential, or repeat yourself. We all know writers who basically write the same book over and over.

CW: But some people can do that—Alice Munro has the same sort of character over and over . . .

AL: She has the same preoccupations, but she always finds a new way or a new perspective on them. Of course you tend to have the same obsessions all your life because that's who you are. I can see the same obsessions repeating themselves all the way through my work, in particular the question of the relationship between private and public morality. What do we owe to ourselves and how does this relate to what we owe to others? When I published *Camille's Bread* some reviewers said it was a great departure from my earlier political novels but the reviewer and academic David Matthews wrote an astute piece arguing that it was more a case of exploring the same preoccupations in a different sphere.

I'm interested in the meaning of life and that life is the life we live now. That's why I write solely about contemporary life and why I don't write or read historical novels. You can nominate an historical novel and tell me how good it is, how wonderful, and how it's won every prize in Australia, or the Booker, and I won't read it. I read historical novels when I was young and came to the conclusion that they are bogus. The critic James Wood is good on this and anyone who wants to follow up on the argument can read him in *The Broken Estate*. Wood argues that the project of the novel is to map the way in which human consciousness works, including significant changes in that consciousness, and this must necessarily be of the moment. In technical terms an historical novel may be very well written, very skilful, but the truth is we cannot access or accurately reproduce the sensibility of past eras, so what's the point?

If I want to read history I can read any number of good historians—I don't need a writer to 'imagine' what some historical character was thinking. Such a manoeuvre has no credibility for me. Did Napoleon say this or didn't he? What do the records tell us? I'm interested to read an historian's speculation on what Napoleon might have said or thought, based on the archives, but that's as far as it goes. Which is why I like, for example, Malcolm Knox's work, because he's telling me about an aspect of contemporary Sydney, a subculture that I'm not familiar with, and in addition he's giving me a male take on it—you know, it's news. The novel should bring news. I want the fiction I read to give me news of contemporary life, the kind of insights I can't get in any other form or available media.

If you really like historical novels, well, you don't need a writer to be in touch with anything but the archives. And historical novels with this omniscient point of view that knows everything are exasperating—it's a bogus authority that doesn't even attempt, speculatively, to present contesting points of view.

Some people might see my first novel, *The Morality of Gentlemen*, as a kind of historical novel, but in fact I knew those men I was writing about, I grew up with them, I knew the way they spoke, and so on. I had, in other words, some access to their sensibility. And even then I felt that it would be bad faith, the worst kind of hubris, to write from an omniscient point of view, so I wrote that novel from multiple points of view. In the end the reader has to make up her or his own mind. Interestingly I got a lot of positive feedback on that. And by the way, I have the same problem with biographers who confidently assert things about their subject that they couldn't possibly be certain of.

CW: Is there a part of a book which comes more naturally or easily to you than others?

AL: No. It's all slog. But the funny thing is, if you get it right, it reads like you knocked it off over a spare weekend, and then other people think they could do it. They have no sense of the time and effort and the craft that goes into it.

CW: That reminds me of my favourite Patrick White quote, about people who gush at him how marvellous it must be to write. And he says, 'As though one sat down at the *escritoire* after breakfast, and it poured out like a succession of bread and butter letters, instead of being dragged out, by tongs, a bloody mess, in the small hours.'

AL: Oh yes. That's true most of the time, but there are times when if you get out of your own way, to use an old Zen piece of advice, you let your unconscious have a word and often it will pop up and give you a few really good pages that do just flow. For me it doesn't happen very often, or go for very long.

So the trick is to get out of your own way, which is not easy. You have to stop trying to plan everything. Stop trying to be in control. Not be attached, be prepared to fail. If the book doesn't work, it doesn't work, okay, I'll do something else. Which is easier as you get older, because you have more confidence. You know, you've finished a couple of books, so if this one doesn't work, okay, you'll do something else. And you're not going to make a lot of money from any of it anyway, you're not going to make your fortune . . . [laughs]

CW: I see many new writers being interested in the machinations of the publishing industry, in a way I find worrying.

AL: Yes, but in a way you have to go through it, don't you? It's part of the model. It's part of the rite of passage, to be young and desperate to be noticed. It's the whole growing-up process.

First of all you're desperate for attention, then you get some, then you realise it hasn't actually solved all your problems, either personally or professionally. And you can't tell a young writer that—you can hold their hand and support them while they cry bitter tears, and tell them they're really talented and one day it will be fine, but they actually have to go through it.

CW: How do you think you've changed as a writer?

AL: I don't think I've changed at all, not really. I'm a ruthless chucker-outer and I keep my manuscripts for a year after a book is published and then I send them to the tip, otherwise I'd be drowning in a mountain of paper. But a few years back my husband was doing work in under the roof and came across a box of very old papers. In the box were some of my school examination papers and I sat and read them through and was struck by the fact that my style was exactly the same then as it is now. I think your style is like having big feet or black hair. It's you.

CW: In one of your stories a character says: 'That was just a rationalisation, transient structures of thought that clear a space for some deeper instinct or intuition to do its work.' Can you say more about this?

AL: Well, what we call 'education' is about having a lifelong conversation between reason and intuition and maintaining a productive dialogue, and balance, between the two. That's why you have therapy, isn't it? Because you are maybe too much a captive of one mode or the other, too cerebral or too impulsive. Not that I've had much therapy, I've never been able to afford it. I'd love to do the Woody Allen thing and have it forever. What a luxury!

I do think that you have a deep intuitive knowing that's always there, but you get in your own way and you obscure it, or you argue with it and you rationalise it. Because we live in a culture which is hyper-rational, and is always trying to teach you to rationalise your intuition. So you keep getting in your own way instead of just, you know, asking the inner voice. But then, it's not quite that simple. The big question is: how do you know to trust the inner voice? How do you know the inner voice isn't a rationalisation of your primal drives and desires? It's a maze, isn't it? And when we talk about 'life experience' we are talking about the strategies we've developed over time for dealing with that.

This is why I think meditation is such a good practice, because it helps to clarify these issues, helps you to behave intuitively in a way that just seems to work. This is getting into a whole area of metaphysics—but you're trying to access another dimension of meaning, and you've got this cultural conditioning, this armour around you that's screening out other sources of knowledge and insight. It's very hard to talk about, because it sounds airy-fairy and New Age. It's actually not New Age, it's a physics—and a biochemistry, a neurology—that we don't yet understand. All I know is that if I stop meditating, I make bad decisions and I even become physically more clumsy.

CW: So meditation helps your writing?

AL: I think meditation runs a process on your nervous system that purges a lot of the dross. Somehow it melts away. But as to whether it helps my writing, well, I wrote a lot before I began to meditate.

CW: I love the exchanges between the two men in the meditation story.

AL: It's liberating to write about men. I like writing about men.

CW: Are you writing about yourself in them?

AL: Yes. There's much more of me in my male characters than my female characters. But also, I was raised by men for the first five or six years of my life. My mother worked and the men in my family were shift workers. So often during the day I was looked after by my father—which meant that he just carted me around wherever he wanted to go. The pub, the bookmaker's club, the wharf—there was no concession. He'd take me over one of the big boats that would come into the harbour in Hobart, or have a few drinks with his mates while I sat out on the hotel steps with my raspberry lemonade, and the drunks would come out and give me a shilling. It was quite a good life, really! And it meant I grew up feeling comfortable around men.

CW: By far the most autobiographical I have been is in the male character of my last novel.

AL: I guessed. You were so comfortable in that character. Another writer can see that. I thought, yep. Writers are always reading another writer in terms of strategies. 'Oh, that's a good trick. Ooh, she did that well, oh I wonder how I would have done that?'

I read a story of Robert Drewe's in *The Rip* where a corrupt financier retires to the Byron Bay area. And he's renting a house that's got a swimming pool, and he finds a snake in the swimming pool. Okay, no big deal. But then a second snake appears. And I thought, this is brilliant! Two snakes! How risky a move that was and yet he pulled it off. I wanted to say to him, 'Fantastic, what a cheek to even attempt that second snake but it worked!' [*laughs*] Now, a reader wouldn't have that response, that's a writerly response. A writer doesn't read the way other people read.

But it is liberating to write about the other gender. That's why Henry James' heroines are always Henry James. And when people say, 'Patrick White is a misogynist, all those awful women'—those awful women are aspects of White. It's obvious.

CW: I don't find them awful. They're trapped.

AL: Well, Jung has an interesting take on this, a belief that the individual Self is androgynous in its essence. Every man has a female side, if you like, that Jung calls the anima, and a male writer's female characters are projections of his own anima. And vice versa for women writers. Jung's not so good on the woman's animus, he tends to have a wholly negative construction of it, but his disciple, Marie-Louise von Franz, improves on his original insight.

CW: You once said: 'People talk about writers' egos. I don't know how any writer can have any ego left after a certain age.' What's the role of ego in writing?

AL: What I meant was that writers are usually their own harshest critics and the more they write the fewer illusions they have about their own talent. And in addition they have hostile and sometimes downright insulting reviews to help keep their egos from becoming inflated. Moreover, Australia is a small market and the rewards, financial and otherwise, are limited.

But as to whether writers, or artists of any kind, are more egotistical than others, well, I see no evidence for that. What writers have to be is driven, and dogged, and these attributes are usually inborn and have nothing to do with 'ego'. It's a calling, and to some degree it's out of your control. At some point in your youth you learn that you have to do it in order to stay sane. I've had postgrad writing students who were very talented but didn't have the drive to go on with it. They had other things they wanted to do more. Of course, the ego is wounded by criticism, but that's true of anyone. You put it behind you and get on with the next project.

My old friend and colleague Jan McKemmish used to say, 'Writers write. That's what they do. Some do it well, some do it badly, some succeed, some don't—but they write. They don't talk about it, they write.'

Mind you, I can talk under wet cement!

CW: How do you know when your work is going well?

AL: If I'm not bored it's going well. I have a low boredom threshold so I think that's what I would call going well—that I remain engrossed in the process, regardless of the final outcome. That doesn't mean it's going to please other people, or it's even going to get published or be successful or any of those things. But 'going badly' is when I'm bored.

CW: Have you ever wanted to give up?

AL: Oh yeah. I've had a few tantrums. I had a major tantrum after *The Philosopher's Doll* came out. I thought nobody had got it. Well, some people did, but—not enough! [*laughs*] But that was to be expected because in narratological terms I pulled a few risky moves and a lot of readers didn't like them.

For a few months there I thought, 'That's it! I'm wasting my time, I'm going to write non-fiction where I can make a decent living, blah blah blah.' And then before long you're making notes, thinking 'Oh, this'd be interesting . . .' You're back there writing another novel. Which shows, among other things, that it is a therapeutic process. It's your way of processing something, but it's also a wonderful form of play. There's a click when the thing locks into place and a form emerges. Exploring the form, that's the thing—the form is always greater than the sum of the parts, and this thing appears, this form! In the past I've used the analogy of the magician's trick where the magician pours random ingredients into his top hat (flour, milk, eggs in their shells, but also lolly wrappers, sawdust and talcum powder) and utters the magic formula to produce—a perfectly baked cake! Of course, the cake is not always perfectly baked. So many novels are less than the sum of their parts.

CW: Why is this 'locking in' important?

AL: Well, this is the big aesthetic question, the one philosophers chew over. Have you noticed, by the way, how unsatisfactory most writing on the subject of aesthetics is? I'm drawn to the Platonic notion that there are ideal forms, that truth exists in a series of perfect forms and that whether we are artists or physicists we seek to explore those forms, to connect to that truth by aspiring to map or to emulate those forms. The closer we approximate them, the more revealing the work and the more satisfying. It's that 'aha' moment we have when we experience a fully realised work of art. If you see a photograph of *Blue Poles*, it's like, oh yeah. But when you *see Blue Poles*, the form comes out three-dimensionally to encompass you, and you have this sense of some perfect realm or sphere where everything comes together—it's aesthetic satisfaction, and no-one I've read has ever successfully defined what that means. We just know it when we experience it. It's why *The Great Gatsby* is an almost perfect book and *Tender* *is the Night,* wonderful as it is, is not a perfect book. It never found its form, and Fitzgerald knew that. He kept shuffling the beginning and the middle around and it bothered him for the rest of his life.

CW: But the form also has to be natural too, doesn't it? You can construct a shape and write to fill it up but if it's not coming from within the material then it doesn't work.

AL: Exactly. That's why you have to trust the process and not get stuck in a plan. It's hard to write good fiction. That lovely thing E.M. Forster says, that to write good fiction you have to be able to do ten things—'and unfortunately you have to be able to do all ten of them at the one time'. It has to work page for page, sentence for sentence, and then it has to work as a whole. It has to realise its latent form.

Sometimes you'll pick up a book by someone who writes beautifully, and you'll read fifty pages and think, 'This is terrific!' But then as you go on, nothing's developing, nothing's happening, it's just more 'fine writing' and there's no shape emerging. And you know you're never going to have that opening-out experience, where you feel connected to something larger than yourself. It's like—I have to use the word—it's like a communion. Good writing is a form of communion and maybe that's because there are these ideal forms, and art is one of the ways in which we can connect most directly and meaningfully with them.

CW: A painter friend of mine says people think they don't know what good art is, but that in every show he's ever had, the best pictures sell first. You don't understand it, but you know it.

AL: You do know it. It's instinctive. But at the same time I think that's more true of the visual arts than of literature. For it's also true with fiction that there is no single standard of excellence. A book is a meeting of subjectivities and the subjectivity of one writer will speak to one reader but not to another. There are some writers who don't speak to me at all but I can see why they speak to other readers, can see that they are in the same zone in terms of their preoccupations, and their conditioning, what's important to them. It's just not important to me and I'm not interested. So I don't mean to say—I'm not trying to posit an idea of excellence that everybody responds to. I think literature is very much a one-to-one conversation, which is why I cannot argue with someone who says *The Alchemist* is their favourite book when they've obviously got a lot out of it.

CW: Do you think about readers as you write—do you write for anyone in particular?

AL: I think about the reader in a general sense. But you discover from experience that your ideal reader is often the most unlikely person. It's happened to me often. I think I've written some radical piece of political fiction and some wealthy eastern suburbs matron will come up to me at a book signing—the hair, the gold jewellery, the full package—and she amazes me by getting every single thing in the work, the entire subtext, all the allusions. And so you learn not to try and second-guess your readers because you don't know what's going on in their heads. Whereas publishers, who so often think of themselves as being in the avant-garde, I've found as a group that they are often quite conservative.

CW: Margaret Atwood said something in *Bad Writing: The Movie* that sent a chill down my spine: 'There's no rule that says you steadily get better.' I realised that, foolishly, I had been banking on it.

AL: Oh, no. Just because you can write one good book doesn't mean you'll ever write another one. It's not like going to the gym, it's not an improvement program. You do learn some things, though—you learn how to hold your nerve, and that just because this thing doesn't work it doesn't mean the next thing won't.

And you have to be careful in talking about bad writing. In the past I have run some community writing courses, which can produce a lot of bad writing. But they are tremendously worthwhile because they are therapeutic for the person doing it. The writing becomes a conversation that the self has with the self, a conversation that can only be had when the self sees its thoughts externalised on the page. So in instances where you or I might think 'that's bad writing',

I've seen people get a powerfully positive response from their maudlin poems.

I would never dream of telling them 'that's a bad poem' because in that situation it's a case of writing for therapy, which is a perfectly reasonable and respectable thing to do, and anyone who begins to sneer at that doesn't get much change out of me. It's actually doing some good. It's just not to be confused with writing as an art—but it's not invalid, either.

CW: Are you ever afraid while you're writing?

AL: Of what?

CW: Well, I don't know . . . failure? Death? [*laughs*]

AL: When you get to my age you've failed so many times as a writer that, you know, what's another one? The things that haven't worked, all that work you've never published because it hasn't worked . . . A crude analogy would be a professional footballer. Every game is not going to be a good one, even for a high-level athlete who's got everything going for them. Look, the mantra is this: just get on with it. Just get on with it. What else can you do? And find an income. Marry a dentist.

CW: Did you marry a dentist?

AL: No, I didn't! [*laughs*]

CW: You sound very pragmatic about things.

AL: How could you not be?

CW: But your work is more than simple pragmatism.

AL: There's a dialogue I think is going on in any profession—even if you're a politician, or a carpenter. I'm watching a neighbour of mine build a house, he's a professional builder. He's a practical man and at the same time a creative man—and maybe that's a false distinction—and I see that dialogue going on in him, between his practical skills and his creative side.

There's always a conversation going on between instinct and ideas; you have an instinct that you should do this, and then your editorial side begins to critique it. I don't see how you could work any other way—not just as a writer but in anything you do. Otherwise you're just a child splashing paint around, aren't you?

Sometimes your greatest attribute is your doggedness. Your sheer, bloody-minded perseverance. Sometimes I've rewritten a whole manuscript in another voice, from third to first person. This novel in progress about the man—it bothered me that the main character was a man, so I rewrote him as a woman. Didn't work! I'm a woman, so why didn't it work? There were too many other issues running interference, female issues that I felt I would have to incorporate, that I didn't want to have to deal with in this particular narrative. So in the end, what works, works.

CW: I want to ask you about the rich dream lives lots of your characters have.

AL: Does that annoy you?

CW: No! I used to worry about using dreams, as a writer. I loved having rules, and one of the rules is 'Tell a dream, lose a reader', as Henry James is supposed to have said. But now I think the more sophisticated a writer is, the more they can use dreams in interesting ways and lots do—Richard Ford does, and there's a little brief beautiful bit in a story by Amy Bloom, and Ann Patchett's *State of Wonder* is full of dreams. It's such a potent part of life, if one is a big dreamer, it now seems wrong to me to leave it out of books. Are you a vivid dreamer?

AL: I am a big dreamer. I'm a poor sleeper so I'm always waking up and waking out of a vivid dream. But the dreams in my fiction are rarely the ones I've had myself. It's unlikely you will be able to reproduce the inner charge of your own dreaming and it can be a trap even to try, so like everything else in fiction you have to fake it up. It's funny you should raise this because I've often wondered why other writers don't use dreams more often. They are a rich way of allowing the unconscious to have a voice in the narrative, to open up a space of mystery and to gesture towards the complexity of some action that may on the surface appear simple or obvious.

Part of the reason I use dreams is that I don't like reading writers who give me a sense that they know everything. Margaret Drabble is a classic example: she's magisterial; she knows everything. She knows what her characters have had for breakfast, what colour eyeshadow they wear, how often they burp or fart, she knows everything. I can't bear it. Her novel about the Thatcher era, *The Ice Age,* is a good novel but it could have been a great one if she hadn't overloaded it with so much naturalistic detail.

A text has a literal surface—the 'story'—and then it has its own unconscious, a poetry that you the writer can either obscure or reveal, or if not reveal, hint at. If you're giving characters dreams, it's a way of saying to the reader, 'There is some mystery here, I'm not quite across it, what do you think?' It's a way of setting up more of a conversational or speculative relationship with the reader. Some readers respond to dreams in fiction, some don't. For me they add another dimension.

CW: And dreams have a sort of watery quality—a part of the person that they themselves don't understand . . .

AL: Yes. It's a little puzzle for them to maybe figure out. But also, there's that literal surface of life, and then there's that oceanic meaning underneath, and dreams are a message from another realm that we don't understand. Any narrative that doesn't have a few messages from that realm is, for me, deficient. Too mastered, too known, too literal. Too naturalistic. I hate naturalism.

CW: What do you mean by naturalism?

AL: *Neighbours. Home & Away.* Just about any Australian television drama. I spent the first ten years of my writing life thinking about forms of realism. How can a writer begin to represent the real through the very limited medium of language? How to avoid bad faith? Naturalism is a one-dimensional aesthetic that gives us the 'obvious'. The world is taken for granted in a way that creates a complacent banality. Ultimately the effect is like being under a bell jar. The air becomes stale. What people mean by 'realism' is often a formulaic naturalism, a taken-for-granted set of conventions about what is 'obvious' or 'common sense' in interpreting and representing the world, with no—or minimal—awareness of the degree to which all forms of narrative distort as much as they reveal, and no reflection on new and innovative—or even old and forgotten—techniques for creating a fresh way of seeing things.

I've always been interested in exploratory and inventive modes of realism, not for their own sake but because each new project demands its own aesthetic. I could get very technical on the subject but this is probably not the time or place. I would say, however, that one of the important functions of university writing courses is to encourage students to interrogate taken-for-granted modes of representation. If you decide to write in a conventional way, at least know why you've made that decision. Traditionally, film-makers have been much more concerned with issues of representation and more innovative. And to be fair, the camera gives them more scope, but that doesn't mean that we as writers shouldn't think about it. You don't have to be obviously 'experimental', you don't have to write like Gertrude Stein or James Joyce—small unorthodox manoeuvres can have potent effects.

CW: I want to ask you about ambition. I think Raymond Carver said every writer needs a bit of luck and a bit of ambition, and too much of one or the other is fatal.

AL: You do need both of those things. That sums it up. You need enough drive to do it, but too much of the wrong kind of ambition—the desire to be famous, for example—will distort the work. No luck and you are likely to get discouraged. And you have to accept the degree to which so many things are beyond your control. I've known writers who were relentless networkers but in the end it didn't pay off for them. I've known others who scarcely left the house and fortune was kind to them. All the best things that have happened to me have come completely out of the blue. Like winning a prize. It's either never crossed my mind I would win a prize, or I've won the prizes it never crossed my mind I'd win.

It teaches you. There is actually a lesson in this: *forget it*. Forget ambition, other than aesthetic ambition, the desire to write something interesting, to try something new. Get out of your own way, get on with the work. The work is your domain. You are not in control of the rest.

JOAN LONDON grew up in Perth, Western Australia, in the 1950s. She graduated from the University of Western Australia having studied English and French and then, like many of her generation, spent time travelling through Asia and Europe, an experience that affected her deeply and gave rise to some of her work.

London is the author of the acclaimed short-story collections *Sister Ships* and *Letter to Constantine* (published together as *The New Dark Age* in 2004 and 2010), and the novels *Gilgamesh* and *The Good Parents*. The Nobel Prize winner Alice Munro—one of London's literary heroines—has praised her stories as 'fluid, alive—such grace and sharpness together', and her books have won or been shortlisted for many prizes, including the Miles Franklin Literary Award, the Orange Prize and the Christina Stead Prize for Fiction. Since her thirties London has lived in Fremantle, Western Australia, but during the five years prior to this interview had commuted to Melbourne every few weeks with her husband Geoffrey London, who was the Victorian Government Architect.

Despite this split home life, London is deeply anchored to Fremantle and Western Australia—her two children and grandchildren also live there—and speaks lovingly of the landscape of the west.

I have always deeply admired London's writing, which the *Washington Post* described as 'a seamlessly shifting blend of poetry, pathos and humor', and I have recently come to feel that *The Good Parents* is the only book I've ever truly wished I had written myself. She writes, seemingly effortlessly, of the intricate and complicated bonds between families, lovers and siblings with great compassion and stunning precision. She says of her beloved Chekhov: 'There is no ego in his work; he is complete observer.' The same can be said of London's writing.

We had met once or twice before at writers' festivals, but it was not until I spent a month on a residency in Perth in 2013 that I got to know London better. As soon as I accepted the residency I wrote asking her for an interview, and over the month of my stay, London and her husband welcomed me to their large old Fremantle terrace several times. I enjoyed many conversations with her about writing and reading, about our mutual love of Hilary Mantel and Alice Munro, and her passion for film and Russian literature. She is generous and collegial, and was particularly encouraging as I struggled with my own novel in progress during that time. Often through this interview she would stop speaking to turn my questions back on me, asking about my own views on what I'd asked her.

Whenever I left a conversation with London I came away buoyed by the possibilities for my own work.

Although she's in her mid-sixties, London seems a particularly youthful woman, with a mass of thick dark hair that swings wildly when she bursts into loud, delighted laughter, which she does often. She is extremely self-deprecating and articulates a deal of self-doubt, yet at the same time displays the deeper will and self-determination of the serious artist. She has discovered and made her own path through decades of experience, and appears to be no longer concerned with what others may think of her or her work. While she clearly has no interest in a literary 'career' in the public sense, the work itself, with its depth and imaginative scope, displays the highest literary ambition.

For this interview, conducted in 2013 and first published in 2014, we sat in London's kitchen, eventually moving to her small, light-filled writing room at the top of the stairs where she showed me her walls covered in notes and the shoebox of collected postcards she uses to spark characters and scenes. She had just sent her new novel—set in a children's polio convalescent home in Perth in the 1950s—off to her agent, but was still seeking to resolve the final scenes of the book. The book was *The Golden Age*, published in 2014 to great acclaim and winning the Prime Minister's Literary Award for Fiction in 2015.

One of the most appealing things about talking with London is her deep curiosity, her open sense of wonder about the world, and about reading and writing. Perhaps it's this questing nature, always seeking to discover and understand and distil, that makes her work so penetrating, so fresh.

CW: You've just finished your new novel—congratulations. How do you feel in this phase?

JL: Well, I feel lighter. And that—for a short time—I can leave it. It's like giving a child to a babysitter or something, because I haven't fully resolved the ending, and I know it's best to leave it. I need a short break from it. So completing it is still ahead of me, working with an editor, second thoughts . . . But I feel like I've done the job as much as I can for the time being, and I'm a little bit free.

However, there's also an emptiness there now—I mean, I love working. I love working hard. I hate it when I'm beginning something and it's slow and tentative and clumsy, and I'm not sure at all that it will work ... But when it is coming together, then I love it, really. I can work all day.

CW: What is it that you love about that stage?

JL: It's satisfying. And it's something a little beyond you. Towards the end, I can have those moments, you know, of feeling, 'Oh, of course! That goes *there*!' Or 'No, this is what happens!'

It feels almost as if it comes from somewhere beyond yourself—but you've first had to earn it over the years. It takes me years to write a novel. We started going to Melbourne four years ago, and I was researching it then. So it's been about five years.

CW: Is the place where you work important to you?

JL: Where I work is important—it doesn't have to be right here, but I am tremendously attached to Fremantle and to living close to the sea.

At first I found it quite hard going to Melbourne—although it's only two weeks on, two weeks off, often less, but it was like dragging me out of my burrow. But I've come to enjoy it. Melbourne has also become a little burrow, I have a desk there, and I can work there. I have to have my station—I can't just set up anywhere, I don't think. I need to feel private and quiet, and after a while I accumulate quite a lot of visual things. I like having postcards, I'm a postcard collector. A deltiologist. I have shoeboxes of postcards of people's faces.

Or I have postcards of things that are redolent to me. I sort of shuffle through them and think, 'Hmm, that looks a bit like Frank', that sort of thing. They're like cues.

CW: Do you do this randomly, or do you need to find the right one?

JL: I need to find the right one.

CW: Do you have an established routine?

JL: No, but I'll sit there as soon as possible after various things have been done. I always get my duties done first—phone calls, send off emails and stuff, and then I'm free. And then unless I'm interrupted, or have to do something, I work as long as I can. By about three in the afternoon I'm tired, and then I can get dispirited. It's better to knock off then.

It's amazing, actually, how important energy is for writing. There's no time like the morning, really.

CW: It's hard to explain to people who don't do it how physically tiring it is, to spend all day thinking really hard. But it is, isn't it? It physically wipes you out.

JL: Mmm—and once you're tired you do get dispirited.

CW: Some people write quickly and then pare it back, or some write word by word, carefully . . . what's your working style?

JL: Oh, I've been plagued, always, by knowing I do it wrong. I know you're supposed to just *go for it*. But I try and get it right as I go. I mean, I do sometimes say, 'Oh, enough!' And I just put down everything. And it is quite useful, I might get a few things out of that—I'll try anything to get going! [*laughs*] But then I fix that bit up. Because I feel I have to get on the right foot, and I have to find and dig into a seam that's interesting, a little surprising, unexpected, or I'm bored. I can't just write stuff. I have to get a hook, every day, of something that has a truth, or something real to me. And some days I don't get a hook . . .

CW: What would that be—an image, or a bit of story, for instance? What does the hook consist of?

JL: Well, something I just like, I suppose. Actually, more and more, I just like to be surprised. In the beginning, when I have nothing, when I start with a desert-plain kind of feeling, I start getting ideas and I write them down, and I sort them, and sometimes I number them in the way they should appear and stuff like that. I do think in terms of scenes. Characters—I really find characters have to emerge. It's no good constructing somebody because I need them. I often do need somebody, you know, the secondary characters who make something happen, but they too have to start taking on a life of their own, even if I've conjured them up. The main characters are themselves from the beginning, and they have to come to me really.

CW: Do you feel you have to wait for them?

JL: I think they're there from the beginning. The subsidiary characters not so much. They can be harder to find. Some characters burst onto the stage and they're who they are, and they may not be the major ones but they're really enjoyable.

CW: At the end of the day when you've had a good day, what does that mean?

JL: Well, I love to have written a page. Or a page and a half. I know you're supposed to do 250 words a day —

CW: Who is this supposed-to person saying this stuff!

JL: [*laughs*] Nobody, really . . . but for a long time I felt I was probably doing it wrong because I was so slow, and I had bad habits that way, you know. But it just seems to be how I do it.

CW: How do you know when a book is finished enough to hand it to your agent or your first reader?

JL: I think when you've gone as far as you can go. And sometimes you feel, 'Yes, that's it!' But sometimes I know, like I know now, that I haven't quite clinched the deal, which could be as little as a sentence, actually. I remember really hunting for the ending of *Gilgamesh*. In those days I used to work in that room out there [*gestures to garden studio*] and I'd watch the life of the family here inside, going on, and I'd sit there and come up with something, and I'd come in and tell them and then go back. I remember finally getting to it. But it took me a long time. It's like the final piece going into the puzzle. But I haven't got to that this time, not yet.

CW: But you will.

JL: Yes. But also, I look forward to working with an editor. If the editor's good, what a joy that is!

CW: It's a very intimate relationship, isn't it? Can you say more about what happens in that relationship? What does a good editor do that another kind of reader can't?

JL: The really good editors are objective, look at the work without knowing you personally, see the work in the context of all their experience of literature. It may not be to their personal taste, but they can understand how much it fulfils the vision that the writer has for it, and where it falls short of that. They understand the potential of this work, its place in the current culture. They have faith in it, like a good teacher with a promising student. And then they apply themselves with unstinting concentration to the sense and logic of your sentences, the unconscious contradictions or repetitions you have made, and commit themselves to the voice and point of view of the writer.

I can feel very grateful to someone who has so conscientiously and sometimes brilliantly applied themselves to my words.

CW: You've told me before that when you finished *Gilgamesh*, you thought it was no good and you put it away.

JL: Yes. I thought, 'Oh God, what a pile of made-up—nonsense!' I just turned against it. It was almost like looking at your face in a mirror and thinking, 'Ugh!' Perhaps you're sick of it . . . you need a break . . .

CW: So what convinced you to take it out of the drawer?

JL: Well, Drusilla Modjeska came to Perth, and she came to dinner, and Geoffrey said, 'Joan's got a novel and she's put it away.' Drusilla said, 'Show it to me.' And I did, I sent it to her. So she saved me. I do have this feeling of indebtedness to her. Because I had thought, 'Well that's it.' I thought, 'I'll write stories again instead.'

CW: Did you believe Drusilla instantly when she said it was good?

JL: Yes! All you need is someone *else* to say, 'It's fine, it's good.' I mean, also, I knew her well enough, I knew she was a straight talker. And that she might say, 'Oh, you know, yep. You're right.' Or, 'Perhaps if you chopped out a bit you could . . .' But no—she liked it.

CW: And it did so well. Readers just love that book.

JL: What about you, how do you feel when you finish something?

CW: Um, I'm usually somehow ashamed.

JL: Yeah. That's a terrible feeling! Why do we feel like that?

CW: Maybe it's because we've exposed something very important to us. It's the risk, perhaps.

JL: The English novelist Tessa Hadley says something about this. She said: 'What you're writing should hurt and make you feel slightly anxious, and almost ashamed.'

CW: And Jonathan Franzen talks about shame quite a lot, about how he spends more time now investigating the shame and fear involved in writing. I recognise that. It seems very self-punishing in a way I don't like, but I do know my own best work comes out of a place that scares me in some way. What do you make of all this shame?

JL: I think we are always trying to avoid banality, the pleasing, the second-hand. We aspire to be explorers really, uncovering some previously unknown corner of the human psyche and experience, however small and familiar the context of our narratives may be. We can only do this by being completely accurate, completely honest, to the emotion of an experience, so that whatever happens in the work is shown to be inevitable.

And all you have to go on in this exploration are the scraps and fragments of your own experience, sometimes from your deepest guilts or humiliations. Or sometimes the pain you've witnessed in others, taken and used for your own narrative . . . Whatever, you've stopped being the one wincing and become the one making others wince.

Or perhaps this shame comes from the insubstantiality of what you've created compared to actual experience . . . and the shame of self-revelation: *'Don't show off!'* Suddenly the writing all seems so obviously marked by your own quirks and predilections, like looking at your own face in the mirror. 'A poor thing, but my own' sort of feeling . . .

CW: Do you think characters need to be altered in some way by the end of a book? One of the things I loved about *The Good Parents* was the scoured-out feeling I had when I finished it. I felt that I was different, and everyone in the book was different. They had all come through something, and they were altered. And I felt altered.

JL: I'm glad you felt that, that's wonderful. I wanted that, of course, one always does—that's really what we want, isn't it? Readers to get lost in, to identify with, the deep movement in a story. And since I'm mainly about internals, it's got to be movement in that way. Internal change.

CW: It's complex—it's as if the people in the book don't quite understand what has happened but they know they have been changed. That's what I felt.

JL: Well I think change *is* complex. We don't always change the way we think we have. Sometimes you realise that you have changed, but maybe it's not something very dramatic.

I love it, actually. I love, personally, feeling that I've opened up in an area where I might have shut a door. There's nothing

I like more. And nothing I respect more in people than to see them open and change. How wonderful it is, when you're young, to see older people who come around, and understand why you're doing something your way. When I see that happening now, I think: *Bravo!* Because that's what life is, really. Changing and opening, if you can. It's very hard, to yield or give up something you might have hung your hat on for so long.

CW: Do you think the writing—or reading—of a book changes you?

JL: I could say, 'No, of course not, I'm always who I am on one level.' But—oh, where would I be without books? Without writers? The worlds, inner and outer, that they've opened up . . . The music of their language. The evidence of human imagination and experience, the courage of their explorations. The force of their thought. Identifying with experience extends you. The writing of a book changes me in that I think finishing anything that you've tried your hardest at moves you on a little bit, whether it's painting a house or making a journey or teaching a course. It affirms you for a little while. And then you start at the bottom again.

CW: Tell me about your love of Russian literature. This love of writers like Tolstoy and Chekhov comes through in your work very strongly. What do they give you?

JL: Tolstoy, Dostoyevsky, Chekhov are . . . well, they're in *another sphere*. Giants. I'm just one of the millions who love the wonderful, wonderful experience of reading *War and Peace*, or Chekhov's stories. Chekhov is a master. I had a real Chekhov thing for years. There's no ego in his stories. He's complete observer, in control, but at the service of the unexpected, of his art. He is very tough, unsentimental. And his canvas is so broad that everyone has their story; it might be the coachman, or a bishop or a princess, as well as the middle-class characters. I love that. And in the twentieth century there is Vasily Grossman's *Life and Fate*, the great Soviet novel, set during the Second World War. It has the same piercing psychology, insight and honesty, yet huge, humane canvas, even including the interior life of a German captain.

CW: In *The Good Parents* you have a very intimate, very Australian novel, but with this epic sweeping quality I admire so much. In the same way as you just mentioned, you have all these peripheral characters whose lives are all going on as richly and deeply as the main characters' lives. And by the end they too are all changed. As I was reading, I thought, that's what you've got from the Russians.

JL: Maybe that's what I've *attempted*. But with *The Good Parents* I really did want to explore—or present—a time of idealism that was part of my particular generation. That terrible thing of trying to live in communes. [*laughs*]

CW: Communal living really interests you, doesn't it?

JL: Only because I hate it! I had to find that out, because our youth was a time when many people were attempting it.

CW: Is there some part of you that still feels idealistic about that communal way of living?

JL: Not at all. As for most families, it's lovely having guests come and stay, but it's nice when they go . . .

CW: There's a privacy you need, perhaps. Do you think all writers are deeply introverted?

JL: I don't know. But some part of them must be—the job requires you to be alone eight hours a day, really, and to go inside yourself.

CW: Do you find it lonely?

JL: Sometimes. There was a time in Western Australia, about thirty years ago, when Fremantle Arts Centre Press started up. It was when I was beginning to write, and I met some other writers starting out, and suddenly we had a chance of getting published. We were friends, we were supportive. And it was lovely for a little while. But a group can only go so far—you're on your own, actually.

Fremantle Arts Centre Press, started by a visionary West Australian, Ian Templeman, was terribly important to writing here. It gave a start to so many writers, including Elizabeth

Jolley, Marion Campbell, Sally Morgan, John Kinsella, Phil Salom. Some writers from that time have gone on, some have been defeated by illness, the changing world of books, of writing fashions, all sorts of things.

It's a hard life, and I feel I've been lucky that the circumstances of my life have allowed me to continue as a writer. I haven't had to go and teach creative writing as so many writers have to do. I worked in a bookshop, part time, mainly at night, for many years, and I really loved it. It was a good job, and it kept me in touch with the world while not depleting my energy. But any other job . . .

I tried to teach English as a second language, I had a go at teaching creative writing. I hated it! [*laughs*]

CW: Why did you hate it?

JL: No doubt if I'd had to support the family I would have had to get my head around it and make it interesting to me and settle down to it. But at the level I did it, it bored me, all that '*And now you read out your piece*'—I'm afraid it did.

Plus, some of them just weren't *trying* hard enough, they thought of it as an easy option. I'm sure you'd get a student or students who thrilled you, and you really would have that wonderful conversation when you're both getting something out of it. But a lot of them were just going through the motions, at least in those days. And somehow I was unable, or too inexpert or unwilling, to inspire them.

CW: It can be so shocking for writers to come across students who don't seem to care about it.

JL: Yes! It's so central to us.

CW: I want to ask you about your interest in relationships between generations. You write beautifully about parents and children, over and over again. Middle-aged children with elderly parents, or middle-aged parents with teenage children, or parents with babies . . .

JL: Well, it has been a pretty major part of my life, and a fascinating one. I think I've enjoyed growing up, growing older.

There was a time when my parents were sick, until they died, when for ten years their four daughters were fully occupied, very, very busy helping them, looking after them. It was a big lesson about growing old, and in filial duty. Because you know, I'd had my arguments with my parents. It was a lesson in love, really. And then the lesson of children is enormous—the enormous, humbling lesson of bringing up children. It's been a big part of my life.

CW: Has writing from Western Australia given you a different literary perspective? It seems to me people here feel very different from people in the east, but it's not something I would notice.

JL: Good! Well, I have felt like that, but I don't anymore. I think it's been helpful living partly in Melbourne for four or five years now. It's very much a different place, and I really enjoy it and have a good time there. I think it is a big thing, the WA feeling of being far away from everything, and it can lead to a feeling of being overlooked, and a bit of paranoia. I did get sick of that.

I do feel attached here, though. As everybody does who is interested in their landscape, I suppose, I feel it has its own geographical specialness. I'm sure I would feel that way if I lived anywhere—I would get attached. I think quite a lot about it, how this attachment probably comes from your earliest childhood.

Just the nature of the light, the sort of landscape and vegetation around you, probably the habits that climate and geography dictate—going to the beach, sitting outside on summer nights, those kinds of things.

There's a feeling of space here, not just in the immediate surroundings, but in the vast distances from other places, in the map inside your head. Depending on your circumstances, it can feel like a sort of freedom, or even refuge. But along with it can also go a kind of us-and-them feeling: *Oh, they overlook us . . .*

CW: So with this feeling of isolation or separation, is international publication important to you, or not so much?

JL: I think the desire and hope for readers and recognition is universal for writers. But I try not to count too much on such things. It's important to me to have readers, and it's important to me that some of them have connected with me. That's lovely. That's all you can hope for. And I don't care where they're from.

Too much ambition can distract you from the work, or from the real nature of your material. It's truth that matters, it's finding the seam that reveals what is most deeply important to you. Thinking about publishing and publicity when you're writing is constricting, distorting. I think you have to be as honest to your own impulse as possible. The more original you are the better. Write it and then see what happens . . .

CW: It brings to mind what you said before, about opening, instead of closing down. We've all met writers who are bitter at their lack of success—it's awful to see. And it's instructive, because it shows you what you mustn't let yourself become.

JL: Oh yes, it's a terrible thing. I'm sure I've been there too, sometimes. But not in later years. I actually hate that feeling. I think you just don't go there. For me, anyway, the healthy thing is to forget about the public stuff—I find all publicity very painful.

CW: Why?

JL: There are probably a few reasons. I suppose I was brought up not to show off. And certainly as the youngest, I could often be told by my sisters to stop showing off. It's the puritan streak in my family, I suppose.

But also, it is always somehow a distortion—your photo, the things you say that can be quoted in a way that sounds like some other person altogether. As well, I think there are too many issues going on for me when I speak, on stage, or in an interview. There's the constant awareness of the interviewer, or of the audience: then a sort of silent panic takes me over like a rabbit caught in headlights that makes me leap onto one track and find myself bogged there! Then the regret at all I didn't say . . .

CW: Something I have noticed on rereading your work is how good you are at very smoothly making things happen that are surprising and unlikely, but never feel implausible. And it's thrilling in a narrative sense, because it's got pull and power, and risk.

JL: Oh, thank you! I work terribly hard on the mechanics of plot and movement. Over and over and over I write these things, trying to find a way to make it plausible or acceptable. That's really an area—the mechanics of that stuff—I work very hard on, to smooth it. How to make it work, to make this sort of bolt from the heavens acceptable!

CW: You do it in a way that makes it seem inevitable and destined—'Oh, of course this would happen.' Do you think certain things are fated in life, so therefore you can accept them easily in the writing?

JL: Well, I can't say I *believe* in that. But in my own life—maybe in any life—there have been accidents that have been good, there have been blows that have turned out to be good. I mean, I've had a good life, touch wood, so they're not bitter lessons, but I have had things happen that take me on to byroads, and I have had to get back on track.

I did have cancer, for example. I was very, very lucky—I had early breast cancer, and I just had a lumpectomy, and radiotherapy. Nothing terrible, but it *knocked me out.* I was *completely* shocked. I never thought it would happen to *me,* you know.

And in a way *Gilgamesh* came out of that experience, that extremity. It became an enormous journey for me, that time. A determination to pull myself out of this, to survive.

It also was time out. I didn't have to do anything. I still went to the bookshop, but apart from that I didn't force myself. I didn't have any deadlines. I said, 'I've had enough. I've had enough of striving and of ambition and the literary world.'

Getting cancer really shocked me. I remembered that Rilke injunction: *You must change your life.* That's what really happened to me. It was a very solitary period of time off, of reading and thinking.

And I thought I was going to change my life, but out comes *Gilgamesh,* and I still go to writers' festivals! [*laughs*] And I still don't really want to. But on the other hand, I do want readers, recognition . . .

CW: What about short stories; do you feel you're not going to write them anymore?

JL: Every now and then a story pops up. I have a little feeling of a story at the moment, but then I start thinking, 'Hmm, it could grow.' Otherwise, I don't often get ideas for stories now. 'The New Dark Age' was a cancer story, that came out of the blue. And *Gilgamesh* was a cancer novel too, really. A journey of reparation. I guess all our books are symbols of psychic states that we've passed through in some way.

CW: Is it a psychic state you know at the time, or do you look back later and see it?

JL: Both, I think. *Gilgamesh* came from a dream, which always tells you something about where you are. It's about being lost and making a journey to find what you have lost, and writing it was in itself a sort of journey to affirm myself after the blow to one's being that is having cancer.

CW: Tell me how *Gilgamesh* came out of a dream!

JL: Oh, gosh, I'm beginning to forget the initial dream, how terrible. It was something about being on a journey—oh, I went to a country, that's right. I went to a strange country surrounded by mountains. It was dark, like a time of war, and I was carrying or leading a small child. There was something I was looking for. And the dream ended with the word 'Gilgamesh'.

I didn't even know what Gilgamesh was, or where it came from. I'd heard of it, vaguely, as a sort of myth. So then I started to research the myth, and then I began to ask, who was that woman with the child, and where did she come from, and what is her place in this myth? What was this country surrounded by mountains, foreign, but not eastern, nor European? I described this country to an erudite Englishman of my aquaintance, and he said: 'It's Armenia.'

At that time my sister had a place down at Yallingup, in the Margaret River area, and there is a beautiful old hotel there where our parents had their honeymoon, and that became where it was set. I did some writing down there.

CW: When you woke from the dream, were you aware of how important it was?

JL: Yes, it stayed with me. Generally if I dream I've forgotten it by the morning—but this was one of those dreams that stayed with me, it was significant in some way and I wanted to find out what its significance was. Where did I get Gilgamesh from? Had I read about it? It was mysterious. I think that probably only happens once in your life.

CW: I was thinking of *Gilgamesh* the other day, because it revealed what I think is the problem of my book in progress.

JL: All books have *a* problem.

CW: Yes, I think they do too. The problem of mine is that it's sort of made itself allegorical but I don't want it to be allegorical, I want it to be real. And the problem is how to have both of those things—I want it to be true, in the way I feel *Gilgamesh* is real, yet it's also mythic.

JL: Yes, it's got to be real, doesn't it? Or you won't accept the allegory. I think the key is the characters. I think characters are everything in writing, actually. It's got to be the characters, and they've got to be as real, as present, as of their time as you can make them. Because you have to feel for them to get involved in the narrative.

CW: Well how did you do that in *Gilgamesh*? Get this grand, epic quality and yet the intimacy as well?

JL: The epic quality was the structure imposed on me by following the myth of Gilgamesh, because it's an epic. So it had to be a journey to a strange dark country. And then, you know, it's that slow accruing of things. I knew it wasn't contemporary, so when was it? I sort of followed my loves, which included that period around the Second World War, that bit of landscape in Yallingup, and the idea of a woman and a child. Which is a journey in itself, actually, a woman alone with her child.

I do love research. And if I'm switched on to that subject, I love reading everything I can about it—I read all about Armenia, and what the train, the Orient Express, was like in those days, and how could you get, just possibly, from here to there, all that kind of thing. Then I actually went to Armenia . . .

CW: Do you think you could have written it without going to Armenia? What did that visit give you?

JL: Apart from the amazing experience of being the only tourists in Armenia at that time, I was much more confident about creating a certain atmosphere that every place has, especially for the traveller, the newcomer.

CW: Your early stories were set in the contemporary world, and then *Gilgamesh* was in World War II, then *The Good Parents* was contemporary again. Are you conscious of what drives you to set a book in the present or the past?

JL: I think that often the older you get the more you write about the past. I notice that with Alice Munro. Her stories were once coming right out of the recent past, or at the time of writing, of children and marriage and lovers and things like that. Now, more and more, they are set in the past, in her childhood in the 1930s and so on. Or occasionally a story is set even further back, in the nineteenth century . . .

Perhaps the individual events in one's own life stop being so momentous, and one's interest switches to those events in the past that are the origin of where we are now, individually or socially. Or you see your experience in its own historical context.

Penelope Fitzgerald is another writer I love. She wrote historical fiction, she's a great model if you want to think about historical research. She's a wonderful writer. Her novels are so alive, it's as if you are there. There's no feeling of 'This is historical fiction'. It absolutely *is* Cambridge in 1920 or 1930, or Russia at the turn of the century. She's very important to me actually. Very.

CW: What time are you writing about now, with your polio hospital?

JL: It's the fifties, 1954. I was six then, and for some reason that time has a sort of light around it. A bright glaring light, of having to go to school and the huge gravel playground, and so many children, classes of fifty or more children, the baby-boomer generation. I guess I am partly drawing on the memories of a child, of what Perth was like then. I suppose we all write from where we are.

CW: And you are *who* you are because of where you are.

JL: Or are we all the same? I mean, Alice Munro, in her small Ontario town, is universal.

CW: Who was it who said that only in the particular is the universal? Chekhov, wasn't it! I wonder if some of the particularity is about coming from a small place, so you always feel an outsider in some way. Do you think writers should be outsiders?

JL: I don't think there are any *shoulds* about what makes a writer! But by the nature of their work they are cut off from others, sitting long hours alone in a room. They are outsiders because of the risk they take—every book is a risk. Because of their vulnerability, exposing their inner worlds. But I've noticed that many writers have a wound, big or small, that they write from. Or a situation, a set of circumstances from which they have to free themselves, which becomes the material of their fiction.

Penelope Fitzgerald, who came from a famous English intellectual family, and was a brilliant student at Oxford, married a man who couldn't succeed at anything, and she had to spend years teaching at a 'crammers', in poverty, supporting her children. She published her first book when she was sixty. Yet many of those experiences are the source of her luminous, frequently comic fiction, and of the depth of the conviction behind it that the world is divided between 'the exterminators and the exterminatees'.

CW: Let me ask you about titles—yours are so declarative. And big. When do you get your titles?

JL: Early, usually. *Gilgamesh* had to be *Gilgamesh*. *The Good Parents* came with its title, because that is something that hangs over you as a parent—are you *good* or not?—and in the end it seems to be the most important thing you do. But it was also about a time when some people were so idealistic, ideological, so it was meant to be about that too. Being good. The titles that come like this just seem to be irrevocable.

CW: So getting the title early helps you write the book?

JL: It can do, but of course, you don't want a good idea for a title to influence the direction of the narrative in any way—that has to be organic.

But perhaps the way the title comes, all of a package with the initial idea, means that it is part of the main thrust of the novel.

CW: I can't get them early. I tried to get one early, once, but it just locked me in and didn't work.

JL: Yes, and then it all becomes a big metaphor, and you don't want that. But sometimes it does help to have one, I think.

CW: Your new title is *The Golden Age*—does it relate in any way to *The New Dark Age*?

JL: No, it came from the name of an old pub in Perth that had been converted to a polio convalescent home for children in the 1950s, an actual historical place, long ago knocked down to make way for a freeway. But of course it's a resonant name, and it has an edge to it, that may or may not be ironic . . . Is that time in the hospital something that the young boy and girl at the centre of the novel look back on as special, important to them?

CW: Do you have certain mental states or mood states that you feel are most creative?

JL: I think the ideal state is one in which there is not too much joy or too much sorrow. A good ordinary-day state. If there's too much joy, I'm too happy, I want to go on a bike ride, I want to go outside and look at the sky . . . I do distrust being too excited about my work. I prefer a medium, sort of just-keep-going, don't-go-up-and-don't-go-down state.

I also have times when I feel down about it, and have to knock off really, because a good night's sleep, or a weekend off, can help. And then you get your energy back. I think energy is very, very important. I can understand why Alice Munro says she doesn't think there'll be another book. She's in her eighties, you know. It's too exhausting.

CW: Do you consciously prepare yourself the night before writing?

JL: I can do, almost. I don't want to read something that's so strong in a certain idiom or voice, or has such an engrossing narrative that I wake up with it in my head.

This reminds me of something I like that Edmund Wilson said: 'Keep going, never stoop, sit tight. Read something luminous at night.'

CW: Oh, that's beautiful . . . Do you think you've changed much as a writer since you first began?

JL: I write longer things now. I'm able to commit myself to something that may take me a few years—and still might not work.

I'm calm about that. It's a part of me that I'm more trusting of now—the way I do it. I've stopped being so fearful. I was in my thirties when I really began to do this thing that I'd always wanted to do more than anything else, and when I started, for a while I was afraid that it would go away, that it wouldn't happen again the next day.

CW: What exactly is it, do you think, that you trust more now?

JL: I think I trust the energy around a project more now; that if there's a little seed of fascination, a little picture or a character, or even the name of a character, that intrigues me, then it has potential, it can be brought into existence, it can find its form, its place . . . it just needs work, time, application.

More and more now, I love surprise. Even on the smallest level, when you're writing something and it's a bit ordinary or mechanical or something, and then suddenly a character does something and it wipes out all that boring stuff . . . *action*, I love action. I love a character *doing* something.

My son read me a line from Gide over the phone the other day that relates to all this: 'Art is a collaboration between God and the artist, and the more God has to do with it the better.'

I wrote that down. I write these notes to myself. Quotes or thoughts or ideas for the narrative, the characters. Increasingly

I write them on small sheets of paper. I used to have big heavy notebooks, and I used to write and write in them.

But now, I only want to catch them very lightly. I've got lighter and lighter. I get these notepads that you can buy for a dollar each. I've got pieces of paper like this pinned up or stuck on the wall or lying in little stacks everywhere.

CW: So you don't want to keep them carefully ordered.

JL: No. I want them to be caught on the wing, not to be treasured. Because the main energy should go into the work. I never go back to them after I've brought the project to completion. I don't look at my old notebooks. I'm going to burn them all one day . . .

CW: Don't burn them. Have you ever wanted to stop writing, just give up?

JL: I don't know if I've wanted to stop, but I have felt I should stop. I've felt despair. And I've thought: 'If you're not going to do something that's really good, what's the point?' What about you? Have you ever wanted to stop?

CW: There have been times, yes. When I've thought, 'I'm never going to have the kind of mind that's required.' It's been at times a great source of pain and grief.

JL: Yes! To feel that you're never going to rewrite what writing can be. That you're a handmaiden at the foot of art, plodding up the hill. But then I think, 'Never mind, that's my path'.

That's what keeps me true. And it's how I entertain myself, I suppose. It's my joy, actually. It's the deliciousness of reading, and the deliciousness of that *click-click-click*, when things start to come together. The pleasure of making. And it's the only making that I do. Sometimes I think it's held me up, out of life, really, because it's so preoccupying.

I realise this now, because I've sent my novel off, and I think, 'Right, well now I can do a few things.' Especially towards the end of the project, I can hardly make a phone call—it's too much, I can't switch off, I need everything I've got just to get there. It's ridiculous in a sense—and many writers are not like me—but it stops me gardening or doing anything. It's stopped me cleaning the house for about three weeks, I've really got to do that! [*laughs*] But I haven't developed other parts of myself. You'd think, with that devotion, I'd be a twenty-volume writer, but that's what it's taken.

CW: What do you do when you get marooned in your work? How do you overcome it?

JL: Oh, isn't it awful? You get in a really bad mood, very depressed. I hate it. Actually, I think it's usually solved by time. Let go, leave it for a little while. If you leave it, sometimes something happens, someone says something that helps—someone who's not a writer will say something quite simple and practical and you think, 'Oh yes! I can do that.'

I have something written down from Kipling. He said, 'When your Daemon is in charge, do not try to think consciously. Drift, wait, and obey.'

That's what I think, too. The more you let go the better, in some way—but you have to earn the letting go, really, don't you? You've got to be deeply involved, and then if you get stuck you can go for a walk, or you wake up the next morning or something, and then it comes: 'Oh! Now I see.'

CW: Do you have a sense, at all, of what the larger project of your work might be? Is there a sense of purpose uniting or guiding all your books, do you think? I suppose this is a question about why you write.

JL: No, I don't. I have a sense of the next book, and what it's about, and even a tiny prickle about the subject of the one after that. I like the security of having these projects 'booked up', so to speak, but they are about responding to the idea for each novel, finding out what it is about this particular subject that I want to explore.

In fact I don't want to think too much about certain tendencies in my work, or what unites them, because I want to respond to each work on its own terms as fully as possible.

Why do I write? Because I love reading so much I suppose, and because from early childhood I've had a great enjoyment in making things up.

Working things out in fiction is very satisfying. I love having the chance to enter different worlds, to explore different issues as fully as possible, and I try to give myself fully to that. Although I'm aware of certain tendencies in my work, and of their origins, I try to focus on what I call 'the given', the source of the work, to explore it, make something out of it, bring its significance to light.

WAYNE MACAULEY is the writer of blackly funny, often disturbing, always daringly original fiction. His short fiction has been widely published in literary magazines; he is a former winner of *The Age* Short Story Competition and his work has appeared in the *Best Australian Stories* and *New Australian Stories* anthologies. His debut novel, *Blueprints for a Barbed-Wire Canoe*, was published by Black Pepper in 2004 and was included on the Victorian secondary schools' VCE English reading list. His second novel, *Caravan Story*, was nominated a 2007 Readings Book of the Year while his collection *Other Stories* was shortlisted for a 2011 Queensland Premier's Literary Award. His highly acclaimed novel *The Cook* was released in Australia by Text Publishing, and was also published in Canada, the UK and Turkey. It was listed as a fiction book of the year by ABC Radio National, *The Australian*, *Sunday Herald Sun* and Readings Bookshop and was shortlisted for a Western Australian Premier's Book

Award, a Victorian Premier's Literary Award and the Melbourne Prize Best Writing Award. It won the inaugural 2012 Most Underrated Book Award. His latest novel, *Demons*, was released in 2014. Macauley tutors in creative writing at the University of Melbourne—a role he admits to feeling a little conflicted about—and has also worked extensively in the theatre as a writer, director and dramaturg. He lives in Melbourne with his partner, the actor and theatre director Susie Dee, with whom he has a daughter.

Macauley has had a cult following for years, but not until his novel *The Cook* did his work begin to reach a wider audience. In this interview he speaks frankly about artistic success and failure, intellectual freedom and his love of classic literature. The influences he cites are decidedly political and male, from Plato to Cervantes, Defoe to Swift and Voltaire, and on to Orwell and Beckett. While he has mentioned Coetzee and Sebald in other interviews, in our conversation the recurrent names on his lips were those of the past.

Macauley has an easy manner and projects instant warmth; he's the kind of man who seems completely at ease in women's company. This interview took place at the kitchen table in the Brunswick house he shares with Dee, and he often mentioned her theatre work as an influence on his fiction. His own past experience in the theatre is also, I learned, a powerful influence.

I was first drawn to Macauley's writing by the inventive language and sharp observations in *The Cook*, a satire about contemporary affluence and our cultural obsession with food as entertainment, but during research for this interview I discovered that *Caravan Story* is my favourite among his books. This surreal, sinister and blackly comic tale examines the relationship between art and the state: a city's visual artists, writers and performers are rounded up by bus and delivered into an ailing rural community, where they are housed in caravans, fed and put to work 'creating art' under the auspices of a vague government agency and the specific instruction of a harried arts administrator. The main character is a writer named Wayne Macauley, who soon discovers that his efforts to please with his work are doomed: rejection slips for all writing produced in the community are already pre-printed and waiting in the administrator's drawer for distribution. It could be that *Caravan Story* came to me at just the right time, as we discuss in this interview, but it also seems to me to give full rein to Macauley's personal literary project—a caustic examination of sociopolitical relationships in contemporary Australia.

I first met Macauley at the Perth Writers' Festival when *The Cook* was released, and was impressed by his thoughtful responses when I saw him take part in a panel discussion, where the form and limited timeframe often makes complex conversation impossible. He struck me as an independent and humane thinker, an impression confirmed in other meetings since. Each time I've spoken with him, I've been impressed by his intelligent modesty, willingness to challenge and his playful sense of humour.

CW: Can you tell me a little about your background in theatre?

WM: Well, I came to writing probably in my late teens when, like many, I first started to write bad poetry. I began writing under the influence of a teacher in year twelve. I was already writing a bit of secret poetry, but then she introduced me to a whole bunch of books and plays I didn't know about, and this sort of energised whatever was in my head. I didn't really like school, it was just that one teacher who turned me on to literature.

I started to write prose, but theatre was always around. After we left school my best buddy, a writer who now lives on the other side of the world, was going to what was then Rusden State College, a drama-teaching college. So I had that influence from pretty early on, and I was also reading a lot of plays.

I travelled a bit, worked in labouring jobs. Then I applied for the Victorian College of the Arts. At that point it was quite a prestigious college to get into, but I really didn't know much about it—I just saw a block ad in the Saturday newspaper that said, 'Arts'. That's all I remember. It said Victorian College of the Arts, and I just knew that's what I wanted to do. [*laughs*] That word. *Arts*. I knew it. I'd already done one year at university and dropped out, then I travelled and worked. I entered the VCA as a writer, but I only lasted two years of a three-year course. I don't think institutions and I have ever really got on very well, aside from that single year at high school.

CW: At VCA you were writing plays?

WM: Yeah. The first year at the VCA was a very influential year in every respect, because at that stage it was one-in-all-in, so I did acting classes, movement classes, voice classes, and I did production: stage management, lighting and these kinds of things. That was an amazing experience. I got to act, to sit in on all kinds of rehearsals and workshops. I got to work as an assistant director with one of the key lecturers, and then direct my own stuff. I was writing on the side as well. It was a really stimulating time, and I've definitely hung on to some of the stuff I got from acting. I gave up on acting pretty quickly, actually, but what I learned in those couple of years was influential.

CW: Is there a relationship between acting and fiction writing?

WM: Probably in recent years I've recognised it more, the idea of inhabiting a character, of speaking with a particular voice. Also in acting classes I learned the stuff of just being utterly in the moment, of being present in the moment. That is very strong for me. The perfect piece of acting, when I've seen it—it knocks your socks off—is when you know the actor is utterly present in the character, and utterly present in the moment, but they are also aware of the energy of the space, and the audience. Do you know what I mean? When I'm deep in writing, I think I'm trying to do that. I'm trying to find that place, being completely present, but I'm also aware of my audience or reader.

In my second year of college I met my partner Susie, who is a theatre director. That interchange has been going on for thirty-something years, and this table we're sitting at is constantly peopled with actors workshopping, and reading, and talking, and analysing, and putting on voices. All that stuff obviously goes in, the way you formulate a scene in the three-dimensional, fictional space. I've watched Susie do that in the theatre, I've observed the spatial awareness that a good director has.

It's fascinating, and it does feed into my writing. If you think of a novel, the location of the place, the characters in it, in a sense everything is performance. Even the most realist work is still somehow performative—you're winding up your actors and getting them to do stuff.

CW: The idea of the stage seems quite present in your work. All your novels are set in very contained spaces, mostly in an almost closed society.

WM: I think I've only recognised that recently too. There's no question that's something I've subconsciously taken from writing for theatre. That's not to say there aren't great plays where the action takes place in multiple locations, but really the best theatre for me, the theatre that's most memorable, is the stuff that happens in a single location across real time. Like a great interpretation of Chekhov, for example. A great production of Chekhov would classically be that situation, a single location, and in it we just watch the world unravel.

CW: This 'single arena', as my screenwriter friend David Roach taught me to think of it, is very useful for the building of pressure in a novel.

WM: Yeah, I think that's it, the building of pressure, and that's been my natural inclination. Obviously there are novelists very different from me who build up a Rubik's Cube kind of world, dislocated in time and locations—a kind of jigsaw puzzle. I admire the technique of that, but it's something I've either never been able to do or I've never been interested in. I just want to see what people do when you put them together under pressure.

CW: Your novels are interesting, because your characters often seem to be trapped in a place, but actually it's not against their will. They choose it.

WM: That can relate, I suppose, to the theatre again. The old fourth wall, and the choice an actor has about whether to walk up into the audience and break it. The tension of that. But I also think it probably comes from a thematic concern about my problem with Australia, with this country. The idea of freedom and what you do with it. It's what all fiction is really, I suppose—exploring the limits of possibility. In other words, it's like when you open the door for the bird that's been caged all these years—does the bird really want to go out there? I feel we have unlimited potential for freedom here, but we're so trapped, so fixed, so un-explorative. We don't go beyond the door of the cage. We are allowed to go anywhere we like, and do anything we like in a way, but we don't take that chance.

CW: What does our cage consist of?

WM: I think it's complacency, in the first place—just outright complacency. But what breeds complacency? I don't know. I suppose it's the problem of: in a world of unlimited possibilities, which one do you choose? I mean in the psyche, in the brain space of the country, if there is such a thing. You see that reflected in politics all the time. But even on a micro level, I feel Australia is a country of unrealised potential, and I suppose that's where it comes from thematically . . . I put my people in a closed environment, but I'm always leaving the door open to see if they are able to walk out. And some characters do. Some suggest that perhaps there is a better way to do things than this. But mostly they're locked in by the complacency.

CW: You're often described as a satirist. Is that how you see yourself?

WM: That's a really hard one. I admire great satirists. I love Swift, and I don't begrudge it when the label's applied to me. But I think in a contemporary world, the notion of satire has been pretty devalued. After the advent of sketch comedy, TV comedy, TV satire, commercial FM radio satire—I don't know. If they added 'classical' before 'satirist' I would be very happy with that label.

I like to do as Swift did, to deeply investigate the political culture, the headspace of the country. The trick with satire is to do it by taking on the uniform of the enemy; adopting a character you may not necessarily like, but you must inhabit totally. I mean that's pure satire, when you can take on someone you don't particularly like, and expose their foibles. That's what Swift did, and I think that's great satire.

In actual fact, I don't know what I am. [*laughs*] I have signposts, writers I like, like Swift, to set my course by. But my reading and my literary loves are very eclectic, eccentric even. So I can't really attach a label to myself. I still don't know, because everything's a bit of an experiment. I do think every novel is an experiment. Sometimes it might turn out that I'm a straight-up satirist, and some passages of those novels might put me in that basket, but overall I think I'm just trying stuff out.

CW: Do you think you write dystopian fiction?

WM: It's never by choice, it just works out that way. I seem to be not-a-happy-ending guy, and I can't say I really understand that deeply, I don't know. I guess I tend to have a pessimistic view of the world. That's something I understood early on. A lot of writers are like this, a lot of us start writing because of a dissatisfaction with the world. We're not actually happy in the place we're in, or the clothes we're in, or the skin we're in, and we're pushing against this. Some basic pessimism or opposition is often the big driver for anyone to start writing, and I guess that was the case with me.

Sadly, after thirty-five years of doing it, I haven't changed! I'm still rubbing up against this world, so any dystopia I write is simply a result of that. There is also a slight speculative-fiction aspect to my work. In other words, there's not a lot of the past in it, but there is a lot of present, and a lot of future.

CW: Can you talk about this speculative element? How do artifice and reality relate in your fiction?

WM: Well that comes back to theatre as well. There's an incredibly constructed artificiality about the theatre, and yet it can be transformative. It can represent reality, and *be* reality—the actor on a stage—all in the one instant. The actor is a living, breathing human being. They have lungs, a heart, limbs. They're there, they exist, and yet they're pretending to be someone else in a different place. This awareness of the artificiality of what I'm doing has prevented me from being a straight-up realist.

But then, I don't even understand what realism is. I recently read *Madame Bovary* again, in the Lydia Davis translation. It's a fantastic book—and yet it's so constructed. It's a remarkable piece of realism but it's impossible not to see the artifice in it, for me.

I think the way my brain works is to examine the things in my head really closely. I tend to look at the ideas, images, characters or whatever in my head, really intensely. And if you look closely, intensely, at the real for long enough, it starts to become something else. It reveals its profundity and its complexity to you.

CW: And its absurdity?

WM: And its absurdity. Because you are looking at it in a way you simply can't do in daily life, in what we call the quotidian, the real. I've thankfully managed to walk the tightrope now, the art–life tightrope, so I don't go mad. But for certain hours of the day when I'm working, I am looking into the world in a really intense way, and by doing that it's hard not to turn it into something else. It is almost transformed into something else purely by the act of looking at it hard. I think that's what happens. I don't think I consciously construct other worlds, it's not my thing. I've never read science fiction, for example. I've no interest in it at all. My belief is that, in a sense, there is another real on the other side of this real.

CW: That's a beautiful way of expressing it. Do you think you'll ever write a straight realist book?

WM: Part of me would like to. Again, the old experiment thing—just to find out what that would feel like. I'm not sure I could. Some people have said, I think maybe in a backhanded way, that '*Demons* is Macauley trying to be a realist'. I wasn't conscious of that. I mean I see it as such an artifice, it's such a construct.

CW: To me *Demons* still has a sense of the theatre, of people coming on and off stage to tell their tales.

WM: Yeah, precisely; that's what I had in mind. But strangely enough, for some readers the comings and goings of those people in that space say 'realist novel'. Absurdities are contained in the stories—but it's set in a house, and the house is named as being in a real place. The characters in the place are given names and descriptions, and they act in such-and-such a way, so therefore it all must be real. But from my point of view, I'm making that arena, as you said, and putting my performers in it and seeing what they do.

CW: When you're starting a new book, how much do you know?

WM: Not a lot. Well, I know a lot subconsciously, and many writers talk about this, about how an idea bubbles underneath for a long time, and then bubbles up to the surface. That is true for me. I'm very superstitious about writing. I'm very conscious that it can all just go to shit at any moment. So that's why I'm loath to over-plan.

Somewhere deeper back there I actually know everything that's going to happen, but I refuse to acknowledge that I know it. Then it does come to a time where it bubbles up, and I'm like, 'Okay, I'm going to write this one, I'm going to try this one out.'

Then, in practical terms, I do have a plan, which would run to about one or two A4 pages. With *The Cook*, the week before I started writing the book I wrote out a page and a half—I still have the document—describing how it would go. I actually attached page numbers to these sections: 'That's going to be sixty pages, that will be about eighty. Then I'll get to there, then you'll go to the house, and that'll be about da-da-da, and then that little coda will happen.'

And pretty much that was it. I didn't know what was going to happen in the units really. But I have . . . what would you call it? A theme, a reason. I suppose that's where the satirist comes in. I have a reason to write. I'm engaging with my culture, with my time. I have a reason to begin.

CW: Let's go on with *The Cook* as an example. How long did it take you to write this page and a half?

WM: I just did that in an afternoon, about a week before I started writing the book. Now, I'd been sketching little notes, not a lot, but just little notes in a notebook for some time, possibly a couple of years up to beginning the book. Then at a point I've said, 'I think I'm going to write this book, so I'll start on . . . oh, February fourth.' So the week before February fourth, I think, 'How am I going to do this?' Writing a novel is partly about mathematics, I believe. [*laughs*] Pages multiplied by days. I mean, I'm shit at mathematics, but that's what calculators are for. I think, I'm going to spend nine months plus writing the first draft of this, let's say about two hundred pages. So how would that work, how would it fit? By now I know I'm writing a satire about food culture as it relates to capitalism. I know that. That's the thing that's been chewed away. That's the bubbling. And writing the novel—those days, those pages—is to ask, what's going on here? What's this weird thing in the world? What's happening? Why is it like this?

CW: So that theme is what's going to sustain your interest?

WM: Yes, that's really important. A character is not going to sustain my interest for three years, but the question of why food decadence seems to match economic turmoil is going to sustain me. The question of what's happened in a post-Cold War world with the rise of late capitalism—those things will keep me interested for three years. So I have to have that going for me first, otherwise I'm just not going to get up in the morning. That's the engine that's going to drive this book through to the end.

CW: What about the discovery of characters? Is it hard work?

WM: Well, that's the spontaneity part, the part I don't want to over-plan, and I trust that. Maybe it's the theatre thing again—the way you develop a character over a long workshop and rehearsal period: a character doesn't arrive into the world fully formed. It needs to be worked, it needs to be found, which is what actors do, they find their characters. I really trust that, and I think pretty well all my characters have developed as they've gone on.

Even Zac in *The Cook*, I mean he was there in outline, and he was going to achieve certain effects for me, I knew that. But what he would do in a scene, or how he would react with another character, and how he would grow on me as well through the course of the book, was unknown. And actually, being a first-person book, part of the beauty of writing it was getting to know him from the inside.

CW: The voice is really particular in that book, it seems to me, more than the others.

WM: Well that comes out of experiment. I had never written in that way before, and to some extent I've always mistrusted the idea of completely inhabiting a character, and letting them speak. I couldn't come to one of those books until I figured that I actually wasn't going to write Zac's spoken words, but I was going to write Zac's thoughts, and that's a very different thing. A totally different thing. To track a person's thoughts, chase a person's thoughts down, is really what I wanted to do, and that's different from trying to imitate his speech.

CW: You said before that you were superstitious about writing. Can you say more about that superstition?

WM: Well, I went through a long period in my twenties when I wrote a novel—but I ended up destroying it, I got rid of it. I certainly didn't have a grammar-school education, I didn't have a university education, I really was learning myself, and I wasn't ready. Then I went through a period where I didn't write much. I read an enormous amount, took copious notes, and kept a journal throughout that time. But I didn't write. I mean, we might call it writer's block, but actually I think it was just a growth period I needed.

But that period did stretch on, and I began to get quite scared that maybe I was getting all this knowledge, all this stuff, but I had yet to put it into practice. So when I finally began writing again it was a long story that got me through; almost overnight I finally found my style, my voice, my feel. But once it was there, I've just been totally paranoid ever since that it might go away. Less so these days, much less so, because I've become a better manager of it, and understand the tricks we all need to perform to make us keep doing it. So I'm better at it.

I'm teaching now; this is my third year of teaching, but I still find it confronting. I enjoy it actually, I love it, and it's fun—but if I just take one half-step back, I think, 'Oh, you can't teach it!' And I'm not trying to teach it, I'm just trying to inspire people to do stuff. I do say this to my students. But all this blah about creative writing courses going through the roof, writers' festivals, interest in writers, interest in the way writers write . . . there's something about all those things that diminishes the sacredness of it, which I still hold to in a way.

CW: Writers are very shy about saying this kind of thing, but I feel the same way, that at times there's something almost holy in the pursuit of it.

WM: There's got to be, in order to keep doing it, and to keep doing it with meaning. To do it with art, not just craft. To be able to really put some of your humanity into it, it does have to be a headspace that's not flippant, not facetious, that's not cynical, not throw-away. It cannot be diminished by saying, 'If you put this word there and that word there, you'll have a great sentence.' It is more than that. Of course it's more than that.

I suppose the superstition is part of a feeling that any morning in which you can go to the desk and write a couple of really good pages is actually a gift. It's a good, fine thing. I suppose I still surround that with a certain aura and sacredness and superstition, because it's the heart of who I am and what I do. I'm sure everyone has degrees of that. Everyone must.

CW: Let's talk about going to the physical space where you write, to get into that headspace. For me there's always some resistance, some niggling fear, every time I go into the room. How is it for you? Do you have a very strong routine?

WM: Yes, I do. Thankfully I don't have that fear so much now. I try to go in there with the idea of neutrality, of allowing something to happen, of being totally in your body and so on.

I suppose I prepare by not preparing—that's my superstition at work. Of course it's about habit and routine, everyone knows that. I'll get up early, have the shower, have the breakfast. I read the paper. I find I need to read a bit before I start working, but I don't necessarily want to read something that's going to be too much of an influence on me, so first I read the paper. That's just a nice way of getting the brain from a slow ticking over into a faster tick-tick-tick!

Then I go to my study, I'm down there by eight o'clock. There have been times when I was down there at six thirty and earlier, for example back when I was writing *The Cook*. I've got a nice armchair down there, just fits in there, and I usually sit and read just a few pages of the book I'm currently reading, which might not necessarily be the same book I'm reading up in the house.

I'll be careful not to read too far, though. I mean, I'll maybe bring that book up to the house later and read on the couch for an hour, if it's at an interesting point or something, but before starting work I'll just read a few pages, just to get the brain tuned up a little bit. Just to hear the rhythm, see the sentences. Then it's, 'Okay, right. That's enough.'

I'll then do three to four hours' work. I write longhand, in notebooks—those cheap red-and-black notebooks which OfficeWorks still sell. I think they're all going to disappear one day; I don't know what I'm going to do then. My longhand pages run to about four hundred and fifty words, something like that, and two pages a day has been my routine this year.

I'll have written two pages the previous day, and then I've just left them, closed the notebook and put it aside. So first thing I'll do is open up the notebook and go back to yesterday's beginning. Possibly read back a half page before that just to get the flow, and then I'll read into what I've written the previous day, and I'll do a first edit on it.

CW: So you're revising that before you write anything new?

WM: Well, if it was very good I wouldn't, but chances are I've tried to get into the state where I'm not going to question too much, I'm going to let things occur, so that means often that the sentences are very hurried, and pretty messy, and I've possibly even forgotten a character's name or something. It's always possible. So I'll do a basic clean-up, just so I know those two pages are set. They're obviously going to change heaps in drafting, but they're set for the moment. I'm happy. But also, what this does is refresh me. It tells me where I am, who I'm talking about. Just putting my toe back in, and saying, 'Well, what was I on about?' Hopefully, at that point, that's exciting, because you go, 'Oh, this is really good!'

Then I arrive at the blank page. I write on the right-hand side and on the verso page I keep notes. Then, at the end of every session, the last thing I do before stopping is tell myself in dot points what I'm going to do tomorrow, or where it will go next. Then I'll close the notebook, and that's it.

CW: This sounds very orderly. So you write chronologically? You start at the beginning and work towards the end?

WM: Yeah, I do, very much so. It's mad, I mean it's fucking mad really. I write it all longhand, and I write it chronologically. That just forms a pattern, and some days when it's all breezing along there'll be barely a note on the verso page.

Often, though, what I will do on that page is write the first phrase or sentence for the next day, because sometimes you don't want to stare at the blank line for very long. You know that thing of stopping yourself just when it's getting interesting? That too. Even if it's just a phrase, I'll actually write it in quotes with a dot, dot, dot, like, 'This is what the writer would have written if he hadn't got hit by a bus.' So that's there, I know what's coming next: there's my first line, let's go. [*snaps fingers*] And hopefully that's how it goes.

CW: Why is it important to write in longhand?

WM: Look, every time I start a new book I question this idea of writing longhand. With some books, I have written everything that way, right to the very final full stop, before I've gone anywhere near a keyboard. It's very messy, but I have traced and tracked all the little marginal extra sentences and things. I know I can read those pages because I've read

276

them over each morning before the work. Then I just type up, almost like a stenographer really.

CW: So no redrafting before you type?

WM: Not yet. Very slightly, obviously. But at this point my mission is really just to type up this mother and get it onto pages. That's a block of work which just goes on frantically day after day, just typing, typing, typing. Then the miraculous day arrives—because it's all been just Wayne's head, Wayne's weird handwriting—the magical day arrives where I hit the print button, and it comes out, and it sits in front of me, and that's the beginning.

It's a fantastic feeling, because that is when my real craft begins.

I actually really believe in this hand–eye thing. I don't think twenty or thirty years of computers have taken away the idea of man and tool. I just really do trust this more—that it's true, it's truer to me than if I had typed it. But the other thing is, we just spend so much of our lives in front of these fucking screens! So for that period of the work, which might take nine months to a year, maybe more, I'm not waking up in the morning staring at another fucking computer screen.

CW: There does sound to be something very pure about it.

WM: Yeah. It's very quiet, it's just the scratching of the pen, and seeing it. Sure, that's old-fashioned, I understand that, but seeing the marks on the page—to me, really, it's very beautiful. It's very messy actually, but very beautiful in a way. When you turn to that in the morning, it's textural, it's there, like it's beginning.

CW: You're converting me. I'm being converted.

WM: [*laughs*] Oh dear. The thing is seeing the traces, seeing the way it's evolved out of the muddle of the brain, through the muddle of those first pages, and as you type up, you start to see the way the chemistry between sentences came together in a much clearer way than you do when you're typing, I think. And I find that really valuable.

CW: I want to talk a little about the content and structure of your work. Let's talk about *Demons*, and the story-within-a-story concept. What interested you about that?

WM: I really wanted to explore the idea of the storyteller in fiction. I wanted to see what it would be like for a character to start apparently speaking, and then transform into a storyteller. To have a cast of characters, to let them say, 'I'm going to tell a story. I heard this from someone who told it to my second cousin. You might have heard it, it sounds like this.' Then to convert that voice into a genuine storyteller's voice, which I use a lot in my own short fiction. Most of my short fiction has a teller behind the tale.

CW: I'm interested that you're so passionate about storytelling, when it seems so co-opted now by capitalism, and corporatism.

How is it possible to still believe in storytelling when 'narrative' is now a marketing tool?

WM: Well, partly what I'm trying to do with *Demons* is to show that storytelling is artifice, but as long as you can acknowledge that it is artifice, then it actually can tell the truth. I wanted to at least run that up the flagpole, and let a reader look at it, and think about that, so that next time they hear Fuckface on the television telling porkies, they might go, 'Okay, storyteller. Got you. Right.'

CW: There was that whole discussion about Julia Gillard's government not having the right 'narrative', and every advert-isement, even every business now has to have 'a story'.

WM: Oh God, that word is just so abused! Absolutely. It's manipulative. I guess that's what I'm trying to say. I think back to those extraordinary road-accident campaign ads that were done as hyper-realism. A crash, a girl at the side of the road bleeding, horror, horror. That's classic storytelling, those ads really began the idea of how a mini story works, a really tiny story, maybe two minutes . . . I mean those were good campaigns, but they were using hyper-realist storytelling, so there's apparently no artifice in there, but if you listen to the violins, and you hear the voice-over at the end, you realise how incredibly manipulative they are. To good ends, sure. But we take that package—and they have—over to big business putting out its corporate ad, and it has a narrative of all these happy people. In hard hats. Lots of happy women in hard hats working for the coal company. I suppose all I'm saying is, I'm claiming back the artifice. I'm taking it back. [*laughs*] It's mine, it's ours! And if we *know* it's artifice, we can use it for good, not evil.

CW: I'm intrigued by how much physical decay there is in your settings—the buildings are falling apart, there's a sense of breakdown. What is that about?

WM: I don't know, how do you sum up the world at the moment, except through the word decay? [*laughs*] I mean it's hard to see regrowth and renewal where every patch of the earth has been explored, if not exploited. I guess if I glimpse the future I do see it as like *Blade Runner,* you know. The amazing art direction of that film. I mean, I want to see a different future, but I see one that does have decay around the edges. That's a provocative question, because I guess you're right, I do see decay and collapse, it's a common theme in a lot of my work.

CW: It has an interesting effect—even though, as you said, your stories are always set almost in the future, this decay implies a past that everyone is emerging from. There's a sense of waste—of resources, of aspirations. A sense of broken ideals.

WM: Well, I think that is what I'm trying to say. Going back to our conversation about this country, and who we are—all the lost potential. I suppose that still beats at me. In other words, maybe I'm saying, 'If we keep doing this, what's it going to look like?' I can't help returning to that theme. I can't put the rose-coloured glasses on, it's too hard. It's not something in my personal life that I could say triggers that, I think it's seeing myself in a particular society at a particular point on the historical line.

CW: Have you ever been idealistic?

WM: I think I'm actually incredibly idealistic. That's the problem! [*laughs*] If I didn't think about all the potential, if I just went, 'Oh, it is what it is. This is fine, it's great. What else?' I'd be very different. But I do have idealism—ridiculous, ludicrous idealism when I think about it. Obviously, idealists are always disappointed, and I guess I'm one of those disappointed idealists. Other people might call me a pessimist. I'm not saying that I have acted in a way in my life that proves my idealism; I haven't chosen to be a community worker, or a politician. That's what I should have done. But I'm a writer. Looking at it through that lens affects what you see.

CW: I wonder if all writers are disappointed idealists.

WM: Well, that goes back to the original driver. We look at the world and we're disappointed with it. What do you do with that? You try to analyse it, I suppose. That disappointment might not be with the world. For a lot of writers, it's because of a brokenness in themselves, a fracture, or a scar or something that means they're not happy, either in their skin or the place they're in. I don't know if I was born a pessimist. I'm certainly . . . I lost my dad when I was quite young, when I was twenty.

CW: I was nineteen when mine died.

WM: There's a common thread here among writers. We're not the only ones . . . Clearly that affects your world view, when you lose someone really close just when you're starting to think in big-picture terms about the world, and the meaning of life. And then God says, 'There is no meaning. Fuck off.' [*laughs*]

So there's obviously a personal thing that has coloured my outlook—because thinking about death too much will definitely do that—about why we're here, and how long it will last, and what the point is. And I suppose we as writers project on to the world our disappointment with this human folly.

But if the world was a perfect place, it would reflect back to me and say, 'No, Wayne, don't be disappointed and broken. It's a *beautiful* world. It doesn't matter that your dad died young!' [*laughs*] But it doesn't look like that to me. It's not that world. I mean, I live in a happy, free place, but if the eye goes out to the global picture and sees Australia's place in it, I'm not happy with what I see.

CW: Returning to your dystopias, I was quite discomfited when I read your early novels in the last couple of weeks, especially *Caravan Story* and *Blueprints for a Barbed-Wire*

Canoe, to find in your work quite a few images similar to ones I've been writing in my current work, which is sort of dystopian too. Things like rabbit shooting, and buses delivering people and taking them away, and the electricity failing. And I wondered if these are symbols in our national psyche, somehow, internalised images of an Australian dystopia.

WM: That's so interesting. Because after I wrote *Blueprints* I've seen that rabbit-shooting thing done by a number of other Australian writers, as some edge-of-the-world picture, some sort of end-of-civilisation image. And buses! Buses feature heavily in my work [*laughs*], which is interesting. I'm not necessarily a big bus-catcher. Yeah, but buses feature as well.

CW: There's a cattle-train sort of feeling about them in this context; it's quite threatening, especially in *Caravan Story*. Now, that novel has a lot of pretty caustic things to say about art and artists. At one point, your character Wayne Macauley describes artists as 'over-educated trash'. Do you think that's how we are seen by mainstream society?

WM: For a portion of mainstream society, yeah. But not all. I'd say maybe the needle has shifted a little bit since I wrote *Caravan Story*. I think maybe our reputation's been a little on the rise since then.

I hate saying, 'Look overseas and see what happens there,' but compare the way writers are treated in many European countries, for example, to the way we are here. By 'treated',

I mean supported financially, or in other ways. I think there is a gap. And obviously that's where the satirist part of me, the Swiftian part, kicks in. Exaggeration is a big part of what satire does—looking into the real so closely that it blows up at you, and looks absurd and weird and strange. But it's only one step away from us.

What's happening in *Caravan Story* is that on the one hand there's the view of artists as a wasteful product of society, an excrescence.

CW: They're a sort of plague.

WM: Yeah. But there's also the idea that this plague has been created by do-gooder arts administrators, right? Who basically use art to sell product. By product, for them it just might mean political capital, or tourism, all that shit. I wrote *Caravan Story* around the early 2000s, and this idea was at its height: that art is not useful in and of itself, it must be attached to economics, otherwise no art for you guys, okay? A shift in arts funding bodies happened, and businesses started to use art as a way of warming up their product, of giving a bit of mushy niceness, because 'we all like artists'. All that stuff's on the nose. But out of all that cynicism of *Caravan Story*, I do sell the idea that maybe art can exist just because it does, and it doesn't have to justify itself. But if you've ever written an Australia Council application, you'll know what I mean. [*laughs*]

CW: Well, I have to tell you that in the last week I've been appointed the Australia Council's new chair of literature.

WM: Have you now? Well, that's good. *Caravan Story* came along just at the right time for you! [*laughs*]

CW: Given this strange new place I've found myself, one of the things I loved about *Caravan Story* was the close examination of the banality of government language around art. And of the relationship between government and artists. In *Caravan Story* you're saying that there shouldn't be one—that artists are only free without this relationship.

WM: Well, sometimes I really strongly think that the way it works, certainly in this country, is that they should be uncoupled totally. Now, I've just got an Australia Council grant this year. In thirty-five years of applying, I've had two grants. But there is definitely a build-up of anxiety that all of us go through in these applications—I know a lot of theatre people making their own applications around that time, and there is this anxiety, a desperation to find the language, to write the language, to understand the language to write it. So you learn this language over many years, you become really good at it, and then one day, which is around the time I wrote *Caravan Story*, you look at it, and you think, 'What is that language? What? I wouldn't speak that language under pain of *torture* normally.'

So that's the relationship between artists and government, I think, in this country. Is it a good relationship? No. I mean, if you have to jump through that many hoops and land exhausted on the other side, then is it a good thing? I'm really not sure. That's the provocative question *Caravan Story* asks, and it didn't go down very well with some of my friends. The question is, well, the government wants to keep supporting us. They want to love us. They love us, but what is that love worth to us really? What is it worth?

I've seen people become sort of twisted by it. And if you have to become a different kind of artist to be an Australia Council-supported artist—I'm sorry, but I've seen it. These are the questions I was asking myself, and using to satirise myself. I think one of the biggest victims of the satire in *Caravan Story* is the guy called Wayne Macauley. I had to ask those questions just to be able to go on, in a way. Just to be able to clear that fucking noise out of my head, and move on.

CW: You also write fascinatingly in that book about the relationship between artists and critics—and you imply that being ignored by critics represents the greatest freedom. What's your intellectual relationship with criticism?

WM: Look, all of this—like you interviewing me now—this is all new to me, this is all post *The Cook*. I was just flying way under the radar for a long time, being mostly ignored, with the exception of maybe two or three critics who really loved me. But, really, completely ignored. *Caravan*, as originally published, only got two reviews. Both of them were fantastic, but it was two reviews. And it sold about two hundred copies.

So what's my relationship to criticism? [*laughs*] It's all very new actually. When *The Cook* was almost universally well reviewed it was odd, because I didn't expect it. I was used to being able to hoe my own row, because of being ignored.

CW: This is all quite confronting to think about. I used to have what I now see as quite an embarrassing preoccupation with shortlistings and prizes, because at the beginning I got shortlisted for this or that all the time. And then my third book got absolutely nowhere in those terms, and it was quite a shock because I'd stupidly thought I was on some kind of trajectory. I remember one specific day, this feeling of bitter disappointment about some announcement or other—but then almost immediately feeling a great, powerful surge of freedom. A sudden realisation that not pleasing other people could, actually, be fantastically liberating.

WM: These are really interesting questions for me at the moment, because you're talking to an artist who's in his mid-fifties, who up until five years ago was a very marginal artist. I had some readers, and very, very small critical attention, but only here in Melbourne. I was definitely not a nationally recognised writer by any stretch, but suddenly I was getting all this attention.

But I started *The Cook* with the feeling, 'I don't give a fuck about anyone anymore. I'm going to write a book with no punctuation, and it's going to be two hundred pages long, and no one's going to want to publish it. It's a big up-yours,

I don't care. I just don't care.' So I just didn't give a shit. And of course that was the book that gets the agent, gets the bigger publisher, and off it goes. Isn't that funny?

CW: It's a common story, though, the breakthrough coming when a writer finally—genuinely—gives up caring about success.

WM: When I was writing *Demons*, it was absurd, because I started worrying. I remember thinking, 'This is second-album syndrome, but it's not the fucking second album!' I started to get paranoid about it, thinking about the critical reception of *Demons*. And then I'm thinking, 'What the hell are you worried about? The only reason you're here, the only reason you've got a contract with a publisher, the only reason you're going to *have* any critical attention or readers, is because you wrote that book when you didn't give a shit about what people thought.' [*laughs*] So that's been my weird little journey over the last few years.

CW: But it's hard to maintain the not giving a shit, isn't it, when you start getting the thing that you thought you didn't care about!

WM: Yes. The only way to maintain it is to start a new book before the current one comes out, which I have done. That is the only way, and that's what saved me. I knew I had to really get this new book underway before *Demons* came out, so I have something completely separate from it.

CW: It's like you have a home to go to.

WM: Yeah, that's right. That's exactly what it is.

So that's all fine: I'll go out and do this interview, and do the talk, and worry about reviews and all that, but actually there's a nice, safe place to go to, which is the work I am doing, and the work I would be doing if it all went to crap tomorrow. That's why it's homey, because it's the place I know very well. It's the work I do, regardless of hullabaloo or catastrophe.

CW: Can I ask you then about ego and art? What's the role of ego, and where is it helpful, and at what point does it turn bad?

WM: I absolutely think you've got to have a healthy ego. Ego's a strong word . . . but all artists have to believe in themselves. You've got to believe in yourself. You're saying, 'I think the work I'm doing is worth it.' So there is an ego push in that, but in another way, I think I approach my work really humbly, as I was saying when I was talking about the sacredness of it.

I don't think I have a rampant ego, and I think I approach the work humbly. You know, just going through that story about my journey as a writer, I've had no reason to be egotistical. I've not been a successful writer until very recently. I think I had a much stronger ego in my late twenties and early thirties—I thought I was the best writer who ever wrote a word! But clearly that tapers off when other people don't agree with you. [*laughs*] However, there's a certain selfishness that's necessary to be a writer. I think it's hard, though. I'm trying to understand that ego question, because in what way does an ego work in the world? I mean, if it's me and my ego down there in my study, I'm not hurting anyone, then what does it matter?

CW: But it might be hurting your work.

WM: That's a bigger question. History is littered with really, really egotistical writers whose work it didn't hurt at all. Hemingway, Joyce—these are guys who really believed in themselves to the point where you could call them almost egomaniacal. But that didn't lead them to make bad work.

CW: All right then, but they were successful. What about the bitterness of the 'failed' writer, that can be associated with ego?

WM: Yeah, I think that's different. That's a feeling of 'the world owes me something', and I just don't think it owes me. I'm being really honest with you. But that's because of my steep learning curve, the curve that went down, not up. [*laughs*] I simply have no reason to think the world owes me anything, quite frankly.

Sometimes you do see that sense of entitlement. You bump up against it at writers' festivals, you know. International Guest A who thinks they're bigger than God, and you see that aura coming off someone. But if you get treated like a rock star you act like a rock star.

Bitterness, surely, is the lot of someone who has achieved a certain amount of success but doesn't think it's enough. I guess you see a few of them around too, particularly on the Australian scene. It's a small world here, and it's hard to achieve rock-star status as a writer, isn't it? In fact we'll all probably end up being pretty bitter and disappointed. [*laughs*]

CW: I look forward to being lavishly bitter in my seventies. I obviously recognise that potential in myself, because I'm so horrified by it when I see it.

WM: But how does it manifest itself?

CW: In resentment at others' success—you see that displayed all the time, the bitchy remark about a successful book. I hope I'm less like that now, I don't know. But I think my project for myself now is not so much about what other people think, whereas for a bit of time it was entirely about that.

WM: Is that just mellowing, or the journey?

CW: Maturing, hopefully. And discovering where the real value in writing is for yourself.

WM: Yeah, absolutely. I can understand how very quickly you get jaded with the circus, and how that would lead you to understand what really does matter. And I suppose that would help relieve some of that ego anxiety which is all about your relationship to the world, the reading public, the critics, and all those things. I had more ambition when I was younger than I do now. Or at least, now I have ambition that's much less related to public recognition than to the literary project that I'm on.

CW: I'm nearly getting to the end of my questions now, let's see if I've missed any important ones. I've done disillusionment . . .

WM: Disillusionment, pessimism, dystopia. What else? [*laughs*]

CW: Humour. I want to ask you about humour.

WM: Oh, good!

CW: I've heard you say something like that to be taken seriously as a writer in Australia you can't be humorous—and yet funny writing can be serious literature at the same time.

WM: Really great humanist writing—the writing that deals with the human, with what it feels like for me to be here, now, say, in the early twenty-first century in Australia—can't be fully humanist unless it says that we are also funny people. We are funny things. It's just true.

Look at us, how much of this conversation has been serious, and yet how much laughing has there been? You're interviewing the writer about the big themes in their work, but actually a lot of it's been humorous. That's life. Totally, that is life. Seriousness and humour is the warp and weft of humanity. Guys like Chekhov, like Beckett, would say that the two are inextricable, that actually the two are one idea. I'm not saying they always are in my writing, and I'm not saying I always find that beautiful moment, but when I do find that moment I feel very happy and proud. I think that's honest writing.

CW: Yet it's not comedy, is it?

WM: I think comedy's a really deliberate thing. Charlie Chaplin slipping on the banana peel when the shot has shown you the banana peel on the footpath, and then the next shot shows Charlie walking towards it. That's comedy. I think humour, in the sense that it is a part of the human makeup, is much less deliberate and contrived. You're smiling internally at how fallible we are, how absurd our actions sometimes appear to be. Those things. Which I suppose is closer to what I try to do with my work—not to deliberately interfere and turn the comedy dial up, but to simply allow humour to emerge out of what's happening.

Humour's a great ice-breaker between people, so why couldn't it be between a writer and a reader, or a work and a reader? I'm aware that I deal with heavy subjects, and sometimes the work's dark, but I'm really happy if I've found some humour in that, because it's going to allow my reader in. It's saying, 'You are allowed to laugh at this if you want.' I certainly giggle at my work sometimes. [*laughs*]

CW: Well, that's the other aspect. It makes it pleasurable.

WM: Yeah, sometimes just getting through a book, day-to-day, is also about keeping it interesting, not getting bored.

Sometimes it just gives me pleasure to know I'm going to write a scene over the next few days that will have some level of levity, or lightness. That keeps it interesting anyway, just for me.

CW: It seems to me you have an unusually strong sense of what your literary project is. Can you describe it?

WM: I think I do have a strong sense of it, and I did from the very beginning. That's egotistical [*laughs*] but I've always had a really clear sense of what kind of writer I wanted to be, the things I wanted to deal with, and what would be the literary outcome of that.

One thing is to just write really well. This is a massive part of my literary ambition, and my early failure, and going back to the drawing board for almost a decade without writing much. Because all I could see was that the great writers I admired were *great writers* [*laughs*] and I saw that it doesn't matter what you're writing about, it doesn't matter where you're setting it, who your characters are, what your themes are. You get recognised as a writer and find readers if your work's really well written.

CW: But you don't, always.

WM: Ah well, you don't, that's true! [*laughs*] I learned that pretty quick too. But I guess once I set myself on that path . . . I've got a note above my desk which comes from Diogenes the Cynic. He was talking about the philosophical project—this is BC Greek—and he said, 'It should be as it is with the trainers of Greek choruses. Set the note a little too high. It is only in this way that the right note can be reached.' I've still got that above my desk: set the note a little too high. So even though I felt it was going to be a big fucking struggle to become a good writer, somehow, regardless of whether people recognised it or not, this idea of setting a high note has always been the thing that can keep me going.

The project is to leave a good body of work behind when we die.

But part of the project too, from very early on, has been acknowledging that I am an *Australian* writer. I might not put on the cork hat and fly the flag, but finding my own way into being an Australian writer has been part of that project as well. To say, 'How do I use the skills I learn to interpret what's here?'

When I think about it, the writers I've greatly admired have been those who made universality out of the local. It took a while to twig to this, but I want to just dig down a little deeper into what's already here—to stare at it hard enough that it becomes something new. You don't have to go far in the literary canon to see other writers who've done it in other cities, and other countries. I mean, the suburbs of Melbourne are my thing, so why not here? At some point in my life I thought, 'Well, this is the landscape you were brought up in, and whatever it is, it's that interior landscape you carry around with you, so why not?'

So without putting bells and whistles on it, yeah, I'm an Australian writer. Of course I am.

EMILY PERKINS is the New Zealand author of four novels and a collection of short stories. Recently, she also began writing for theatre and film.

Perkins grew up in Auckland and Wellington. She left school to act in the TVNZ drama *Open House,* and trained at the New Zealand Drama School, but claims she made a better waitress than actress.

She switched from acting to writing in 1993, studying creative writing with the renowned poet and writing teacher, Bill Manhire, at Wellington's Victoria University.

In 1994 Perkins moved to London, and Picador published her first book when she was just twenty-six, in 1996. *Not Her Real Name,* a collection of acutely observed stories about the drifty, disaffected young, introduced her clear-eyed gaze to the world and announced her as a 'writer to watch'. *Not Her Real Name* won the Faber Award in the UK and was short-listed for the New Zealand Book Award, winning the

Best First Book (Fiction) prize. In the following London years, Perkins published two novels—*Leave Before You Go* and *The New Girl*—and also wrote book reviews and personal essays, including a long-running column for the *Independent on Sunday*.

She returned to New Zealand in 2005. The next year she held the Buddle Findlay Frank Sargeson Fellowship, during which she wrote her London novel: the taut psychological thriller *Novel About My Wife*, universally praised for its 'biting social satire', 'dark portrait of contemporary urban life' and 'elegantly unsettling' characterisation. *The Believer* called it 'a novel about middle-class anxiety that is actually terrifying'.

I first met Perkins at Adelaide Writers' Week some years ago, where I was instantly drawn to her warmth, intelligence and sharp wit. Listening to her speak on stage, I was fascinated by her original approach to writing and the deep spirit of inquiry she showed in talking about her work. She is modest about her achievements, but the strength of her literary ambition glows from beneath this modesty. I straightaway read as much of her work as I could find and loved it, especially *Novel About My Wife*, whose depictions of middle-class delusions and vanity I found excruciatingly accurate. I was also thrilled by its utterly gripping narrative drive.

On her return to New Zealand from London Perkins hosted *The Book Show* on TV1, which morphed into *The*

Good Word and ran on TVNZ7 until the channel closed in 2012. During this time Perkins also began teaching writing, first at the University of Auckland—where she also returned as a student—and later as a senior lecturer at the International Institute of Modern Letters at Wellington's Victoria University, where she works today.

When Perkins' novel *The Forrests* was published in 2012, I felt her work leapt to a new level of literary risk and achievement. I fell completely in love with this book for the intensity of its observation, its ambitious scale and narrative wildness, and for the deeply compassionate moral presence at its core. I was not alone: *The Independent* called *The Forrests* 'extraordinary' and 'a magnificent novel'; Malcolm Knox described it as 'a daring experiment that comes off', while Michelle de Kretser called it 'bold', 'canny' and 'imaginative'.

This boldness of approach is what will always make me want to read Perkins—the risk inherent in all her work fills it with energy and life. This courage is also what compelled her, in 2015, to take on the daunting challenge of writing a new adaptation of Ibsen's *A Doll's House* for the Auckland Theatre Company. She has co-written a film adaptation of Eleanor Catton's first novel, *The Rehearsal*, and is now at work on a new novel.

In conversation Perkins is charming, funny, self-deprecating and passionate. For this interview we spoke

by Skype from our respective homes, mine in Sydney and hers in Wellington, where she lives with her husband, the artist Karl Maughan, and their children.

CW: It seems to me that right from your first published work you've been experimenting with form. Would you agree?

EP: In my first short stories, a couple of things probably influenced that. One was that I was finishing the stories in the context of a writing class I took at university, in which there was a great openness of conversation about form. Among the ten students in the class were people who considered themselves poets and went on to be poets, and people who considered themselves fiction writers, but we all had to mix it up and that seemed quite natural. When I had my first short story published it had poems in it, for example. It came out of an environment that was ignoring categories.

I remember being conscious not that I was doing anything particularly experimental with form, but that the form of my work was arising from my own limitations; things I was bored by, in reading and in my own writing, things that bored me when I started writing them, so I just didn't do it. So there was nothing consciously experimental—but it's one of those things that you discover after the fact when people say to you, 'Oh, this is you playing around with form.'

But I'd say it's something that then remained an interest, and as my novel writing has gone on, I've found the choices you make about form are an integral part of what you're doing.

CW: I love the idea that formal experimentation comes out of boredom.

EP: Well, it's that limitations thing where you think, 'I'm not going to do a good job of this. Another person might do this and they might be in their element and it might be really gorgeous but—I can't do it.'

CW: You trained as an actor before you started writing, didn't you?

EP: I was writing at high school in the same way I was doing drama at high school. Then I left school to be an actor, and then I went to drama school after that—so it was all a little bit of a funny way around, just because of how the jobs came up.

I had two years of drama school and then a year or two of failed acting, then decided that I couldn't stick with that anymore but I didn't know what else to do. I was still writing, trying to write little scenes and little playlets, monologues, nothing finished. It was all very, very scrappy. But I started meeting people who had done this writing course, I knew a couple of guys who had done it, and after a while I thought, 'Why am I just hanging out with people who've done this course? Why don't I actually apply for it?' [*laughs*]

So I did, and that was the first time anyone was giving me regular feedback, setting writing exercises, and saying 'You have to finish something by the end of the year.' I still think that's what a lot of people come to writing courses for—structure. And you have to hope that something really healthy and provocative in a good way goes on inside that.

CW: What do you think you've taken from acting into writing?

EP: It wasn't until quite a lot later I realised, really, how influential it is in an ongoing way. I'd say one influence is an interest in the kinds of things that drama does, which is to take human interactions and present them in an intensified state, and dive right into the crux of things. But also, very importantly, acting works with subtext and that's a big part of what fiction does too.

From acting I've also brought a way of thinking in scenes—which it's good to then break out of—and an interest in the way people speak. There's also an interest in process; in drama school we were often encouraged to take risks and be foolish and fall on our arse. That's probably the biggest thing I got out of drama school: a preparedness to fail. I don't think I was able to really engage with it then, in that context. But afterwards, in writing classes and in the writing life, I could. You can't play it safe. You've got to take yourself to the edge of your edge. And sometimes you have to go over that edge in order to know that you're there.

CW: What does that preparedness to fail, that risk, bring to writing? Sometimes I feel the risk I'm taking as a writer won't be noticed by a reader, yet it propels everything for me.

EP: Yeah. That's an important risk, that one which is like there's a cost involved in some way. You have to have blood in the game, that's really important. Otherwise, why do it?

Then there's the type of risk which is where you think, 'Oh my God, can I *do* this?' I'm very drawn to those moments. Sometimes cowardice or taste or better judgement has me backing out of them. But they are fun to get to. It's to do with surprise as well, I think. Then there's the risk of attempting to do something you *can't* do. We were having a class discussion on humour the other day, about how with jokes there's further to fall. And that is an interesting and important risk to take—the feeling that if I don't pull this off it's just going to be really *awful*.

I feel like all this sits on one side of the limitations I might have as a writer, and on the other side there's the idea that you can make your limitations your territory. Your own way of expressing the world.

CW: Can I just go back to something you said about acting— about needing to break out of working in scenes. Can you elaborate on what you mean by that?

EP: I suppose I'm talking about scenes in the show-don't-tell school of realist writing. But there are so many other modes of narrative, and it's a shame to limit everything to simply what can be seen. The short story works really well in scenes and often, in class, people will want to *see* something in a scene that is being otherwise reported or narrated in some other way—summarised, or whatever. But I just love it when there's a balance, when a rhythm works well between the two.

I always think of *The Fifth Child* by Doris Lessing, which is striking in that way. How she covers a whole lot of time and dives in to these scenes and then lifts out again.

CW: That sounds to me like *The Forrests*.

EP: Well—no. *The Forrests* is very much scenic, though the summary bits of it are important for relief, for allowing time to move faster. But when I was writing *The Forrests* I was having a big fight with exposition. I had this idea that I could surgically remove any exposition from the book, not write anything with exposition in it—I wanted to write a novel without *any*. But rules only take you so far. I admire writers who set themselves a task and a rule and they rigorously find their way through it. But I haven't done that. I set them up and then at some point I probably have to break them in order for the thing to have its own life. You don't want to strangle the book because of some imposed rule you've decided to follow.

CW: I do feel you're quite rebellious, as a writer. Which gives all of your work this huge energy.

EP: That's very nice, because I'm so conformist as a person! [*laughs*]

CW: I want to turn to something you said about *The Forrests*. You said Dorothy has a talent for 'hot noticing'—I thought that was such a fantastic phrase, and it seems to me that *The Forrests* is all about hot noticing, in great detail and with great precision. Can you talk about what hot noticing is?

EP: Well, I suppose it was a driving force of that book. I just felt that suddenly there was in me a new awareness of surroundings. I had this strong desire to render in language, and to pay attention to, just the sheer fact of physical existence.

It's a cheat to ascribe that to Dorothy, which I probably did to avoid addressing what the point of view in that novel is. Because it's a sort of weird, focused and then dispersing point of view—sometimes it does belong to Dorothy, but sometimes it doesn't.

I just wanted to let that be, and not try and tidy it up. My tendency could be to have point of view obey some rule of consistency (rules again). That book's point of view is quite inconsistent and yet the one consistent thing is that particular type of noticing. It's a way of being sort of *in love* with things. I was interested in trying to render sensory effect through that noticing.

CW: It's interesting, because that book is extremely sophistic-ated in its narrative. A beginner writer can observe the sensory world very beautifully—but that on its own isn't enough, is it? But in *The Forrests* you've somehow internalised a very strong narrative drive that is almost invisible, and yet it's all through it. If you had tried to take this noticing approach to a novel when you first began writing, do you think it would've worked?

EP: No, I don't think it would've worked and I don't know if it works to everyone's satisfaction now; in fact, I know it's not a book for everyone. I tried to keep the narrative really simple. That was something I realised I'd have to do quite late in the writing process—I saw that if I wanted to do this other thing with the way the novel looked at the world, then the actual core of the story had to be as simple as possible.

So on the one hand, you've got time, which pushes the narrative along, and on the other hand you've got these relationships which are really a very simple structure. A love quadrangle, that's all it is.

CW: But you also have the narrative frame of the arc of Dorothy's whole life. To me, almost just the fact of that is somehow incredibly moving. Part of why I love *The Forrests* so much is that there's something majestic in covering the span of a whole life.

EP: Well, that's lovely to hear. Maybe that is where there was a risk involved for me, which felt like an important one to take. What happens if you reach back and reach forward in time? I started to enjoy the way that things sort of loosened up for Dorothy in her older life, and there was a nice energy for me in the writing of it.

CW: It does have a beautiful looseness, I want to come back to that. But I want to ask, when you start a book, any book, do you know what it is you're attempting? Do you have some kind of job for yourself, at the start?

EP: I start off with a job, but it has to be one that shifts and redefines itself. There's always a tension—I don't know if you feel this, but on the one hand I have to start with incredibly grandiose ideas. [*laughs*] I need to have *massive* ambitions for the work, right? And then, on the other hand, I have to think, 'Okay, this is just a tiny little something I'm going to stitch away at.' So there's this constant internal conversation with myself.

CW: It sounds like a tension between seizing a sense of absolutely authority and confidence, and yet remaining vulnerable to discovery and mistake-making.

EP: Yeah, because you want to sort of reach for the stars, to use a terrible cliché, and at the same time, you can only get anywhere by crawling along.

Being vulnerable to the mistake-making is part of the process, and you need to be prepared for it—but the stuff that feels awful is the stuff you *can't* prepare for, it's the stuff that's bad in new, unexpected ways. But I do think that the more you write, the more you recognise that feeling and go, 'Oh, it's alright, I'm going to get through it.'

CW: It's amazing though, isn't it, that there are so many new ways! You think, 'Well, I must know this by now.' And yet here is a whole new humiliation.

EP: The word 'humiliation' is interesting. I feel there's some weird connection between writing and shame that I don't want to necessarily look at too closely because I don't know how useful it is.

It's more useful if you just get used to a low-grade level of shame and accept that, but there's something in there, I don't know.

CW: So many of the writers I've interviewed very quickly come to that word, shame. It's related to the risk, I think.

EP: I think it's related to the risk too, but there are so many different parts to it. I mean, there's the cultural shame and all of those other things, but the acceptance of shame is related to your connection with humanity—because everybody feels it, apart from psychopaths. So there's something about going with it that *is* useful.

CW: That's very beautiful; it's our connection with humanity. Alright, so when you're starting out on your magnificent world-changing project—in a practical way, what do you start with? When you start typing, what are you working on?

EP: It's usually an incident—and character and place come out of that. It's rare for me to start with character, though I'm doing that slightly more at the moment. Apart from *Novel About My Wife* where London, the city, was very much a feature, place is not so important to me. I just want it to serve the mood, that's all I care about. Place for me is something that works towards the mood, the atmosphere, the constraints, the freedoms, the texture of the story.

Place used to be a kind of obsession in New Zealand writing, though that's changing now—it's too connected with the idea of writing as a nationalist project. Actually, one of my favourite New Zealand writers is Pip Adam, and I once read a piece of hers that said something like, 'Oh, Wellington, you placy, placy *place*!' [*laughter*] I think that's the best thing anyone has ever written about Wellington.

In recent decades the concept of a coherent national literature, or a literature that is fundamentally to do with expressing nationhood, has receded greatly, although there are periodic attempts at revival. But how much do we live in nations now? It's all changed. A lot of people think Robbe-Grillet was full of it, but in *Towards a New Novel* he was at least trying to address how the novel might thoughtfully reflect fundamental social changes, and this might happen inevitably, but it's also necessary to think about where you are coming from in all ways—culturally, historically, geographically, et cetera. Not to necessarily write into that space but to acknowledge that you're writing from it. The interaction between imaginative freedom and all these influences. A lot of really good writing from Aotearoa, whether by Pākehā or Māori or Pasifika writers, is not straightforward social realism, and maybe that reflects a complicated or multi-layered relationship with place.

I suppose I'm still stuck in some feeling of teenage rebellion against those ideas I came up through university with, about what New Zealand writing is supposed to do for us. It's complicated, because we are tiny and we need reflection but that is not always the job of literature. I mean, I want to read a great novel set in Wellington as much as the next Wellingtonian does, but the idea that a Wellington writer *should* write a novel set in Wellington is something else, and has a lot less currency these days.

Another thing about a small country is our reviewing culture. There's blindingly good literature coming from this country, as well as mediocre and bad writing, just like anywhere. But in the effort to encourage New Zealanders to read work by fellow citizens, the public conversation about NZ books can get muddied or diverted. I mean, everybody wants good news, and that's totally understandable. But sometimes the imperatives of a small industry have this middling effect on the way we talk about books. This feels like a transitional time: there are always going to be people who want to have an in-depth, informed critical conversation and we need to foster the platforms that will contribute to that.

CW: The difference between writers' and critics' thinking about national literature is interesting. In Australia there seems to be this continuous anxiety, manifesting in the question, 'What is Australian literature?' But as a writer, I basically couldn't give a shit.

EP: Most writers couldn't, really, don't you think?

CW: Maybe. I do think too much self-consciousness about that sort of thing is bad for writing. But let's move on. I want to ask you about your recent work in the theatre, in adapting A *Doll's House*. It sounds like a fascinating and scary thing to do.

EP: It really was. It was a commission; I just agreed to it. It was too enticing an invitation to decline.

CW: Did you know the play well?

EP: Yes, I did know the play, though I had never seen it staged. I found it so hard to start with. I was very conscious of the risk involved, and because it was a commission and the theatre committed to it quite early on, there was this massive opportunity to fuck up. And I knew I couldn't give in to that cowardice, which was all about public risk, really, not anything else. It would be really awful—nobody wants to have a massive public failure—but, equally, you don't want to let that stop you doing anything.

But it did mean it took me a long time to make the crucial decisions that you need to make to get a first draft of something. 'Oh, this is what writer's block feels like.' I don't know if you've ever felt it, but I just couldn't make a decision. It's also a bit what depression is like, I think—you simply can't make a decision.

There were so many possibilities, it wasn't like I had a blank wall in front of me, there was no shortage of possible ways to tackle this project—but I could not, for the life of me, fix on one.

Partly that was because it took a long time to settle on precisely what it was that I was most interested in exploring, what it was that the DNA of that play would allow me to think about. The play contains so much about relationships, love, myths about love, betrayal, money, survival, responsibility, personhood—as well as having a cracking plot. Finding a way to explore these ideas for a modern audience, but also trying to succeed in keeping them as intricately interrelated as the original does, was a challenge. Each idea seemed to drag me in one direction or another.

And I am embarrassed to admit—but I will because it was a good lesson—that for a while, my ego was in the way. I had a feeling that, as Ibsen did with the naturalism of the original, I should be able to write something in a new form that would be like no play anybody had ever seen, that would just set the world on fire! Which was getting me precisely nowhere. So then I was able to come down to earth and think, listen: you're a beginner dramatist, you're adapting something from a master dramatist, all you can do is just try not to fuck it up too much. I had to listen to the play, and listen to myself.

I talked it through with Karl, my husband, which is a great thing to do when I get to a point of wanting to test an idea out. So it all started to clarify. And I had a deadline, so I had to get on with it. But really, I had to do what we advise students to do, and just write a shitty first draft. And I now know that it's really horrible to do! I'm not saying my other first drafts are not shitty, but I haven't had to *show* them to anyone.

Of course the more you write, the more invested you become, and the more determined to not give up on it. So, it got to the point where I had to press 'send'. And I thought, well, if they want to pull the plug on this, they can, but at least I've fulfilled this part of the contract. Later, they confessed to me that the first draft was kind of a mess. [*laughs*]

We read that draft through with actors—different groups of actors all the time, so you're getting different views on it—and I wrote most of the second draft. Then we had a two-week workshop, which is part of what this theatre does to develop new work. That was great. The actors were working off a draft that I was updating daily. And it was up on its feet, so we were finding out what was working and what was impossible.

CW: Do you think you would've been able to do it if you hadn't been to drama school?

EP: Well, people do, obviously. But I just loved being in the workshop room. I loved it. It was an amazing combination of these different parts of my life—there I was in a rehearsal room with actors, the director, the set people, the dramaturg, all that delicious stuff, people working on making something together, and I was writing! It was a very fulfilling process. What was lucky about the offer of that particular work is that I was very alert to the play itself, very ready to get into it and explore—it spoke to me about this moment, now. So that's where so much of the energy came from, it was a place for a bunch of my thoughts about living to be explored.

With drama you can have an idea as a starting point, but then the great and exciting thing is to *embody* those ideas and test them and put them in impossible situations and oppose them and tear them down and then see what happens. All of that was really enjoyable.

CW: It sounds quite terrifying to me! Just staying with that idea of risk for a minute; as a teacher, how do you teach students about it when what constitutes a risk for each person is so particular?

EP: In some ways, all you can do is create a place where they are not going to die if they do risk something and it doesn't work. It's not going to be the end of the world. There's a wonderful essay I sometimes hand out called 'On Risk and Investment' by Tim Etchells, who is a theatre practitioner.

And sometimes I'll say something like, 'If you don't feel excruciatingly embarrassed at some point in this class then you're not doing it right.' It's letting them know that it's just a part of the process, it's part of the deal. If they want to get the most out of it, they have to be prepared to put that into it. But as a teacher you do have a big responsibility to make risk and failure okay. You can't invite people to take risks and then leave them hanging. You know, there has to be a safe environment in which to do it.

CW: I'd love to be a student in your class. Which brings me to ask about you going back to writing school yourself, when you returned to New Zealand and had already published several books. Why did you do that?

EP: Well, I came back from London and I finished writing *Novel About My Wife* and I was doing contract teaching. I knew that if I wanted to keep on with my teaching beyond a term here or there, I was going to have to get a qualification. So that was a practical consideration.

Also, the timing was right. I'd finished one book that had left a strong internal impression on my writing—it was taking me a while to shake, everything I started sounded like another version of this book. I was ready to start something else but felt quite open about what that might be. Then within the MA, by force of environment and deadline, I started working on *The Forrests*.

The unexpected gift of being in the course environment was thinking, 'I'm not writing this for publication, I'm just going to have a play around and think about some things and see what happens to the writing.' That was really liberating. Then I finished it and handed it in—I mean, it was in a slightly different form, although the core of it, the structure and drive of it was absolutely there. And then the writerly ego kicks in and says, 'Oh no, I do really want to publish this. So, how do I make it work?'

CW: It does have such a lovely freedom about it. I'm interested in the transition from *Novel About My Wife*, which is so tautly controlled, to this enormous, beautifully loose construction. Do you think the looseness of *The Forrests* partly came about from the control of *Novel About My Wife*?

EP: Yeah, I do. I was able to allow it to be loose because *Novel About My Wife* had been this tightly structured thing, which had been something I'd wanted to do. But then I was able to let it go. But also, the looseness was important to me in a way that . . . it wasn't a reaction against structure, but against tidiness, maybe, or niceness or *politeness*, or palatability.

I guess I was trying to follow that looseness on every level with *The Forrests*: on a sentence level and a language level, as well as a characterological and structural level. I just wanted to see where that could take me. Partly it was about wanting to embrace as much *texture* as possible—which means ugliness and jarringness and jaggedness, as well as beauty and fragrance and all of that stuff.

CW: I so relate to the desire for . . . mess. Personally, I feel I've spent so much time trying to learn how to write a proper book. And then after a while I thought, 'Okay, I've got some skills in controlling a narrative and all that stuff, none of which I had when I began. But now I've got some of that control, I just want to blow it all up.'

EP: Yeah, right.

CW: In *The Forrests*, your narrative control seemed to me to be really deeply internalised, but it didn't feel like the main game anymore for you as a writer. I've lately begun to feel that very controlled, event-driven narrative is a manifestation of authorial insecurity. What do you make of that?

EP: This is something quite fascinating that comes up in class, because we're responding to nascent work that is becoming itself, and part of that is often looking at what our expectations of the story are as it goes on. We often have to get over the first stile of conventional expectation, those things we've been indoctrinated with by our culture, before we can really move.

In my own work I want to fool myself, I want to trick myself. I don't want to simply do what I'm *trying* to do, because that's only going to take me so far. That was another thing about *The Forrests*. I thought, 'I don't really understand what I'm doing. I don't know what this is coming together to be'—and it was important not to know. It was important to just go on gut feeling and literally not be able to control its effect because I didn't know what it was.

CW: If there's a spectrum with intuition and gut instinct at one end and really deliberate control at the other, where do you think you lie as a writer?

EP: Hmm, God. Probably at the intuitive end.

Control comes and goes. It's vital to have control, but also to let go of it. This is not to say that intuition is always right because it's not. But . . . it's about listening. In drama training the essence of the learning is to move with your instincts. Don't block, don't second-guess, follow your impulse, react, make something happen. Something honest, not something calculated. You've got to lose yourself enough to have the intuition, and then the control—the useful, good control—can only come from really listening to that.

If it's coming from something outside you, from some idea of what something *should* be, then that's the bad, second-guessing, manipulative kind of control. I don't know if there's a hard and fast rule about that, but maybe that's true.

CW: There seems to be something about humility in what you're saying there.

EP: Well, as I was saying before, you need this funny combination of total humility and soaring hubris. You need humility because you have to accept how things are, but we're all *making* something, right? You can't actually be an entirely humble person and still make something and put it out into the world. It's an interesting tension. It's quite a fun tension. I mean, you can be feeling all humble and be making away, dah de dah, and then you get something pushing back against you, against the work. That's when I think, 'No, fuck you, I'm doing this.'

CW: When I've done teaching and mentoring, especially with women, there's so much talk about confidence—not having any, needing to build more, blah blah blah. But what I've discovered over time is that confidence is a decision. Nothing will earn it for you, you actually just have to decide to have it, you have to demand it of yourself.

EP: I completely agree. I can remember the kitchen of the flat that I was standing in, in Mount Victoria in 1993 when I was doing the writing course, and I was suffering from all of that: 'Oh, what have I got to say? I've got nothing to say,' dah de dah de dah. And I suddenly realised—I remember this so vividly—that so many young men I knew were making short films or playing in bands or making art of some kind, and they didn't do what I was doing. I thought, 'They don't do this. They're not worrying about whether they're any good, they're not crippled by self-doubt or whether or not they've got something worthy to put into the world—*they're just making it.*' It didn't even occur to them to worry about it. I mean, maybe that wasn't entirely true, but that's how it looked from the outside. And I thought, 'It's time to get some of that.'

It was absolutely time to get some of that, whatever it was—testosterone, confidence. So I wholeheartedly agree that it's a decision to make. And I find now that I have . . . well, I know there's a social context, and I have sympathy, but I get frustrated on behalf of women who can't make that decision for whatever reason. One thing that drives me crazy is going to readings when—and I'm sure I've been guilty of this myself—when women undermine their own work at a public reading, by being all shruggy and apologetic. They might be reading this electric prose or poetry or whatever and it gets swallowed.

Public events can be excruciating, but if you're going to do it then ideally you back yourself, even if you're playing a part. And in the end those events are about giving the audience a good experience—to revert to the people-pleasing hostess model if we must. It's for them.

CW: It's such a crucial point of development for writers, isn't it? And like you, maybe I react so strongly against this in younger writers now because I was so much like that myself. But you have to just get over it.

EP: In class we have a no-disclaimers rule. Because a lot of this doubt stuff is actually not really about writing, it's more complicated—it's about being liked, and not being too big for your boots and all that sort of stuff you probably got slapped down for when you were a kid, or even now by the culture at large. When I was writing my version of A *Doll's House* I became painfully conscious of how much women can unconsciously work to protect the egos of others. In all kinds of ways.

CW: In a weird way, when it's out of control, insistently vocalised self-doubt is more hubristic than anything else.

EP: Yes! It's a sort of narcissism, a desire to control what other people are thinking of you.

CW: All this criticism of poor young writers, when I was exactly guilty of all that! But I love that your memory of that moment, that decision in the kitchen, is so vivid. It sounds like a breakthrough point for you.

EP: Well, it was. Then of course the work keeps on testing that decision, because your nerve can fail you at any time. Or mine can, anyway. And life is full of all sorts of tests for it. But the core moment of that decision about the confidence, that's necessary.

CW: Let's talk more about some of the content of your work now. It seems to me that you've always been deeply concerned with explorations of memory and time. In *Novel About My Wife*, Tom is trying to reconstruct Ann and his own memories are unreliable or have proven to be false in some way. And then of course in *The Forrests* there's so much slippage of time and memory. What interests you so much about time?

EP: Well, it's something I've become increasingly interested by, and it was a presiding curiosity in writing *The Forrests*. Time is amazing to play with in novels because in fiction you're off clock time—you can do whatever you want with time. Probably that's one of the most pleasurable aspects of writing for me. And also it's so core to our experience of being human and being mortal, that it seems essential to investigate it in different ways.

CW: And your different ways are so fascinating. It seems to me that your sense of time moves not just forward and backward but somehow outward and inward. It sort of pulses.

EP: That's really nice. It's something to do with scale—and scale is something that fiction can play with very well. By scale I mean, say, to ask where are we on our compass point? For example, if we're looking down at where we are from up in the clouds, that puts us in a particular place. But if we are looking at that place on a microbiological level, it's something else entirely. I don't know, but scale to me is really about the infinite, infinite variety of the world, about perspective and contrast, and I find all that stuff energising in writing. I like writing that moves from the very small to the very large. Maybe that goes to what I was saying earlier about trying to break out of thinking too much in scenes, or habitually writing in scenes. Because scenes can lend themselves to a rather dull consistency of scale. And it could be more interesting if you blow it up, or shrink it down.

CW: So fascinating—I've never thought about that before. Speaking of time and movement, how do you think you've changed as a writer from when you started?

EP: I guess my relationship with writing has deepened, and my acceptance of the weirder parts of it and the more frustrating and difficult parts is greater. The delight is still the same when there's something surprising, or you feel you're taking a risk. That feeling when you make yourself laugh, or you think, 'Oh, can I really do this?' That's the same.

It's deepened in the sense that your relationship with life deepens as well. I feel like my life is more vertical now, more reaching downwards somehow, than when I was in my late twenties or when I started writing—back then it all seemed more horizontal and on the surface. That could be a trick of memory.

CW: I once read you referring to what you called Brian Eno's doctrine: 'Honour thy mistake as a hidden intention'. And you said, 'hidden intention is the key phrase'. What did you mean by that?

EP: You can't intentionally make a mistake. You can't intentionally surprise yourself—'Oh, I'm going to do something spontaneous now, and here it is.' You can only arrive at those things by not knowing. I mean, we're such strangers to ourselves in so many ways—and for writers, thank God that's true. That's the golden stuff, where you might be thinking you're writing one thing, but actually it's presenting itself as something else. I see this in class a lot. A student will often get caught in a dilemma between their intention and what the work is turning out to be. They think, 'But hang on, it's meant to be *this*, so I've got to fix it, I've got to change it and make it more what I want it to be.'

And sometimes that's the right thing to do, but often it's not—often the right thing to do is to look at what you've got and listen to it. Ask, 'What is this? What does this *want* to be?' You have to let those *hidden* intentions lead it.

CW: But it can be frightening to do that, can't it? This book I've just written, for a long time I was absolutely resisting what it was trying to be because I didn't want to write a book like that, and I still don't want to write a book like that.

EP: But you have written a book like that.

CW: I have written a book like that, I had no choice. Because resisting it was just making nothing happen at all.

EP: It's hard. It's hard, isn't it? Why is it hard?

CW: Because of what we were saying before about humility, I suppose. I had to come to accept that well, this is saying things about me that I don't like; things that are dark and ugly. I don't even want to know I'm like that, let alone have other people know I'm like that! But there I am.

EP: And it's a fantastic thing to just say, 'There I am.' Because if we don't do that, in life as well as in our writing, then we're on the run. On the run from what we are, or who we are.

CW: Yes—and I think now that's where art actually originates from: that centre which is there, whether you like it or not.

EP: Yeah, that's right. That specificity—and being honest about it. Ooh, it's hard.

CW: It's horrible! Anyway, let's get away from that stuff, into logistics. Do you have a working routine?

EP: I've discovered that every project generates, or results from, its own routine. Right now I'm nearing the end of a trimester of research leave, which is a true privilege and I'm very grateful for it. To get as far with a new novel as I could, I've had a daily word count, only one thousand words so it's doable, and my mantra has been Isak Dinesen's 'write a little every day, without hope and without despair.' So now I'm reworking a very rough first draft and trying to get as much of a second draft done as possible before teaching resumes. The first draft was about the story the second is about the voice, which is completely the reverse of the way a book like *Novel About My Wife* came together. We'll see. I'm just so happy to be writing. I hadn't been writing fiction for a long time, apart from in little snatches. Partly because of these drama projects; I've co-written the adaptation of *The Rehearsal*, Eleanor Catton's first novel, with Alison Maclean. Alison's directing it and it's nearly out in the world, which is very exciting. And there's been teaching too.

But even if I'm writing something else and working hard, and being a good girl, I still feel a bit off if it's not fiction. Like I'm cheating something.

I find deadlines crucial. Of course I always go past them, but they help bring me back into the reality you need to be in when you're making work.

CW: Do you put those deadlines on yourself, or—

EP: Oh no, they need to come from outside. My own deadlines are bullshit. No, they need to come from people who I'd be just so ashamed of letting down, who I might end up owing money to, and where doing that will really fuck with a whole bunch of other stuff.

CW: And when is the best time of day for you to work?

EP: I've been starting early with this novel, but if I had endless amounts of time, I feel like this is not what we're meant to say, but I like working in the late afternoon. I have to have spent the rest of the day gearing up to it.

In a practical sense, the single most useful thing for me is—whosever trick it was—to end the day midway through something where I know what's coming next. Even if it's halfway through a sentence. That I find enormously helpful.

CW: What's at the root of that gearing-up feeling? What do you think it's about?

EP: It feels to me like preparing to focus. It's physical, quite physical. So, I have to feel . . . not restless, not distractible. It's like getting into cold water; you don't want to do it but it's going to be great when you're in. You know that feeling of immersing yourself in cold water, how if you fight it and you tense up it feels colder for longer? But if you relax and you actually let it be cold on your skin, it's different? It's like that.

CW: Is where you work important?

EP: No, I really don't care. I don't write very well in my office at work—that's quite a separate space. But otherwise, I like working in my house but it could be anywhere in my house, even bed or the couch.

CW: I believe there's an injunction to yourself you repeat sometimes: 'Loosen the fuck up!'

EP: Yeah, well that sort of came through writing *The Forrests*. It's part of relaxing in the water: just do it. Don't second-guess it.

CW: And what about humour? Your writing is very witty and your characters are sharp and funny in a self-mocking way. There's a lot of skewering of pretentiousness.

EP: That might be . . . fundamental to writing fiction because it arises naturally out of looking at things from the outside as well as the inside. I mean, I'm as pretentious as the next person, but fiction only starts to get interesting if you keep going to the next layer of things. My favourite dumb cliché: *Take it to the next level.* That always makes me laugh. Like *Be here now.* What is the next thing out? What's the next thing outside that, then outside that? Not accepting things at face value. And I feel humour is a part of that.

And also, life is just so absurd so much of the time.

I find an enormous energy, a wellspring of energy and creativity and fun and joy in that absurdity. For me, it's just bubbling away in everything and obviously sometimes it's there right alongside the most serious and tragic stuff.

CW: Your humour also seems a form of self-questioning.

EP: Yeah, that's what I'm trying to express when I say talk about the next layer, and the next one. You're questioning this situation, these characters or whatever. When I was living in the UK, I loved that self-deprecating humour—and a lot of that is about getting in a hit yourself before somebody else can do it to you. So there's a self-protective element as well as a self-questioning one.

CW: What you've said reminds me, this has just come into my head now, of something the screenwriter Jimmy McGovern said somewhere years ago. I remember madly writing it down at the time. He talked about the need to attack your own cause. He was talking about a drama he was writing with striking dock workers, and he said it would only come alive if they genuinely attacked their own beliefs, their own position.

EP: That's absolutely what you have to do. That is where things come alive and get interesting. That's what I finally found in this adaptation of A *Doll's House*. It's not interesting if you're attacking something you're *already* in disagreement with. So I wanted to set A *Doll's House* in a world of people who were actually doing something I found admirable and, yeah, attack it from that standpoint. It's very energising to the work.

CW: What do you find hardest about writing fiction?

EP: Well, that changes all the time, but maybe the hard things for different writers circulate around the same sort of trouble spots. For me, it's hard to set up whatever it is that means you can surprise yourself. And that's got to be a different set-up every time, because the same tricks are not going to keep working.

And the physical doing of it I find hard. I don't mind being on my own, I love that part. It doesn't ever feel lonely to me, I really enjoy that aspect. But I find it just physically boring. I would rather get up and walk around.

CW: That physical restlessness is pretty much the opposite of writing, isn't it?

EP: Yeah. It's something to overcome. I mean, I do sort of stand up and move away from the machine and walk around a bit and say things out loud—do you do all that?

CW: Not so much. But I always feel like I'm having to really work hard to stay in the chair. I mean, I just want to run out of the room most of the time.

EP: Yeah, I know. I'm happiest doing it when I'm in an environment where I've got enough space that I can stand up and stare at things without seeing them, and talk out loud and do all of that. It's a funny physical discipline.

What else is hard about it? Well, it's that hard thing of not wanting to *lie*. You don't want to bullshit, you don't want to short-change a reader on anything. That's where it gets nitty-gritty, where you have to try to dig deeply, somehow, into that space where you're not lying.

CW: Telling the truth in fiction is quite a hard thing to explain.

EP: It is. It's funny, Charlotte, in talking to you now I feel conflicted because on the one hand, we're speaking about something we can understand, so why not talk about it? I'm trying not to say anything that is not true. But another part of me just doesn't want to talk about it *at all*. And this is weird because everything in my life is set up in complete conflict with that instinct! [*laughs*] Not wanting to talk about it comes from a fear of saying stuff that is superficial, meaningless, trite, worthless, trivial—and you know, *what for?*

CW: I get this. I reckon maybe it's because everything we're saying right now we genuinely believe. And yet, when you sit down to work, it's all gone. All that knowledge or belief or whatever, it sort of evaporates—and there you are in this place with something about which you have absolutely no idea. You have no idea what it is. So perhaps it makes all this other talking feel somehow false.

EP: I really think that's right. This is where my unease sits.

CW: Well, let's talk about the opposite. At what point do you feel most free when you're working? Where's the pleasure in it?

EP: The pleasure is so important, it's the juice. It's the key to all of it. There's just nothing better than when a work gives off a sense of pleasure. It can be very serious or difficult work or tragic work, whatever, but there's a sense that fun was had in the making of it. I do feel this is critical. One of the tutors we had at drama school called Stuart Devenie used to say, 'You can get away with anything as long as you're fun.' So that for me really is a guiding principle.

But where is the fun? I mean, for the writer it can be in the tingle of a new idea or a word that arrives, or it can be in the way things are put together—things bumping up against each other in a way that feels like a discovery of some sort, or leads to something unexpected. The element of surprise and the element of pleasure are totally intertwined. Ultimately the requirement is, this has to be fun for the reader: fun in the sense of being moved or surprised or provoked or carried away or shown something new . . . then you are more likely to get away with whatever other shit you might be trying to pull.

CW: What do you think might be three essential qualities every writer needs?

EP: Being a reader, and everything that that means. Also, curiosity. And—to be a writer I want to read, anyway—a sense of humour. A sense that you know full well there's a joke hovering nearby that could unravel everything.

CW: Do you know why you write?

EP: One reason is simply the process of discovery, of thinking and feeling through writing, the fun of testing a voice, finding a story, playing with language and form. And then there's the pleasure of, I hope, giving pleasure. Which is frankly unbeatable if it happens. Another basic reason is that I like having made something. Something new is in the world that wasn't there before. Once the book is out, beyond a certain point of publication I don't feel umbilically connected to it, beyond the first year of publication, say. Before that, I feel very much like it's still sort of flesh of my flesh, but after it's been out there for a while, I don't feel that anymore. But something is there that wasn't there before. It's a sort of fundamental impulse I suppose—it's primal. I like that.

Photo: Sebb Scott

KIM SCOTT was born in 1957. His ancestral Noongar country is the south-east coast of Western Australia between Gairdner River and Cape Arid. His cultural elders use the term Wirlomin to refer to their clan, and the Norman Tindale nomenclature identifies people of this area as Wudjari/ Koreng.

Scott began writing for publication while a high-school English teacher, and has published poetry and short stories in a number of anthologies. His three novels—*True Country, Benang: From the Heart* and *That Deadman Dance*—are poetic, sophisticated explorations of individual and cultural identity. The stylistically unconventional memoir *Kayang and Me*, co-written with elder Hazel Brown, is another literary exploration of identity and heritage.

That Deadman Dance won nine prestigious literary awards in its year of publication, including the regional Commonwealth Writers' Prize and the Miles Franklin Award. *Benang* had earlier also won the Miles Franklin, making Scott one of a handful of writers who have won the award more than once and its first Indigenous winner. His work is widely published internationally.

As well as his literary career, Scott has worked with others for several years to recover and preserve the traditional languages of his ancestral people. Two picture books, *Mamang* and *Noongar Mambara Bakitj*, have so far been published in Noongar and English by the University of Western Australia Press, and Scott continues working with his community on language regeneration. Since this interview took place, another novel has been largely completed.

He is a Professor of Creative Writing at Curtin University and lives with his wife and two children in Coolbellup, south of Fremantle, Western Australia.

I met Scott when I chaired a 2011 Sydney Writers' Festival panel on readers and writers. Like the audience that day I was struck by his lyrical turn of phrase in conversation and his modest but powerful presence—the room was spellbound when, to illustrate a point, he softly sang for a moment in traditional language. It is no surprise to later learn that he is a keen amateur musician.

This interview took place in Scott's office at Curtin University. A bicycle and a large framed plaque from his publisher commemorating the many prizes won by *That Deadman Dance* are two personal touches in an orderly and otherwise unadorned workspace.

Scott is serious and quietly spoken, though he smiles and laughs often as he speaks, and his fiction is suffused with humour even in the midst of suffering. Much of his conversation reveals a tension between the solitary pursuit of his literary career and the desire to contribute to the community; the quest for 'usefulness' is something he mentions frequently. He is open about his unease with some parts of the writing life—such as the world of literary prizes and the sometimes-uncomfortable public role into which they have thrust him.

Scott is not one for slick responses; often after answering a question, he would qualify it with exceptions and counter-arguments, displaying the same refusal to reach for simple conclusions that characterises his acclaimed fiction.

CW: Can you explain the relationship between your language regeneration project and your fiction? Where do they overlap or mesh?

KS: I don't completely know. It's a bit of an experiment—it comes from some sort of personal need, I think.

I worked on *That Deadman Dance* and the project together, and I was thinking—it seemed outrageously ambitious at the time—that if I could get some success with the novel, as I had with *Benang*, I could use it to shine a bit of a spotlight on the language project, and create a bit of momentum. It sort of worked better than I ever expected—except the momentum didn't get generated to quite the extent I would have liked. But the language project is still going.

Moving the other way, there were no intentions, really. I actually wanted to keep them separate, so I could be clearer in my own mind about the possibility of appropriation, or exploitation. But I do believe that working on the language project helped some of the narratives in *That Deadman Dance*. It helped me write something other than just a resistance narrative, with all the dangers of being ambushed by the genre of military history, or providing ammunition for the cause, or asserting your indigenous identity in your writing—they're problems I see a bit, in the niche.

CW: Why are these things problems?

KS: Because they reduce the possibility for what you might be doing, and stop you being exploratory, and stop you going into those dangerous areas that usually end up being the most fertile for creative work. The narratives in the language project are full of confident protagonists. They are non-reactive, non-polemical narratives, and because they're in language they're not talking about what's Aboriginal and non-Aboriginal. It's just full-on confidence, and *being*.

I think that helped me write the novel in that sort of way. Also, in doing that language work, I was paying a lot of attention to things like rhythm, and I think that may have bled into the novel. Certain imagery may have bled into the novel in an osmotic sort of way, which is interesting. And so did certain conceptual possibilities I got from the language, which I try and enact a little bit.

As part of the language work, I also traced quite a lot of archival Noongar language texts. One Noongar song had a colonial place name in the middle of it; another had fragments of English phrases—I thought that was really interesting. Another had the point of view of a sailor looking through a telescope at the composer. These are extremely *literary* exercises, you know what I mean? So I started thinking, 'How might those composers write a novel if they were me?' And so I was encouraged to favour what you might call literary means rather than just the overt politics or polemics.

Then there's the whole audience question—of who you're working with, and for. With the language project it's a small community, and it's a nice way to demonstrate your literary 'muscle', [*laughs*] for want of a better phrase, in a really *useful* way. If you're a person of letters working with language, that's a useful way to help your home community, I think. Whereas the literary fiction thing is a little bit awkward. It's a much longer-term project and you don't know where it's going to go, and it's not so immediately useful, I don't think. But it's got its own perverse pleasures.

CW: On the question of audience, do you think about your readers as you write your fiction?

KS: Not really, no. I don't know if I've thought about readership other than in an apprehensive, fearful way.

I suppose as I write I think of someone a bit like me, hopefully with better taste. A kind of ideal reader, who knows the sort of allusions that oneself knows, and the context, and has read the same sort of books and reads in the same sort of way. That's all you can do, I think. But that reader is probably cleverer than me.

CW: Is this a generous reader, or a more critical one?

KS: Ah, good point. No, it's a pretty critical reader I'm often thinking of, that's what stops and slows one down a real lot. It's definitely a critical reader.

CW: Is that harmful to the work?

KS: It's harmful in getting work *started*, I think. Once you're into it, it's possibly less harmful, it just becomes more like editing. But in the earlier days—and I haven't started another novel yet, so I'm very aware of this—it makes it really hard to get going, because there's all that fear. 'Can I do it again? No I can't. I don't know what I'm going to write about, and I don't know if I can bear to put that energy and time into something that might fail, and everyone will just sling shit at me.' All that sort of thing.

CW: Can you feel another novel coming at you from a distance, or is it a conscious matter of saying, 'Now I'm going to sit down and start something?'

KS: It has been like that—'I'm going to sit down and start'—but usually I have a notion. I've had a notion for my next novel for a couple of years at least. And I make little notes about that without actually writing it. I imagine that in a few months, I'll put all those notes together and I'll get started.

I'm also trying a new ploy. I went to a screenwriting workshop with [Mexican author, screenwriter, director and producer] Guillermo Arriaga a few weeks ago, which was really interesting. So I've written a couple of little short scripts as a way of sneaking up on a longer prose work. Using the same sort of ideas. So that might be a cunning little ambush I'm setting for myself. But maybe not, it might end up being a whole screenplay.

But that also interests me because it relates again to the business of being an *Indigenous* novelist, which is such solitary work. With a screenplay, you can bring a lot of other people into the action, as with the language project. If you had a screenplay that seemed all right you could get a whole bunch of people working on it. And they could be non-actors, even, because you wouldn't have to describe all the body language stuff.

So if I can do that, as well as use it to sneak up on all the visualisation you have to do, and the sounds—I'm already finding it pretty interesting. And the sort of book I'm thinking of writing is less interior—for various reasons, I am thinking of having it not going so much into heads as I have previously—so that also works for the screenplay idea.

CW: So this is glimmering away while you work on your other projects?

KS: It comes and goes. I'm doing a lot of non-fiction writing at the moment, which I'm not enjoying. So it comes and goes.

CW: When you're over the hump of starting and are well into a book, do you have a particular routine or way of working?

KS: It changes depending on my circumstances. Nearly all my books have been written between jobs, when I'm not working—I've saved up and bought the time, or I've got a little grant or something like that.

Most recently the routine was four to six hours at the beginning of the day. Quite often it's good for me to do some exercise [*gestures to bicycle*] early on, to trim off some of the nervous energy and help me get a little bit more mellow, rather than all edgy. It makes it easier for me just to sit, and takes a bit of the edge off things.

So there's a set time, or sometimes it's word count—I keep a bit of a tally—or number of pages, I just keep an eye on that, so I'm not getting too slack, not just spending six hours at the desk gnashing my teeth. That doesn't count, you know. So I have those two things to measure against one another.

I like a separate space but I can work anywhere, and usually it's the worst area of the household. That's probably something to do with the idea that you can't make it all that important, because—you know, it's not a proper job. [*laughs*]

CW: Do you really feel that?

KS: Mmm, I'm afraid to say.

CW: Do you think that about other writers?

KS: No, no no. It's just a little bit of a self-esteem issue or something, and also a bit of guilt about why I'm doing this very solitary, perhaps selfish thing. You know, it's not bringing in the dollars for the family, which you should.

Writing can be a creeping, contraband sort of thing.

CW: So you make it harder for yourself because of that by choosing a busy area to work in . . .

KS: Oh, it's not people busy, it's just junky busy. You know, the lawn mower, and the old carpet and all that sort of stuff all around me. I don't know. If it was the flashest area of the house or something, the anxiety might get even tougher.

I always think I'd like a good little writing space all well organised, but I just never get organised, I suppose. I suppose I have to face up to that fact, at my age. [*laughs*]

I used to write at work, in a secretive sort of way, in the early days. One of my first poems was written during exam supervision. So I reckon I can do it anywhere, once I get the momentum up. Getting the momentum up, getting enough of a start, that's the tough bit.

CW: What would define a successful day's work for you?

KS: Quantity. [*laughs*] That's quite a big thing. Usually a good working time would be four to six hours and then a break. Then you have a look at what you've done and it's not really working, but if you're lucky you end up doing a bit more work anyway.

A really good day is when you've got something done, and you look at it later and it signals where you can go next. And it's *surprising* in a pleasant way. You are pleased with yourself, and it's something you weren't expecting, but were hoping for.

CW: Do you revise as you go?

KS: Yeah, I revise as I go. Often because it stops, so I go back to the beginning and go through and revise, and hope that'll carry me through the next bit.

CW: How would you define a successful book—for yourself, not in terms of what other people think? How do you know, for example, when your book is finished and ready and good enough to send off?

KS: I don't know if I ever know. I just get sort of sick of it. That's a considerable part of it. And I'm always aware of possible flaws, of the bits I just can't quite sort out. I will have had initial notions and diagrams and stuff. And once you get that all done—the ending, the closure or the resolution or whatever—you just have to get it together as a package. But you can have false endings. You leave it and look at it again and you think, 'Oh no, shit, I've gotta keep going!' [*laughs*]

CW: How long did *That Deadman Dance* take to write?

KS: I did it as part of a PhD, within three and a half years, which is remarkably speedy by my standards. But I had that scenario or the situation of that novel in mind for a fair while, so that may have helped. I wouldn't mind if I could do that again.

That's the fastest book, I think. *Benang* was the slowest, that was about five years, and *True Country* must have been three or four years. *Kayang and Me* was pretty speedy, but that was non-fiction.

CW: Did you find that easier than fiction?

KS: Probably, but perhaps not. It's a pretty vulnerable sort of thing as well, you know. It's non-fiction but I was pretty open, and also going against more conventional ways of writing some of that stuff. I was deliberately not prescriptive and was articulating a fair bit of doubt. Which is hard enough on its own, but in the context of politics of identity, that makes it even trickier.

CW: Do you know why you write?

KS: In part I do. I used to be an English teacher and—I've said this many times—I realised a manual arts teacher could build a house, but what could a fucking English teacher do? [*laughs*] That's part of it.

I think temperament—being introspective and solitary and shy and all that sort of stuff—is part of it. I used to draw a lot, and I think that's connected to it. In my childhood I got a lot of pleasure from that sort of stuff, from the absorption. The best thing about writing is this 'ceremony of innocence', I think that's what Yeats called it. I think that's what he meant, the absorption, getting lost in the *makingness* of things.

And then, when you've written a book, it's something to try and do again. That's part of it.

CW: Do you see things about yourself, after you've written a book of fiction, that you didn't know were there before?

KS: Yep. And that's a pretty big factor. I write stories to think, or explore things.

Stories as a way of thinking, dare I say it, is a neglected aspect of the literary endeavour. You get into new territory that you can't get to through other uses of language, or through other discourses. Through the many meaning-making devices that literature makes available to you—the whole idea of literature being a meta-language—you can start to shape what's non-verbal, and you can discover new intellectual territory, I think.

So if I write about identity in *stories*, which it seems I do, I get further than I would be able to, say, in academic or political discourses. In fiction you sort of half-apprehend things, start to shape them a little bit, which leads to thinking more about those things in other areas.

My first novel, *True Country*, starts with an individual voice, and then it moves into a collective narration. And that collective voice *stories* the original narrator, you know? It's a way of talking about collectivity and the individual and the negotiation between the two in terms of identity. And the formal element of the novel opened me up to thinking about that a little more and attempting to articulate it.

And I think that bled into me using a sort of contorted biographical note—that I am 'descended from one among those who call themselves Noongar'. Both those things are about assertion of identity, but not just self-assertion.

CW: Do you think writers should be outsiders, in some sense?

KS: I'd prefer it if they weren't, in my own case, to the extent that I'm an outsider. But I do think those things go together a little bit. It relates to the exploratory thing, the readiness for—as much as the reality of—moving into areas of doubt and confusion and ambivalence. I'm not sure which comes first. Maybe some of the reflectiveness and some of the observational qualities are in the temperament, but certainly in the writing—not for everyone, I'm sure, but for someone like me who fiddles a fair bit with the text. It's not just poured out like a performance.

CW: Earlier you said you have false endings—do you ever have false starts?

KS: Well, you might start and then throw away that start, but the rest of it's okay. It's getting that momentum up, whatever gets the momentum up and gets you about this much [*holds up thumb and forefinger*] then you know you've got enough to be working with. And you've got an idea of when it'll stop.

But I've had a failed novel—the whole false thing all the way through, beginning, middle and end. I knew it wasn't working, though bits of it were. It was after *Benang*—it was a third novel. I was just pushing it too much. I was probably trying, rather than to separate one sort of project and another, like the cultural language thing, to fit them together. It just didn't fit any readers' expectations. Any genre or anything.

CW: I'm getting a sense that it's quite a delicate thing for you in the early stages, that it's important not to put too much pressure on it.

KS: I find it pretty difficult, the whole thing. It's absolutely perverse! I have to trick myself in various sorts of ways. Like saying, 'I don't care what I'm writing', or sometimes it's using the time, the word count, all those things.

I like pen and paper, usually that's pretty important at those starting points. That's partly why I mentioned how I used to draw a lot. I think it's nice, there's something soothing in it, that helps me be smooth, and flow, whereas I don't get that with a keyboard until I have a much better idea of what it is I'm writing. So I'll work longhand and then I'll type that up, and then it will be further revised.

CW: Do you write short fiction much?

KS: I have a little bit. And I've thought about it as a way to work, but it ends up being something bigger, generally. If I'm going to be writing something I'll write a novel—I don't want the chance of lots of little rejections, I'll just put it all on this one *big* chance. [*laughs*] You know, if I wrote a little short story and someone rejected it, I'd get terribly discouraged and I wouldn't be able to work again for a couple of years. [*laughs*] Possibly. It's not definitely the case. Whereas you can hide in a novel, you know. I'll gamble a lot on it.

CW: A sense of playfulness seems important in your work. Even in the midst of some very sad and difficult material there seems present a capacity for joy—do you see that? I wondered if that was a presence in the Noongar stories.

KS: I'd like to think that playfulness is there. I believe so, for all my earnestness. Those Noongar stories are pretty recent to me though, as opposed to just yarns, where there's often a humour in them. You know, it's a sort of cliché virtually, the survival thing of humour. But yeah, that's where life and energy is, in those little bubbles.

CW: Do these bubbles of optimism or joy consciously perform a narrative function in your work, or are they just naturally part of the whole body?

KS: In *Benang*, I think there's quite a bit of humour, although people don't see it. And that was—I knew what I was doing, I was trying to make fun of some of the really shitty stuff. The only way to deal with it was to pick it up and take it along, you know, 'uplift and elevate', so that's where the fella floating around and other things like that came from.

It defuses some of the hurtfulness that's in there, I think, by playing with it. And it also seemed gutsy to *play* in that context. It seemed courageous—not only because it was difficult to sort of psych yourself up to do that, but because it might also be seen as an unworthy way to deal with nasty shit like that, to play with it. It is a source of such hurt and damage, you know, what are you doing playing? You can't play with that, it's not an appropriate response. But it seemed very necessary.

CW: Another joyous presence in your work is that of song and dance. How conscious are you of the role of music and dance?

KS: I'm a frustrated musician. I have great envy of and admiration for those who can improvise in performance, in music and dance. Of the idea that there's a whole body of stuff you know, and improvisation is a little blossoming of that knowledge and skill and expertise. I admire the non-head thing of it all.

I love all that. I think that's what I like in writing, when it gets a bit like that—when you get the surprise and the pleasure and the shapeliness of what's made manifest out of stuff you've got back there somewhere. And dance and music just—[*clicks fingers*] there it is, and then it's gone. And then there'll be another one [*clicks*]. Yeah, I'm full of envy. It's just such a demonstration of what is good about creativity—and more than that, it's non-verbal and so *sincere*, the shaping of spirit or emotion, that seems to come really strongly in music and dance, in performance.

But you can get it in reading to some extent, that utterance. Writing's just so slow with all that stuff, it's frustrating.

CW: I had a painting and drawing teacher once who used to say, 'All art springs from a desire to sing.'

KS: Yeah, that seems about right.

CW: Is that where your interest in rhythm comes from?

KS: Possibly. It's a sensual sort of thing I think, the savouring of rhythm. I like poetry, I used to memorise poetry—I like sound. As I said, I'm a frustrated amateur musician. You can do a lot with rhythm. I like thinking about rhythm generally, conceptually, if that makes sense. But I don't know if I think of whole books as a rhythmic entity. Bits of them I do, and some bits you just glide through.

I think about the rhythm of reading, about where I want to slow people down, where I wouldn't mind if—this must be what people dislike about my stuff I think—where I wouldn't mind if they *reread* it. [*laughs*] Where I want the reader just to step back for a minute, have a bit of a think about what's going on. Or where I want them just to go through a few pages and not realise, I want to make the language transparent. I think about things like that, and I think that's something to do with rhythm.

CW: It sounds almost instrumental, the way you describe it. Like playing an instrument.

KS: A book is an instrument for making someone do something, making them read in a certain way, I suppose. What a delight it is to get all abstract like this.

CW: What about the role of place? It seems to be very enmeshed with humanity in your stories. Do you think about bringing those things together, or are they already like that for you?

KS: I do think about it a bit. In *Benang* I did particularly, even though in that book the place is arguably a text, you know, the archives. But yeah, they are the things I think about because of just being a Noongar person. And there's a bit of doubt and ambivalence in there. I don't live in ancestral country, but I know those areas, and you wonder about connections and how they might be expressed, and that probably just ends up in the stories.

I don't push to put it in there or anything like that. I just think about those sort of things.

CW: Do you think all Indigenous writing is political, whether it likes it or not?

KS: I think so. I find myself encouraging people to not be so overtly political, you know—to reduce the political overtness, because it's there anyway, if you're known to be in the [Indigenous writing] niche, or if you're labelled with that. It might not be, otherwise. But even if you're not labelled like that then I guess that's political as well. That's how it goes.

CW: Do you see that as a burden?

KS: I do to some extent, but I also shy away from the business of coupling indigeneity and burdens. I'd rather say it is a privilege and it's an honour, and how lucky I am. To oppose all the sort of welfare discourses, you know, 'sorry sorry, poor me, and poor them', Florence Nightingales, missionaries, mercenaries and misfits and all that sort of stuff.

I prefer to say, 'Wow. How lucky and privileged I am to be descended from those who first created human society on this, the most ancient continent on the planet. And to have the sounds of that people.' That's really ring-ding. And texts, in rock. Wow.

So that's a stand against all the other shit, though I'm fair-skinned, so it's possibly easier for me to say this. But I prefer to downplay the burden bit.

CW: Can we talk about the incredible success in prizes of *That Deadman Dance,* and *Benang?*

KS: Hmmm, yeah. What about that?

CW: Well, how do you feel about that?

KS: First, I'm pleased. I like to be able to do something well. Then beyond that it gets a little bit awkward at different times. Sometimes it's embarrassing, and I do find myself a fair bit thinking about all those jealous people who will say, 'Ah, fuck it, it's only because of so-and-so,' and I have little arguments with those people in my head.

CW: Have you come up against expressions of that kind of thing?

KS: No no, it's just in me! I'm sort of used to feeling that paranoid thing. I'm sure that *is* there [in reality] as well, but that's just, you know, so what. But what else bothers me?

There's a writer I admire, though I haven't read much of his stuff: Eduardo Galeano. There's a line in one of his lovely essays, 'In Defence of the Word': 'Mistrust applause; it may mean you've been rendered innocuous.' So I think about that sometimes.

So, I do my best not to think about prizes. But firstly it's pleasing; you think, 'Ah well, that's good, I must have hit the spot in some way.'

CW: Presumably there's a practical element in that the money allows you time to work?

KS: Yeah, though I'm working full-time, and the work has been interesting me up till now. And again, that's my own preoccupation about how to be a useful person. The work over the past few years has been important. But yes, I paid off mortgages and all that sort of stuff. It means you get the bite put on you a great deal more, and that can be awkward. But yeah, it's pleasing, it's good, but then . . .

People say to me, 'Oh, you're humble.' But I don't know that I am. I just think there's a lot of luck in these things. It's fairly random. The shortlist is the thing, from there there can be all sorts of ways it goes.

But I wanted to write a very literary book, that was respectful of literature and what I know of books that I like. And the judges by and large, they're people who read a lot, and they're clever readers, so that's all lovely.

CW: What about the way the attention pushes you into the public world?

KS: Some of that's really uncomfortable. Winning the West Australian of the Year was extremely uncomfortable in a whole range of ways. Partly because of what that implies about heritage and identity—that is a little bit of a burden, that one. And I articulate some of my concerns in the novels, but then to convert that into little pithy, short little grabs, that fit neatly in the context of the existing discourses, if you can forgive me speaking like that, feels impossible. So that's really hard.

I even had some grief over—I was shortlisted for the Indigenous category and the arts category, before I won the West Australian of the Year. And I won through the Indigenous category. And I—I wish I'd just won both of the fucking things. Just because of the whole politics of it, and that 'rendered innocuous' thing, and me being a so very convenient face of Aboriginality in a way, particularly from non-Aboriginal people, those judges.

There's a lot of discomfort in there, a lot of things to be said that you don't get the opportunity to say because people's ears—and I mean this respectfully [*smiles*]—are not quite ready for it. And there are ambushes and hijacks all over the bloody place. I'm not a representative, I'm not a spokesperson and I don't like or function in that way. So it's a bit of a bastard, that one.

CW: You have expressed concern in the past about the commodification of literature and of Aboriginal culture. What does that mean to you, and why is it worrying?

KS: It's quite a presence in *That Deadman Dance* actually—in the older Bobby, who steps outside the frame, and in that closing scene, which is about power and possibility and potential being reduced . . . So yes, I do have that concern.

It stems from my delight in the literary areas—that magic, and the exploration and the possibility and so on—becoming just *entertainment*. Then it's just nothing. Then it's just a way for people to lose a bit of time or a scrap of their life, or something. And ditto when it's commodification of Indigenous stories. When Aboriginal culture is commodified it reduces the possibilities for the expression of Indigenous identity.

Let me draw a parallel—when I was writing *Benang*, I was involved in setting up an Indigenous visual arts course, and I was judging the Unaipon [the David Unaipon Award for Indigenous Writing] at that stage. And in both those things you would see inexperienced Indigenous artists expressing their individual Indigenous identity in dot painting and in red, black and yellow maps of Australia.

So there was a funny little loop, of them receiving mainstream expressions of identity labelled 'Indigenous' and reproducing them.

The fellow running that art course, Terry Shosaki, who did the cover for *Benang*, was an installation artist and one of the most conceptual people I've met. He had some really big concerns about this, and he argued that you need to dredge up expressions of identity—it's a little bit romantic, but I agree with it—*from your own resources*. Not rely on what's out there. The commodification just closes down the loop, and it just ends up diminishing and diminishing, and it means nothing.

In literature you want the intimacy of the collaboration between reader and writer—and this is why I like complex stories. Not to make them difficult, but just so there's a greater collaboration in that very intimate relationship. You can build things out of that, out of the little ambivalences and unknowns. You expand your sense of the world then, rather than just being reassured, or things being simplified.

CW: I want to ask you about historical research, because your use of it doesn't seem conventional. How do you go about using research in a way that means you are not captive to it?

KS: I don't know. I'm not a particularly good researcher, I'm a bit fitful and erratic and I lose things. That's not a deliberate strategy, but I think it's helpful. To the extent that I've thought about it, I tell myself, 'Now, you're not fucking passing anyone's exam here, Kim. You don't have to show them what a smart-arse you are, and all the research you've done.'

And then, I'm interested in how sometimes you can get by with really minimal research. With *That Deadman Dance*, a number of people have asked me about the research I did on sailing. But I've never sailed. I've never been on a boat with sails, I just thought about it. So that's reassuring. I'll try and do less research in future! [*laughs*]

But I find research really stimulating actually. I use it in this way: you look into something that interests you, and then some bits of it stick in your head, or some bits will irritate you, and for me that's often been where the fiction starts.

With *Benang* it was a photo out of a book, and a couple of phrases that were really objectionable. With *That Deadman Dance* there were a number of different things like that— scattered things, but one of them was a line in a letter, something about 'breaking up this native gang'. Something like, 'These are the people that have known us best, and now we have to break up this native gang.' I can't quite reproduce it now, but its phrasing was interesting and it was just a really interesting little document. So you sort of start thinking about the world that produced that text, and then you start writing about it and away you go.

CW: I love that you mention not having been on a sailboat, because there seems to be a contemporary idea that you have to do or experience something in order to write about it. Which seems sort of anti-literature to me.

KS: Yeah, that transactional stuff—that's not what we're doing here. I had a review in *The Guardian* of *That Deadman Dance* that was disapproving; at the end it said something like 'there's more style than substance in this book'. And I—well, I found that a bit hurtful, but in fact that's what fiction *is*, isn't it? It's *all* style, really. Fiction *is* style.

CW: And yet you want your work to have integrity. That's the substance.

KS: Whatever that integrity is. But you'd hope so.

CW: What do you do when you're really, really stuck?

KS: Well, there's a whole range of illicit activity in there that I won't speak of [*laughs*]. I do those sorts of things. A drink, or whatever, those sorts of things.

CW: While you're working, or to get away from it?

KS: To get away from it, but you end up back there. And maybe something will happen then. But I work at not doing those sorts of things—it's not productive. Or not enough. I don't know, I just try and persist. I go and do some exercise, as well, but it doesn't necessarily help. You just can't stay at the desk forever. Even when you're doing your hours and your quantity and all that sort of thing. It's just too tense.

CW: Do you get depressed about your work?

KS: I'm prone to those sorts of things, yes.

CW: Are there writers you return to, for solace or inspiration?

KS: There are books I return to that I particularly like. It depends on the task, I suppose, and I'm always discovering new ones—thankfully. There are some I return to just because they're so lovely and clever, or disturbing.

Like *Lolita*, I think a lot of people like that. It's just so *masterful* and it has just full-on control of voice. And the sensuality of it. Though I recently listened to that, and I thought it was filthy! I hadn't picked that up earlier on! [*laughs*] It was kind of disgusting! In that arch, clever way that he's got.

And Ishiguro's *Remains of the Day*, which is—oh man, it's painful, and it's also that the narrator is so unreliable. At the end of *Remains of the Day* you only realise he's crying because someone offers him a handkerchief. That's really interesting, what he does with that first person and unreliability. It's great.

There is an Anne Tyler book, *The Accidental Tourist*, that I like quite a lot. It's sort of a light book, but again it's the voice and the unreliable narration.

CW: Are the early stages of the book a matter of getting the voice, from where you can get some momentum?

KS: Yeah . . . voice, or a certain sensibility. The *sensibility* of that story, of what's behind it, what might be the head behind this stuff you're getting together. I think. It's not always voice, but sensibility—a sort of a state of being that might give this story, tell this story.

CW: If there was a spectrum with intuition at one end and rational, deliberate decision-making at the other, where would you fit?

KS: It moves. I like the intuition part, and I think stuff that's come from there gives me the most pleasure. And enables me to build upon it. But also I do diagrams, and I think about character—not plot, I need to keep working on that. But then there is a rational, technical point of view too. I think about it in quite a technical sort of way, about voice and so on. But I like the idea that it's intuition doing most of the work, and I think that's the case.

Again, that relates to being able to do stuff with fiction, to get you places that you can't get with other ways of using language. And the playfulness, when one can relax enough to do that, is an important part of that I think.

And dreams. Dreams give you stuff that can be as puzzling and alluring as the best fiction.

CW: There's something very potent in dreams.

KS: Yes. And there's a lot lurking behind them that's not in the dream—there's this little thing and then there's all this other stuff, where all the meaning is, *behind* the image or the position or the sound or whatever it is.

CW: Are you proud of your body of work, despite the anxieties you have?

KS: Yeah. Yep. The anxiety keeps me working hard. The anxiety is where a lot of the energy comes from, unfortunately. And I'm an anxious sort of fella. But yeah I'm proud of it, because I know about that anxiety. That's part of the pride, to have shaped something out of that. Generally I'm just sort of proud because I know some of the difficulties I've confronted in a range of ways.

CW: Have you ever wanted to give up?

KS: Yep, yeah. Well, I might have stopped now. It's the solitude of it, and that it makes you more solitary and isolated the more you do it.

And then there's this other sort of—not celebrity, but that public thing all of a sudden. That bothers me. I haven't completely given up on the musical career, though the dancing is beyond me now. [*laughs*]

And writing is an old form, and sometimes I think I'm connecting to a sort of stodgy group of people. Old stodgy people, people who read or who are into literature. I think maybe I should see what I can do elsewhere, that might be a more immediate way to release and use your energy rather than to just sit on it, with writing. I have considerable difficulties with that I think. It's not good for my health.

I suppose partly I've kept going at different points because it was part of a vocation or profession.

And I'd started on things—you write one book, well you better do another one. And even with the last novel, *That Deadman Dance*, I was pretty fully absorbed in the language project, to tell you the truth. I entered a PhD to keep the language project going because I could get a scholarship—the language project is nothing to do with the PhD, it was just to keep a bit of time and a bit of money. And there was a lot of native title work I was doing.

So it was a job and a half and no money in it for quite a few years.

And it came out of the book I did with Hazel Brown [*Kayang and Me*], those obligations and intense interest. As part of the PhD I had to write a novel, and I had an idea for it, so I did the job.

That was a large part of getting that one done.

CW: That sounds very pragmatic, but the book doesn't feel like an exercise in pragmatism.

KS: No, I don't think it is, but also I've got this sort of ethic about it: I started, so I'm going to finish. Or 'I'm meant to be a writer, I better see if I still am'. Those sorts of things. Then again, there are privileges with it: people let me finish a sentence more often than they used to before I was published. [*laughs*] People want to listen to you; you don't have to force them to. And there are those little tiny pleasures when you get little bits coming up that surprise you and you want to get more of them. And you want to get it shaped, you enjoy the aesthetics of it.

CW: How have you changed as a writer since the start of your career?

KS: I'm much more aware of what's going on in books. As I'm reading, often I'm thinking, 'Oh, that's a bit sloppy.' You're rewriting as you read—on a small scale, not the big structural stuff, I don't reread enough to do that.

I'm stiffer and I'm slower than I used to be, with the production. I think I'm more inhibited now, because of the different sorts of pressures that are around. I can loosen up, but it takes me a bit more work.

I used to be able to just [*clicks fingers*] do a voice or a style or something, probably not real good but enough so that you could work on it. I'm much more inhibited than I used to be.

But I think I'm better at spotting what's good when I'm reading. I don't know if that translates to knowing when my own stuff is good. I know when my own stuff's bad, and perhaps I'm a little bit too harsh sometimes. I try not to think about those sorts of things. It's usually just: next job.

CW: Amanda Lohrey has said she doesn't know how writers have any ego left after a certain age. What's your view of the role of ego in creativity?

KS: Hmmm. I think it's a small ego that's required, but it's such a complex thing. It's cunning and slippery. In response to that question I think of some people I know who've got big egos, and they want to be writers. They've written books that no one will publish, and I think it's *all* ego driving them. They believe these are really good books even though everyone tells them they're not, and they want you to read them, they insist that you read them—all that sort of thing. I haven't got that sort of ego, and I don't think that's the sort that goes with actually doing the writing. I think the preparedness or the readiness to make yourself vulnerable, and move into areas that not a lot of people necessarily want to go—I think there's a *lack* of ego in there, and I think there's courage in there.

I think when ego does come into it is in thinking, 'I want to do this really well. I want to do a good job.' I want this to be a really good book that meets its own requirements. There must be a fair bit of ego in that I think. Do I want people to like me because of this book? I don't know how much I've got of that, but it's probably in the mix as well.

It's a slippery thing, ego.

CW: What's the nature of the courage required?

KS: It's in knowing you might fail. It's in knowing you haven't read as much as you should've, and others have read more, and who says you're such a great judge of what a good book is anyway?

Knowing all that and deciding to do it anyway—it's that sort of courage. Knowing how much of one's preoccupations, if not self, are revealed in your writing and still going ahead and doing it. It's knowing, 'No one's written about this and it's difficult and dangerous to do it. And I'm going to do it.'

I think that's courage, or that's what comes to mind. The most difficult thing is starting, and getting enough down so you know how to proceed. It's the courage of facing failure. That's the toughest one.

WHEN I meet Craig Sherborne at his St Kilda home for this interview, he's just finished his second novel and has the jaunty air of a man released on parole after a long stint inside.

An acclaimed poet, journalist, playwright, memoirist and now novelist, Sherborne is best known for *Hoi Polloi* and *Muck*, his tragicomic, beautifully written memoirs of growing up in New Zealand and Australia. He moved into fiction with the 2011 novel *The Amateur Science of Love*, which won him the Melbourne Prize for Literature and shortlistings for other major prizes. His new novel, *Tree Palace*, was published in 2014, and was shortlisted for the 2015 Miles Franklin Literary Award. His journalism and poetry have appeared in most of Australia's leading literary journals and anthologies.

The first I knew of Sherborne's work was his poetry collection, *Necessary Evil*, recommended to me by a poet friend. Reviewed by David McCooey as 'a unique combination of directness and obliquity, urgent and powerful', the collection includes unsentimental yet deeply affecting portraits of Sherborne's parents—also the stars of his memoirs.

Those parents, dubbed Heels and Winks by their child narrator in *Hoi Polloi*, are grandiose, deluded, occasionally grotesque but somehow always human, always sympathetic. *Hoi Polloi* was shortlisted for two literary awards; its sequel, *Muck*, won the Queensland Premier's Literary Award for Non-Fiction.

Critic Peter Craven called the latter 'an extraordinary book, full of savagery and pathos and the screed and cackle as well as the sadness of any young life in the midst of mad-seeming adults who constitute the world'. Both memoirs were instantly established as Australian classics of the form.

In a remark that speaks to Sherborne's fearlessness in writing about himself and others, Helen Garner said of his unflinching (and autobiographical) love story *The Amateur Science of Love*: 'All women with lingering illusions about the way men think should read this fast-moving, sharply focused, fantasy-shattering little thunderclap of a book.'

I had met Sherborne once before when we shared a writers' festival panel on the topic of 'love stories', and was impressed by the passion and honesty he brought to a platform that with other writers can tend to glibness and self-protection. It's a compelling mix of performance and honesty, and perhaps his background in theatre is influential here, for in both public speech and conversation he comes across as a charismatic evangelist for literature, sprinkling his remarks with lines from poetry, occasionally thumping the table for emphasis, arguing strongly for art, and against fakery and disingenuousness.

His love of the playfulness and musicality of language is evident in the way he speaks as well as in his work. He clearly enjoys expressing a provocative opinion, pouring scorn on historical fiction and journalists with equal vigour, and at the same time is candid about topics men often steer away from: love, intimacy, domesticity, family. Indeed, his anger at what he sees as men's cultural exclusion from expressions of complex emotion is a powerful engine for his work.

For me, it's this mix of forthright masculinity and the unashamed embrace of complicated emotion that makes him such an interesting writer. And despite his concern that the isolation of writing makes him 'unsocialised', he's a perceptive and generous conversationalist.

CW: What made you start writing?

CS: Oh, that's going back a long way. As a kid, the only thing I was interested in was poetry, making patterns out of words. It was the only thing I could do, I was no good at anything else.

I found a book of Shakespeare when I was seven or eight. And didn't understand the themes or the sentences but just loved the music of it, the grandeur. It stuck with me.

I didn't start writing until I was in Sydney in secondary school, but it just seemed the most beautiful thing in the world. I couldn't imagine why everybody wasn't doing it. I also loved going to religious services. My family wasn't religious at all, but I used to love it because of the language. The King James Bible and all that sort of stuff. Shakespeare and the Bible—the language, and the ideas, the concepts and the portraits, particularly in the New Testament—I found quite profound and beautiful. Just the gorgeousness of it. Writing seemed something I could do that other people couldn't. To make a lovely sentence was something everybody found hard and I found easier.

CW: Do you remember when you discovered that you were good at it?

CS: I remember writing a poem in my first year of high school in Sydney, and I recited it in front of the class. I was really only at that school to play rugby, because it was a rugby school and I was okay at rugby but didn't have much passion for it.

I remember standing up and reciting it, and everybody kind of thought, 'Well that's a bit weird, him doing that, poetry!' And nobody believed I'd written it. I got ten out of ten from the teacher, who then thought that maybe I hadn't written it, that I'd copied it out. I thought, 'That must mean I'm okay at it.' I was about twelve.

It's been the one consistent theme through my life. Whatever happens, with all the tangle of relationships and where you're living and whatever, the consistent thing is the language—sometimes playful, sometimes very plain. Sometimes you use it as a weapon. It's a good weapon.

CW: When did you become a journalist?

CS: Quite late. I worked on my dad's farm for a while, and I went to university to do a vet course, but I dropped out because I had no interest in it. I wanted to be a writer, but that seemed silly. So I went to live in London and thought I'd hang out with theatre people, which I did, and really liked. I saw a lot of theatre and met some actors, and then a friend of mine was a courier in Ireland, taking letters and parcels from Dublin to Belfast and back along that route. So I went and stayed with him. This was in 1985–86, during The Troubles.

I loved the Irish and the Ulster poets, and I started to take things pretty seriously in terms of trying to write, though I didn't send anything off, and the stuff I wrote wasn't terribly good. This is when I was about twenty-two.

Then I went to Belfast and saw these incredible things, the bombs and the troops, and because I was an Antipodean,

I just found it so . . . *exciting*. I started to write about it, with a view to maybe sending some pieces off.

Eventually I came back to Australia and about two years later I sent something I'd written—basically a dramatisation of some things I'd seen in Belfast—to the ABC's radio documentary and features department. They didn't use it but they encouraged me to write broadcasts and radio plays.

They produced two radio plays of mine. I hadn't sent anything off really before that, and I hadn't felt the pain of rejection, so I hadn't been discouraged. If I'd been rejected I might not have bothered going on. But they seemed so welcoming and encouraging that I kept going.

CW: So radio drama was your first 'published' work.

CS: I think it was. I might have had a poem published before that. I had a play win an award in 1989, and there was a reading in Melbourne and eventually it was put on. But I was interested in radio drama, and I was quite enamoured of Dylan Thomas, the playfulness of his language. He, of course, wrote a lot of radio work. I thought it was a very interesting medium. I never expected to write novels or memoirs or anything. I *never* expected it to turn into a serious career, or vocation or whatever you call it. It's not a career, it's a calling.

CW: You were writing poetry all that time as well?

CS: Sort of, slowly. Slowly chipping away. I was also writing journalism because I had to make a living. I lived in a country town in Victoria and started writing for the local newspaper and from there eventually I became a grains writer for *Stock & Land*, which was my favourite job in the world. And then I came into the city and started to work at the big end of town, which at first was exciting and then just kind of debilitating. It was so horrible, and *boring*. And easy. Just monotonous.

I concentrated on city journalism for four, five, six years. I didn't really write other work very much—any poetry or the like—because I had responsibilities, I'd got into a new relationship where I was a stepfather and I wanted to do the right thing—not that wanting is the same as doing the right thing. And I didn't feel as though serious writing would ever come to much.

And, I suppose, I liked putting on a suit. I woke up one day and thought, 'I really like putting on a nice suit and hopping on a tram and going into work with my little briefcase and being one of those guys who thinks they're somebody in the city.' And I did feel like that for a few years, and then it started to wear off. And that's when I began writing again, which was difficult, because I was still working full-time in journalism. Having to work writing around a job was difficult.

CW: How did *Hoi Polloi* come about?

CS: Black Inc, publisher of *The Monthly* and the *Best Australian Essays* series where I had been anthologised, was keen to get me to write a non-fiction book. I said I would, but I didn't have any idea what I would write about.

At that stage my father was getting quite unwell. My parents were living up on the Gold Coast, and I was spending quite a bit of time there with them. It's really quite a dissipated place. It has got all this glitzy high rise and the beach is okay, sort of, but it's all pretty seedy. And in that foetid environment and with my dad getting really sick, and my mum starting to get quite demented with early signs of Alzheimer's, I started to write *Hoi Polloi*. I think the first lines were written at their kitchen table. And then I'd come back to Melbourne and continue.

Near where I worked, at *The Herald Sun*, there was a bar which made quite nice martinis. So I used to go after work, or sometimes sneak away early from work, and sit there and drink a martini and write a page or half a page and then go home and have dinner and go to bed, and then get up in the morning and see what I'd written the night before. If I liked it I kept it and if I didn't I threw it out. And then I worked on it on the weekends, pretty much from eight o'clock in the morning till two o'clock in the afternoon.

It just worked—it came together quite nicely and the publisher liked it, so I went straight on to another one.

CW: Did you always know you were writing memoir, not fiction?

CS: Yeah. I had the voice so clear in my head. When I started *Hoi Polloi* the voice was so strong, and then it went through into *Muck*, and I had absolutely every intention to keep going. But then I think at the end of *Muck* I found it a bit heartbreaking and I didn't want to go there anymore. The idea of being free to make up a whole lot of stuff, and to change into a different kind of voice was very, very tempting. But a lot of the devices I used in *Hoi Polloi* and *Muck* I brought into *The Amateur Science of Love*.

The book I've just finished, called *Tree Palace*, is in third-person plural but a lot of the stylistic techniques are still there. Because you don't lose them, as you would know. Once you start writing you have this style that just comes—so you don't mess with it.

CW: Can you say more about the voice of *Hoi Polloi* and *Muck*? It's very strong, and yet quite different in each book, though the narrator is still you.

CS: *Muck* was definitely a slightly older voice, because he is older—the 'me' in that book is sixteen, whereas in *Hoi Polloi* you take these very quick leaps in time through very young eyes—seven years old or whatever, up to just before sixteen. I suppose in *Hoi Polloi* the first-person style is mimetic. I'm trying to pretend to be me. To fake being me. So you strike a pose. It was striking the pose of being back inside me, as a boy. And it certainly seemed recognisable to me. You know, you just [*clicks fingers*] *feel* it. It's like, 'Ah, *that's* me.' It's terribly vain and egotistical.

CW: It sounds like that came very quickly and naturally, without striving for it.

CS: That's quite true, and I think it comes from writing a lot of poetry, a very disciplined kind of poetry where you have five beats to the line. There's a sort of sprung rhythm on the lines. So that technique helped, particularly sprung rhythm, because it's so bouncy and kind of playful.

So to get the arrogance of a young boy, the arrogance of youth, I thought sprung rhythm really helped organise the lines, and give life and energy to them. And it created that *outrage* that some youths have, when they are really egotistical little shits, like I was. There's a sort of outrage to everything they think and say. You see it too in adults now, everybody's outraged about everything. But particularly with kids, it's: 'Oh, the world's impacting on me in a horrible way, I'm going to be completely outraged about it,' rather than saying, 'Ah well, that's life.'

That all managed to come together quickly in *Hoi Polloi*. But I think the structure and tight lines come from all my years of writing these twenty-, thirty-, forty-line poems, and rewriting them till they were right.

CW: The outrage observation is interesting, because one of the things I marvelled at, particularly in *Muck*, is how you present yourself as this quite obnoxious boy—

CS: Well, I am. I still am.

CW: —and yet I had such sympathy for him as I read. How does that happen?

CS: Well, you have the benefit of youth. It doesn't work in someone older. If I put that voice into a twenty-five- or thirty- or forty-year-old, and to some degree I did in *The Amateur Science of Love*, there's not the same sympathy for them. Kids can get away with anything. You can write a book involving a child and they may be obnoxious but you're always going to sympathise with them. You're always going to want to mother them or father them, protect them.

CW: I suppose one of the things I was seeing all the time is how he was being fed the delusions of his parents.

CS: And right up until the day they died, they kept them going. My mother got Alzheimer's and she died in 2009, but she skipped from one delusion to another. And she was outraged about everything! The world owed her a living and that was passed on to me.

CW: How did you control the balance between humour and pathos? Even just the names—calling your parents Heels and Winks, and later Feet and The Duke—makes them larger than life. How did you manage to walk the line between that largeness of character and caricature? Because it didn't ever tip into cartoon, but it so easily could have. It pushed right up against the line.

CS: I like that, when that happens. Particularly when you're writing something comic, you're inevitably going to do it. Look at the great masters of comedy—look at Dickens. He gets right up against the line and that's where this frisson happens. It's almost awkward to look at because you think it's going to become a cartoon, and then it doesn't, and then something *real* happens that's quite human. But that's just instinct, just knowing when you're about to go too far.

I could feel it, like a force-field. Some people might say I did go too far, but I never felt I did. I think one of the ways you recognise it is you start having too much fun, like a comedian who laughs at his own jokes. If I started to feel that I was having too much fun with it I would just stop. I'd generally go away and come back to it, or just stop it there, and start something new in the book.

But it didn't happen terribly much. You're writing memoir, so you have to be fair to the genre. You can't start making caricatures and enjoying yourself because it's fun, because then you start making things up.

And the reality is that my parents—my mum and dad were, for all their sins, *not* caricatures, they were very much products of their time. They were also unusual, my mother particularly. But she wasn't a caricature—she was too savage to be a caricature.

CW: There is a kind of tragedy in her thwarted desires.

CS: Oh, desires. They were *fake* desires. They were like a fake fur. They weren't the real deal, because she was too lazy to make them happen. To this day I cannot watch television—except the news—because my mother spent the last thirty years of her life sitting in front of the television, watching the news with a great sense of moral outrage at all these lazy people in the world. Bloody dole bludgers and all that sort of stuff, without any self-reflection at all.

She was completely lazy, just getting fatter and fatter and fatter, eating and watching television, drinking a lot of drink, and watching daytime soaps. And I found it so galling I couldn't watch television anymore. To me it seemed to represent mindlessness and indolence, and a waste. She had such a good mind, she was so bright, and to waste her life like that on mindlessness I found almost violently frustrating.

I suppose that was also an important part of the outrage that I brought as an adult to the young Craig in *Hoi Polloi* and *Muck*, this sense of terrible frustration and anger that she didn't have more *get up and go*—the kind of thing she was insisting *I* had to have.

CW: What about negotiating the ethical terrain of memoir? Did you worry about it?

CS: No. In short, no. I've been given lectures about this by journalists. By reporters who exploit the misery and the tragedies and the follies of others for commercial gain, to supply content for their employer, to justify their wages. I have done it myself. You're faking sympathy, you're faking empathy, you're often getting things very wrong and you're pretending to be an expert on someone's life, or an expert on someone's trauma or tragedy or triumph, reducing their life to a little package of clichés. And we're told that it's in the public interest, that it is of public benefit, and that it is ethical. Ha!

And then you get criticised for actually writing about something that you *can* speak about with authority, and you're not doing it for commercial gain, because you don't necessarily make a lot of money writing books. You're doing it because there is this calling or this need to make a piece of art out of it. Or even a piece of theology maybe, I don't know. But something that gives meaning to the experiences you have in your life, gives artistic meaning and artistic display to it. And to have *that* considered unethical alongside journalism, which is considered ethical, has never made any sense to me. So, no, it has never been an issue. The only times in my life I've really cringed as a writer, and felt dirty, is working as a journalist. Which is one of the reasons I stopped. At least for now.

CW: What about family response? Did your parents know you were writing it?

CS: Yeah, yeah, yeah. *Hoi Polloi* was published the year after my dad died in 2004. As he was dying, I was actually sitting by his bed, holding his hand and writing bits of *Hoi Polloi*—this is no bullshit. I was talking to him about his life and he was kind of stoned on painkilling drugs and about to move into palliative care, and he was just talking about racehorses, because it was his whole life. He was remembering and dreaming about all these horses, horses I didn't even know he owned. So he was hallucinating and reciting these names, and my mother was running around panicking—she was starting to go Alzheimery and she used to forget to button up her housecoat, so, you know, her boobs would be hanging out—and at the same time as all that was happening, I'm writing.

It seemed perfectly natural to do it. It felt that all I could bring to the party, the party of death, was the life of writing. The energy and the creativity of it.

So they knew, to answer your question, that I was writing *something*. My mother always said, 'Well I hope one day you'll write about *me*,' and that was the last she ever mentioned it. Well, I wrote about you, Mum! Boy, did I write about you.

They weren't much interested in my writing, which was fine. They were business people. Writing was this freaky thing that their freaky son did.

My Aunty Vonnie came from New Zealand to see me when my mother was really nutty with Alzheimer's, because she wanted to get this special bracelet, an heirloom, that had been their mother's and that my mother had been guardian of. Vonnie came round to my house and I thought, she's going to be a bit sniffy about *Hoi Polloi* and *Muck*. Because by then she'd said that she'd read the books. I thought, She's probably going to be very sniffy, and that's just too bad.

I presented her with all my mother's jewellery to keep, but the very piece that she wanted, the family heirloom, wasn't there. Aunty Vonnie was heartbroken that my mother, who was a very difficult and sometimes treacherous woman, had obviously given it away. And then Vonnie started to talk about *Hoi Polloi*. She said, 'It's a sad book, isn't it?' She said, 'I didn't like it, it made me feel uncomfortable. But I can't fault it.'

So there's one part of me that was heartbroken for her. And the other part of me, the writer part, was going *yes!* I nailed it! And it confirmed for me that I was right not to worry about that in the first place. Because I didn't have to. It was quite uplifting.

CW: What about the exposure of yourself?

CS: Well, I thought that's what writers *did*! I'm not squeamish about exposing myself or exposing others, providing I do so knowing what I'm talking about, and that I do so with style. I don't like memoirs where there's no attempt to bring some sort of graciousness or elegance and felicity of language and wit to it. Because you're not there just to do an ordinary piece of documentary. You're trying to lift it into some higher realm. Like I said before, art, or maybe theology.

CW: Tell me about the shift you made, after that, from memoir into fiction.

CS: I lost interest in memoir—or it lost interest in me. I wanted to change gear stylistically. I wanted to start to have a more mature voice. I knew that if I continued in the first person, that the sympathy people have with children would not be there for an adult. And it was just going to be an unpleasant experience for everybody, not least me, because I would be reading it not necessarily having much sympathy for myself.

So I thought, I want to break things up. I want to make stuff up, I want to use more sophisticated language, to explore complicated ideas. And I thought that was best done in fiction. *Tree Palace*, the new book, is almost completely one hundred per cent fiction, whereas *The Amateur Science of Love* is still heavily autobiographical. But it was kind of auto-biography grafted onto fiction; still very heavily dominated by autobiography, but fiction stylistically and in temperament and in narrative form. With *Tree Palace*, the autobiography is virtually gone. I think it'll probably come back at some stage, that aspect, but at the moment I'm out on a spree.

CW: How much distance do you need between the living of experience and the writing of it?

CS: Good question. I reckon about fifteen years. I was speaking to a professor of medieval literature the other day, who's an expert in revolutions. He reckons it takes one hundred and fifty years for a country to get over a revolution. And I reckon it takes about fifteen years to get over a childhood sufficient to write about it. Fifteen years to get over every significant experience in your life.

CW: What would happen if you began writing about it too early?

CS: You wouldn't get the pose right. I think it would be flat in tone, like a documentary, too journalistic. If you want to find the art in it you have to find the pose, the tone of the language.

And that has to come completely from your imagination, and then you inject it into the autobiographical DNA to give it its life.

You need those years to regenerate yourself as a human being so you can look back and—what was that line from Yeats?—'Cast a cold eye on life, on death'. You've got to be able to cast a cold eye. And as the narrative happens, so too the meaning will come out of it after that fifteen-year period—because you've learned so much in the meantime.

I think we put things in our subconscious, where they go around and around and around and we sort things out without realising it. And then we awaken it by doing something like writing the narrative of the experience out, in a book, but we've answered a lot of the questions we had at the time about what happened and why it happened, and what it all meant.

CW: Do you think writing ever serves any therapeutic purpose?

CS: It hasn't for me. It's done the opposite. It causes you more problems, I think.

I've never written for therapy, I've written just because it's a calling, it's what I want to do, it just seems unnatural if I'm not doing it. But if it is therapy I'm yet to discover it. It causes you problems because it can take over your life when you're writing, and you're no longer living in the present, you're living in your own past like a ghost.

It would be different if it was completely fictional. But because memoir is not fictional it can churn up a lot of things that you really wish you didn't have to go through again, and you fret about getting things right, you become a slightly different person in the present. And the people you are living with or loving now may suddenly see you inhabiting another, previous life. And it becomes kind of difficult for them to stomach.

The Amateur Science of Love was a perfect example. I never had any difficulties with *Hoi Polloi* and *Muck*, but when it's about relationships—about the marriage I was in during the period the book was set—of course you do. I became a very difficult person for that period of time. I was really glad to have that book pass by.

CW: What's your view of the word 'confessional' as applied to memoir?

CS: I think it was Jo Shapcott, the British writer, who described memoir as 'chasing your own ambulance'. She's right. It is exploitative and ruthless. But as for therapy, it's not like that for me, there's nothing therapeutic in it.

The American poet Dave Smith says about poetry, that it's 'dressing language up for a date'. All good writing is dressing up for a date, to meet with the world, and it's got to look its best. To me, confessional writing just means sitting there using everyday sort of language, with no attempt to lift it to a higher realm. Then it's a meaningless experience. It may be therapeutic, but don't publish it; give it to your shrink. Or don't write it. Because we don't need any more crap books.

CW: What part of writing gives you the most pleasure?

CS: The first line. Getting the first line is a great thrill. You wait for it and wait for it, and then it comes, and then you're *off*, you're completely off. With all the books I've written, the first line of the book is the first line published. I never go back and change it. It's all written in the order that the sequences appear in the book.

The first line is a great moment because you've caught the thought-wave and you're coming down the face of it. It's just wonderful. It's about that pose, you're realising you're in the right garb and have the right stance to meet the world, it's all there. You're ready to begin the language part of what you've been thinking about for a whole period of time. That's a great thrill.

CW: What about the hard stuff? What do you find most difficult?

CS: Knowing the moment to stop. With the book I've just finished it was easy because it had its natural end. But I think that can be hard. Also, when you've written something—a line or paragraph—you really like and you know it can't appear because it's just not the right book for that particular line or paragraph to appear. The kill-your-darlings idea.

Also, I don't like how writing makes me become very unsocialised. You spend so much time alone that it becomes difficult to be in the company of people, because you've just forgotten how. The muscle for conversation has gone slack.

I hardly ever go out, and I just really love living in the work. I call it being a method writer; I just completely go into that world and can't really function outside it until I've finished the book.

I'm one of those people who could quite easily, if all the world disappeared tomorrow and I was the last person left in it, exist quite adequately as a Robinson Crusoe kind of figure. But that's dangerous because you do become a bit odd, as you get older, and you lose contact with people and you lose your social graces. So I don't like that.

CW: Do you think writers have any particular duties, to themselves or to the world?

CS: I like the art-for-art's-sake concept. I believe in what WH Auden said about poetry: 'Poetry makes nothing happen.' Books make nothing happen—if writing was going to make things happen in a really significant way then Shakespeare's collected works would have done it, we would have worked it out long ago. It's not writing's job to make things happen; its job is to exist as an aesthetic idea as beautifully and intelligently as it can.

It can often be confronting and ugly, but that's part of the beauty too. I'm a great lover of the paintings of Francis Bacon. I look at some of them and they are completely ugly but they are beautiful in their ugliness. Our imagination can allow a lot of things to stick to it, and there are some people who only like the beautiful and pretty things to stick to it, but those who are a bit more adventurous also love the ugly things, and see worth and meaning in unpleasant things. They come together often, you know.

If we have a duty, I think it is to write about *us, now*. I think the obsession with historical novels in our time is because we don't think we're interesting enough. *Or*, we think we're so perfected as human beings that we don't have to write about now. And I wonder if in a hundred and fifty years' time people will look back at our literature and say about a lot of it, 'Well, they really weren't that interested in themselves, were they?'

I think historical fiction is a cop-out for writers. You can go into research, and you can use characters from real life and find the structure in the history books that you wouldn't be able to find in a contemporary setting, because you're so on your own in a contemporary book. That's my beef about historical writing: I think it's evasive, I think it's a cop-out, and I think it's because people find it difficult and frightening to find a narrative structure using a contemporary setting. They're not working hard enough. It's much easier to go back and find something from history that has a beginning and a middle and an end, interesting characters far removed from your own culture and experience that we can play dress-ups with, we can be a bit more romantic, and all that sort of stuff. I don't like that, and I don't want to play dress-ups—I want to dress the whole book up, but I don't want to play dress-ups with costumes and quaint old-fashioned manners and moralities and dramatic love tales and hansom cabs.

CW: But people obviously want to read historical fiction.

CS: Oh sure! Good luck to them! *I* don't want to read it anymore—I'm only talking about what I think, I'm not disqualifying that entire genre. Well I am actually, if I could, but I realise that my tastes are different from other people's. It's just something I find very curious.

CW: What about Hilary Mantel? She always seems to blow this view out of the water, because her fiction feels so contemporary.

CS: Well, she's terrific. *Wolf Hall*—I haven't read the other one—was terrific. She *is* the business. But she has also written an enormous number of contemporary books as well, and her memoir is *terrific*. That's her genius—it's not dress-ups with her, because she is such a superior talent. Of course there are exceptions to everything, and she's one.

CW: Are you ever afraid while writing?

CS: No. Well, I'm afraid of really silly things: like there's going to be too much noise that day to work, or some pragmatic things. Or I worry because I have to do something else that is going to take me away from the writing. I'm not sure what you mean.

CW: Well, I'm quite often afraid of my book. I don't want to go to it.

CS: Why?

CW: I don't know. But I'm easily distracted, and find other things to do.

CS: Hmm. Well, I suppose I've got a work ethic—I always feel very ashamed if I'm not doing something. I guess we're looping right back to my mother watching television for thirty years, doing nothing. I think my dislike and distaste for that kind of indolence means I have to do something—I would always be more afraid of not doing it.

Even if I thought, 'I just can't be bothered writing, I'm too tired, or I have a hangover or I just want to be out in the sunshine or in the country or something', I'm more afraid of not writing because I know that at the end of the day I will feel sort of disgusted with myself. So I might as well push through that and at least at the end of the day I can say I sat there and gave it a go. These are just personal demons one is addressing.

I try to get up really early in the morning. Sometimes it's four-thirty. Not in winter because it's too hard to warm up. But certainly in summer, spring, early autumn, I get up at four-thirty and do three or four hours, and then the rest of the time get up at six-thirty. So you're all done by lunch, then you can go off and do whatever else you have to do. Check on your share portfolio, or whatever the hell else you have to do. [*laughs*] Go to work. Or go and gamble, which I rather like doing.

That's what I do, six days a week. And on the seventh day I rest—which means still putting in a couple of hours.

CW: You sound incredibly disciplined.

CS: At the moment, I'm going through a good period that may die. It's the middle of life, mid-career I suppose, and I feel productive and as though I've got a purpose. But it doesn't mean you don't have days when you're out the back with a cigarette at six o'clock in the evening and a glass of booze, thinking, 'I just want to throw myself under a train because I've got no talent.'

CW: So you do have those days.

CS: Oh yeah. Shit yes. It's just a horrible feeling, it's almost like a panic attack. I've had panic attacks, and that's what it's like. But you have to keep going. You've got to think, I'm very fortunate that I can do what I want to do, because there are a lot of people out there working in factories—and I know some of them—working in jobs that they do not want to do, and I've been one of them, doing things that make you feel your life is being wasted. And so to be in a position where I have the opportunity and the ability to do it, and a publisher who wants me to do it—I'm blessed, so I can't whinge.

So that kicks in, the Protestant work-ethic thing. You just grab anything that will give you the fuel to keep going day after day. Because it takes so long, it seems. Writing a book takes years!

CW: How long has the new one taken?

CS: Well I got the idea twenty-five years ago. I tried various forms for it—plays and a film script—but I just couldn't quite figure out how to write it. And then I got the first line about eighteen months ago. Once the line arrived, just like a light bulb, [*clicks fingers*] I thought, 'Ah, now I know what I've got to do. Twenty-five years I've been waiting for you, you bloody light bulb!' And I was on my way.

CW: What a lovely feeling.

CS: It is! And then, of course, you get about halfway through and you start to flag, and you start to doubt yourself, and doubt the work, and then you're off again . . .

CW: When you get really stuck, what do you do?

CS: Well, I know I have to get up and try again—it's like the old thing about having to get back on a horse after you fall off. I'm a horse rider, real horses and the book variety. And of course you're falling off a lot when you're writing a book, you're falling off the book a lot. So you have to get back on. But it doesn't pay to do that immediately I find, sometimes. I like to drink and have a sleep-in the next day. I never leave the book, I'm always still with it in some way—but you go and carouse, and sometimes in the middle of all that the solution will be found.

If it's a calling, if you really, really should be a writer, it will tell you. It will tell you whether it wants you to be there, or whether you should just go and become an accountant or landscape gardener, I think.

Even when you get through those bad bits, when you're out in the garden having a cigarette at twelve o'clock at night because you think your life is worthless and your calling really isn't a calling, that it really wasn't there, it's all just been some dream of yours, a fantasy, you've got to trust that the next day or the day after that it'll call you back.

CW: So it requires some kind of letting go?

CS: It's a letting-go and, in the process, a clinging-on. Probably I shouldn't, but if I run into a big problem I go out and you know, head off to the Gin Palace and drink martinis.

CW: I want to ask you about your wonderful grip on idiom and speech. You seem to select certain spoken phrases which then get repeated through the book in a kind of shorthand. The spoken phrase becomes a kind of internal mental slogan for the narrator, about who he is and what he comes from.

CS: Hmmm. I'm not exactly sure what you mean, but maybe it's a way of infusing the sentences with idiom in a conversational way, but then heightening it. Somehow it becomes lifted up a notch, to become illuminated—and illuminating—in a way that it wouldn't normally be in flat speech.

I think that just came from many, many years of writing poetry in that sprung-rhythm monologue way, with a beginning and a middle and an end, of twenty or thirty lines. And then within that they must loop back and around and inside each other to have a poem. So that's just how I think.

As soon as I started writing poetry, back in my early twenties, that's what appealed to me. That's what interested me, otherwise I wouldn't bother with poetry.

I certainly don't like abstraction. I think that's one of the problems we have with contemporary poetry, which is why it's virtually dead. It's committed suicide, through the pretension of abstraction—it's so lazy to write that way.

Even in journalism I used to write like that—twenty or thirty lines, they loop in, and have between five and nine beats to the line, and seldom more than eleven. I'm not conscious of it in writing prose, it's just what I realised gradually. When I'm writing I can feel the sprung rhythm, it's like I'm jumping up and down on the spot. You think of writing as just being something that happens in the head, but I find it a very physical thing, and even in the middle of winter, if I've been really intensely writing—I'm writing longhand—I find I'm sweating. I'm running a sweat, it's a very physical activity.

CW: Looking back at your books, you don't seem to have a very sympathetic eye for your younger self.

CS: No. I don't like youth. I didn't like childhood. I would have just liked to have been born an adult. I never hung out with other kids, I didn't like them. I found them cruel and terribly shallow.

And it really wasn't until I was starting to become sexually attracted to girls that I wanted to have anything to do with girls, because they were *terrifying*. Childhood was always about mockery—I was terribly crushed if I was mocked, and kids mock all the time, so I then had to learn how to give it back. So I don't think of youth and childhood as any necessarily pretty place to be.

When I was a kid I used to love hanging out with the adults, I used to love going to the races with my parents, that's all I ever wanted to do. I wanted to dress up, and be an adult. Not hang about playing chasies or footy or cricket. If there is a hell, one circle of hell would be being made to stand around playing cricket for all eternity. That's what I think of when I watch cricket; I think, 'Are they being condemned to a life of complete indolence, of just standing around on a green paddock in whites, just playing with a ball? Is that some kind of Dante's punishment here on earth?' It seems organised indolence.

CW: You have a real thing about indolence, don't you?

CS: Yes, I do. I've always found it difficult to have down time. I go on holidays and I work, so I don't have holidays much.

CW: Tell me about your notebook and how you use it. You always have one with you?

CW: Pretty much. I've got a calendar, I write little notes on the calendar. And I've always got a notebook, because you always think you're going to remember things and you never do.

And the calendar—[*retrieves it from the kitchen wall*] well, this is the one for the book I've just done, *Tree Palace*. See? All the stuff's down there. [*columns of tiny notes in the margins*]

CW: Oh! How amazing! But I'm confused. Everything in here is about the book? Or is this just general stuff in your life that you've got to do?

CS: It's everything. Here are the things I have to do in life: haircut on Tuesday. Pay Visa on Friday. There on the dates. But then I've got my other notes all around them. I'm always doing that, making these notes here.

CW: Why do you think you do it on a calendar?

CS: I don't know! I just always have. I guess it's because the calendar's there—but also maybe it compresses it. I don't think your notes should be more than about three or four words. Because unless it's a really great line, you can go paragraph after paragraph after paragraph in your notebook and you come back to it later and it's just all drivel, because you haven't compressed it.

CW: And presumably if it's just three words you can conjure it up in the most useful way for the right time later. It's not set in stone, it's flexible.

CS: Yep. Here's a note: 'I have no ancestors; they're all dead.' I think I've used that in the book, or I might have cut it. But that's enough, that's got it covered. So you do that, or you make notes when you're just hanging round, or fiddling on the piano or whatever.

CW: It doesn't bother you that other people see the notes?

CS: Well, my wife sees them. But nobody can read my writing anyway, and I've got my other notebooks.

CW: Once in an interview you said, 'Autobiography is the bedrock of most literature.' Do you still hold to that, with this new novel?

CS: I emphasise 'most'. With this one, *Tree Palace*, the autobiography is about five per cent of it. The rest is all mind-made. It feels wonderfully free. The five per cent consists of my having been to the areas where the novel is set, and I've smelt the smells, and I've touched the things.

CW: Place is important to you, isn't it?

CS: Huge, huge. This is set in the Wimmera Mallee. So was *The Amateur Science of Love,* but this book is in a very different area of it, and there's a lot of nature in it.

I've often thought I'm not a great believer in books that go on and on about nature, seascapes and landscapes. I think you can always tell when a writer's run out of ideas and uses nature for padding. It's so easy to just write and write describing a tree, or the sea or whatever. If you have any talent at all you can do that till the cows come home, so I've always avoided it. But this time it was so germane to the characters and the story, it's there.

CW: You've said you're interested primarily in power plays in relationships, and that, 'What is at the centre of most of my work is the emotional violence, it's not big wars and politics.' It's not so usual to hear a male writer saying that.

CS: Oh yes. I probably should have said emotional manip-ulation, more than violence. We often think of violence as someone biffing you on the nose or attacking you with a knife. But the wounds heal from that. I mean, I've been hit in the face, your wounds heal. But the emotional violence, it never heals. The wounds are there all the time and they come back and back and back. So to me it's terribly important to write about, because if you're going to write about people you have to write about the small things.

We all get told not to sweat the small stuff in life. But the small things are everything in life. Writers I reckon have *got* to sweat the small things. You find it in the emotional manipulation and power plays in relationships. And that's what all my work, including the current one, is about.

CW: I heard Richard Ford say once, 'Everything starts with two people in a room.'

CS: Exactly! That's the genome of everything a true writer does, two people in a room, he's quite right.

It's interesting you say that it's unusual for a man to speak about the intimacies and complexities of relationships. Because I've had this very strong feeling all my life that in our culture men get consigned to the mental and emotional ghettoes of sport or business, or, if they're going to be a writer, write about footy, or a business book. Or military history—another book on Gallipoli, please, that's just what we need.

It's as if men aren't considered any better than that; that's all men are any good for. They can't understand the complicated intricate emotional psychological details of human life—that's somehow women's territory.

It is such a *shame*, because I think men have fallen for that. I've known a lot of men with very complicated emotional lives but it never comes out, because they just keep it all in there, avoid it. We're expected to keep it all in there. Then are criticised for doing that.

It's as if our culture thinks, 'Oh well, they're just simple souls, men. Just give them a footy game or a business deal to do or a war book to read and they'll be happy.' And that's not true. But we are made to think it is, and it's almost like the culture is misandrist—it hates men. It's as if they are considered insignificant emotional creatures. So they have to be consigned to the mental and emotional ghettoes, let them play around with sport and Gallipoli tales, but just don't let their feelings come out of the bottle. We don't want to know. We want you to be either dumb or noble, but we don't want you to be complicated.

That's what pisses me off about our culture, that we've allowed this demarcation between men and women where emotional and psychological complexity is concerned, particularly as it applies to literary fiction.

CW: And yet it's given you this territory. It's what Franzen might describe as your 'hot material'.

CS: Yes. That's where I've stumbled in, and then I have honed it, I suppose. It's what I do. It seems a terribly interesting and invigorating thing to write about.

CW: Without considering other people's responses to your work, what defines success for you? When you've done your job well, what have you done?

CS: Well, it's probably best to talk about *Tree Palace*, which I finished about a month and a half ago. I had a sense of,

'That's perfect—that's exactly it.' Before, I've only ever had that sense in parts; I think I've written a couple of poems where I thought, 'I can't actually mess with that, it seems to have a perfect shape, it's become a perfect object.'

But when you have that sense about the whole book, that's what I like. I still had the feeling last night, I was out doing a little bit of gardening just as it was becoming dusk, and I thought, 'Oh, I still feel like that!', which is really good. Because sometimes in the past, I've wondered, did I let the book down, is there something more I could've done?

When you send it out into the world, it becomes this thing on its own, but still very much connected to you. People often talk about a book as their child—that's silly, I don't think of it like that at all. But it is this little tendril of you that's way, way out in the world, and you don't like to think that it's somehow malformed. So I had this feeling with *Tree Palace*: I don't think anything's malformed. And I thought, 'That's good'—it's out there, it's going to be out there, and I'm going to be able to say I'm proud of it, it's a beautiful object.

CW: Did you work differently on this one to the way you have before?

CS: Well, this is a slightly longer book, and I have six characters on the go at one time all connected with power plays. Whereas with *The Amateur Science of Love* it was stripped down to two main characters and some bit players. But here I have five main characters and a baby, and a whole lot of bit players all around the place. So to keep them all up in the air was challenging but a delight, because they interested me and invigorated me, but I knew I had to work them hard, because—or they were actually making me work them hard, because they had a lot they wanted to do or say. So I was just pushing and pushing them.

CW: When I first got here you said how much you had enjoyed writing this book, especially using humour in this one.

CS: Yeah, well all my books are funny in their way. I don't go out of my way to be funny, but life is like that. The day my father died was one of the funniest days of my life. I mean, I was *drenched* in tears, but so many things happened that were just farcical. So that's the way it comes, the pain and suffering and tragedy and trauma come with comedy, all the time. Not to include comedy is not to be true to life. The absurd, cruel, comic moments. It's a cruel god. It's not a god of love, but it's a very funny god.

Joe Orton said one of my favourite lines, that I think of whenever I get into strife. He said, 'People are awful, but so terribly funny.' I think about that all the time—that the awfulness comes with the funny. Not to have humour in a book somewhere is to overlook a really massive part of life.

I've loved this book because the characters were so inventively comical, of themselves, when they were going through challenging strife. I didn't even do it.

You know that moment when—I think Keats called it negative capability—you sort of disappear into the moment as you work? When it's as if you've ceased, yourself, to be writing? The moment when the writing happens on its own, and it happens to be a funny moment, that's what I love. That's why I've laughed a lot.

CW: Those moments, when it seems to be writing itself, those are what you live for, right?

CS: Of course. You know that old cliché about writing being ten per cent inspiration and ninety per cent perspiration? No, it's not. The inspiration should be a lot more than that, and sometimes even though I will be sitting there sweating with it, in the end the *work's* not sweating, you know? It's happening of its own accord, yet still very disciplined and structured and following its own logic and my logic, together.

Of course you live for those moments. They're just wonderful. It's the moment when you've gone through the winner's tape.

And then you've got to go round and run again. [*laughs*]

Photo: John Tsiavis

CHRISTOS TSIOLKAS is the author of five novels and a collection of short fiction, and is one of Australia's most accomplished and provocative writers.

His first novel, *Loaded* (1995), announced Tsiolkas as a new voice with challenging things to say to and about Australian society. His second, *The Jesus Man*, followed in 1999, but it was *Dead Europe*—a bleakly disturbing novel about mythology, religion, evil, and race—that cemented Tsiolkas's reputation as a risk-taker willing to go places most writers—and many readers—fear to tread. *Dead Europe* won the 2006 *The Age* Fiction Prize and the 2006 Melbourne Best Writing Award, and it seems this book is the one Tsiolkas believes really formed him as a writer. He found it almost unbearably difficult to write because of the darkness of its terrain; after this, he says, his fourth novel, *The Slap*, 'felt effortless' to write.

The Slap's explosive examination of Australian anxieties about class, race, violence, sexuality and family catapulted Tsiolkas to international megastardom, with sales of 200,000 in Australia and another 1.2 million worldwide. The novel won the 2009 Commonwealth Writers' Prize and the Australian Literature Society Gold Medal, was shortlisted for the Miles Franklin Award and Britain's Galaxy National Book Award and longlisted for the Man Booker Prize.

The stuff of writers' fantasies, the success of *The Slap* took Tsiolkas by surprise and, predictably, brought its own complications. But unlike other writers who might be paralysed by the pressure of following up such success, Tsiolkas took it in his stride and has produced two more books since—the novel *Barracuda* (2013) and the short-fiction collection *Merciless Gods* (2014). Tsiolkas is a serious cinephile and has made several films of his own, as well as writing regular film reviews for *The Saturday Paper* and other publications. Screen adaptations of his fiction are numerous: *Loaded* and *Dead Europe* were both made into films (the former as *Head On,* starring a young Alex Dimitriades), and *The Slap* was adapted for television separately in both Australia and the US. A new series of *Barracuda* screens on ABC Television in 2016.

Tsiolkas lives in Melbourne with his partner of more than twenty-five years, Wayne van der Stelt.

I first met Tsiolkas many years ago, during a visit I made to Melbourne with his and my publisher,

Jane Palfreyman. She spoke highly of him as a friend, but I was nervous about meeting him: his fiction spoke of edgy, inner-city cool, not to mention a deal of anger towards hetero, middle-class Anglo Australia; I assumed I would represent everything he despised. I was shocked, then, to be greeted with one of what I now know to be his customary huge enfolding hugs, and his quietly spoken, courteous demeanour. With his warmth and cheerful attentiveness he reminded me, more than anyone, of my own little brother. Like everyone I know who has met him, I was immediately charmed by his generosity and modesty.

I have always admired Tsiolkas's courage and honesty as a writer: it seems to me his work is not only an artistic quest but a moral and intellectual one, to discover how to live well, how to treat others well, and how to be free. His personal explorations of family and sexual tensions, of race and class divides, are also explorations of those things on a national scale, showing us what kind of society we have become in Australia. It's neither pretty nor comfortable, but Tsiolkas's work is always revealing, always powerful.

For this conversation, just after his return from a research trip to Europe and the Middle East, we met at his regular Northcote cafe for coffee and a cigarette for him. Then we took the short walk to the modest studio where he has worked since earnings from *The Slap* afforded him a private work space away from home.

We talked for two hours; he spoke slowly and thoughtfully, sometimes pausing for long moments while he considered the question, or rephrased an answer to respond with greater clarity. Every now and then he would burst into loud laughter, but I noticed that whenever I asked him about his successes his voice grew much quieter. It seemed symbolic of the humility and honesty driving all his work as a writer.

CW: When you look back over your body of work, what do you think has changed and what has stayed the same?

CT: The things that have remained the same are the obsessions. I think we all have obsessions, as writers, that don't change; they're like old wounds, and you can't help scratching them. For me, one is sex and sexuality, both the pleasure and the danger of it. Then there's family, and race, and what those things mean, all in that potent mix with migration and questions of belonging.

A lot of people have said there's real anger or rage in my work, particularly the early work. That's true, though I'd like to claim the writing has never been without tenderness. But I think that moving into middle age, you become more conscious of both your limitations as a human being and the mistakes you've made. You're much less judgemental than when you're twenty-five or twenty-seven. So I think that's a real change in my writing.

I've said that in a strange way, after the success of *The Slap*, *Barracuda* felt like writing my first novel again. Danny in *Barracuda* and Ari in *Loaded*, they're not dissimilar characters. But *Loaded* ends after a twenty-four-hour cycle with him in the same position he was, staring at the ceiling. Whereas that was clearly something I didn't want to do with Danny in *Barracuda*. I think for me it was a story about how you navigate shame, failure, those terrible mistakes, and find a direction towards goodness. That's become more and more important to me as an older writer.

There's a period of artistic creation where you can be the *enfant terrible*, and a period where you can be the wise sage. And then there's this middle period where you're not quite sure of your position in something called Australian literature. I have a sense that this place, this studio where we're sitting, is the shed or the workshop where I'm just doing my work, and part of my work is thinking through craft: how does story work? How does language work? All those things. That's, for me, what writing is now.

If I'm going to be absolutely honest, I think there was a notion in that younger period of wanting to be the best, wanting to be a genius. But true genius is incredibly, incredibly rare, you know. There's Kafka, and Woolf, and then there's the rest of us. That's what I mean about being an artisan, thinking about what I can do, and hopefully that is to write better with each book. That's actually what I'm looking for now.

CW: One constant in your work is that there is risk, or disturbance, at the heart of it all. There's a sense of danger, you never feel safe as a reader. Which is why it is so compelling.

CT: I was in France recently and I noticed a real difference in the kind of questions I was asked, different from those I get asked in the Anglophone world. One journalist's first question to me was, 'Can we talk about blasphemy?'

I loved that question, because I think my personal trajectory in life has been—and my family is important—struggling against certain expectations of what it was to be the eldest son, certain expectations of what it was to be a Greek son. Not ever wanting to abandon family but not knowing if I could integrate the self, the family and the social. And thank God I discovered reading and writing and cinema, because that saved me. I think it saves many of us.

From a very early age, the writing and the art I was attracted to was dangerous art, outsider art. I was also someone who went through a period of deep religious faith in my adolescence. I look back on it now and it was clearly a way of trying not to be gay, you know. I thought God would save me. I abandoned that, first intellectually and then emotionally, by the end of high school. But I also had this other faith, a political faith, in something called communism. So the Greek family, religion, politics—I'm a product of all of them, and I'm trying to retain what I think is of ethical value in all those things. But they're also dogmas, and my work is about challenging dogma, trying to escape it. So that's possibly where some of the danger comes from in the fiction: from trying to escape, or to make sense of what happens when you place yourself outside of those things.

With the family, the real fear was extreme solitude and loneliness: that one of the most important elements of my life would be broken. And with religion, this may sound to secular ears really bizarre, but I did think, what would it be to be abandoned, to be—in hell? And with politics, though I am so firmly a man of the Left, there's an element of the Left that is not that different from sectarian Christianity. So for me, to challenge some of that doctrine felt like being outside, you were excommunicated.

I don't think I necessarily feel the extremity of emotions about it in the same way now, but I do feel a certain obligation to keep thinking about those things. To keep thinking about what it is to make yourself completely outside. What it is to be the outsider.

That adolescent period of faith for me was evangelical Protestantism. I'd moved schools in year eight from a largely migrant school in the inner city to a high school that was quite Anglo Celtic. So I felt like a fish out of water at an age where I was also realising I'm homosexual, even though I wasn't quite sure if I had the words to say it. So, you know, for the first evangelical Baptist who came along, I was easy prey. But that said, there's something about that Protestantism that I still have an intellectual argument going on with in my head. So the book I'm working on now—I mean, look [*points*] there's the Holy Bible there—is about St Paul.

The way I was raised as a young kid with religion was . . . I wish I had a better word for it; the English word is 'superstitious', and it is. It's very much, you know, you touch wood; if you're feeling melancholy maybe someone has put the evil eye on you. I think there's a pagan element in the old peasant European life that, in a strange way, was still there in early seventies Melbourne because of where the migrant communities came from.

But another thing about Orthodoxy, and maybe it has to do with the history of that side of Europe and the Middle East, is a fatalism. You read it in Dostoyevski, you see it in so much of Russian literature and Russian art, and I think it's there in elements of the contemporary Greek literature and cinema. Which is against Protestantism. Yes, you can work hard, you can try to do all the right things, but there is something called faith—the Greek word is *moirá*—that you can't run from. And I think that's actually maybe had a stronger influence than I've given credit to in the past.

CW: That's fascinating. Okay, let's get back to sex for a moment. I'm interested in the nexus of sex and violence in your work. The tenderness is always just a very fine blade away from a dangerous kind of darkness. What is it about this that interests you so much?

CT: Well, I think the risks you can put yourself through in the pursuit of sexual desires, and the suddenly overwhelming fantasies that can strike your imagination, are terrifying. I mean, you're talking to someone who's been monogamous for a very long time now, but I've been through periods where I've done the most stupid, destructive, ugly things in pursuit of sexual desire. And writing has been this grace—that I have this space where I can work those things through. But I feel we're not very honest about sex and what sex does. Clearly, being gay and dealing with the relationship between what it is to be a man and what it is to have a non-heterosexual desire has been an ever-present struggle in my life.

And there is a difference between Christos Tsiolkas who is having this interview now and can give you the proper feminist and queer analysis of all those things, and the man who has sexual thoughts and sexual desires that are really scary. It's not disconnected from what happens with us in love, especially in those frenzies of love. We can do the most awful things, the most shameful things, in pursuit of it. What is it about those feelings of inadequacy, those feelings that arise from repression and inadequacy, that lead us into the most hateful responses? That's what I'm interested in.

CW: Your writing seems often as though it really comes out of the body. Do you feel like that? It's got this explosive force.

You don't mediate sex to make it nice, or tender, you know. Do you think Australians are squeamish about sex compared to Europeans?

CT: Well, the danger is to romanticise European views about sex. I mean, traditional Greek sexuality is clearly patriarchal, and if you look at the experience of someone like my mother—the choices that woman had were so very limited. When I think back to her life and compare it to what I've been able to do in my life I just feel so fortunate. So I don't want to romanticise it in that way—but I do think that there's a difference. I don't think that in Europe the sex defines the person, and the ethical person, in the same way it does in the Anglo, Protestant world.

The clearest example I can give you is from when I was coming out. I was very, very young and was trying to formulate my feelings to my parents, to their world. And I had two elder male family members say about themselves, plus at least one of my friends' mothers say to me, 'Oh, my father, my husband, my brothers, they've all fucked men. That's just what you men do.' Which is such a very, very different way of conceptualising sex. So, yes, I think there is a squeamishness here—about the body, maybe. Not just sex, but about the body.

The other thing that is dangerous and therefore enticing as a writer is that it's not like there is the good, feminist sexual self and then the bad, antifeminist sexual self. I mean, one of the struggles is that there's no clear line, where on this side is the bad and on that side is the good. That's what's problematic about sex, and what's exciting about it. And—I always say this—why is it that we have a bad sex writing award in the English language and we don't have a bad love writing award?

Whoever we are as writers, we are also our influences, our history. So as an adolescent, the writers I kind of feared but also responded to were writers dealing with sex and sexuality. And a lot of their work was considered pornographic. Now maybe it's called erotica. The argument will never be settled about what is erotica and what is pornography. I mean, that's a very big difference between us and the French, for example. The French have great pornographic novels that are part of their cultural history. I think that tradition of writing is . . . maybe you can help me on this . . . is it more obscured in the Anglophone countries?

CW: Don't ask me, I'm an uptight English-heritage Catholic girl!

CT: [*Laughs*]

CW: I want to move on to drugs for a minute. It seems to me drugs offer such a great narrative possibility, the potential for chaos. I wondered if the use of drugs in your stories is just because they're around in life, or have you been conscious of them as a narrative tool, to build uncertainty and tension?

CT: The honest answer is no, it hasn't been a question of craft—more that it's reflected a certain period of my life. A pretty long period! [*laughs*] Drug use was just a way of being in the world; I'm not going to put a moral judgement on it. But I'm not there anymore, so I think the experience of drugs will be different in the writing I do now.

I do think there's something interesting about the states of both euphoria and ill-ease in drug experiences that I've channelled into my writing. But the reality is that memory fades, so because I don't use drugs anymore, certainly not in that way, I think that absence will come through in the writing. It's too early to tell how.

I mean, it's interesting with my new novel in progress, because if we're squeamish about sex, we're also squeamish about drugs and the history of drugs. But you read the religious literature—writing dealing with experience of the divine—and you know, those people were off their nuts! So it's not that drugs have completely disappeared, I just think it will be different.

CW: This leads perhaps to a question about mystery. How important is mystery to you? Because it's tied up with religion and also with drugs, I think—that sense of a drive to experience something beyond ordinary reality, something big we don't understand.

CT: I talked about blasphemy before. It feels like the most blasphemous thing I could say at the moment in the literary world is that I'm really seeking the divine. Imagine coming out as a Christian! [*laughs*] I mean, Tim Winton's sort of done it . . .

But yeah: the mysterious, the unknowable, the transformative, the transcendent, they're huge things, and to me they're part of what makes the lives we lead worth living. I'll tell you this, about this recent trip we did. We went to Antakya, which is the ancient Antioch, right? There's the new Middle Eastern city, and then you're walking up the mountain and through these little narrow laneways and you're stepping over stones that are Greek and Roman and Byzantine and Ottoman. And there are still working-class people cooking there, and kids are playing football, and girls playing whatever their version of hopscotch is. It's a really steep ascent through history and the contemporary, and full of Syrian refugees because it's only, what, twenty kilometres from the Syrian border. And we got to the top of the mountain just as dusk was coming on and, below us in the city, the call to prayer sounded from what must have been one thousand mosques. It was this beautiful sound that filled the heavens, and all these birds started flying—and I looked at Wayne, and his eyes were ablaze. We were just silent for . . . I don't know how long. And with tears, I realised that that would be one of the most beautiful moments of my life, where I felt something of the divine. I think this is something I may have struggled to run away from for a long time. Maybe even in my writing. But I don't want to run away from it anymore.

Now, that doesn't mean I'm a Christian. But think about the age we're writing in, Charlotte. There is the ascendancy of science and the rational run of technology—and you understand it, it is amazing what they're discovering. But what can we do as writers? We can write something else. We can make sense of the divine or the nightmarish or the dangerous.

CW: Or the transcendent: the movement into a different state of being.

CT: Yeah. Which is what love is.

CW: And it's what art is for, isn't it?

CT: It is, isn't it?

CW: Let's talk about structure, because I know you take things apart a bit. How often would it happen for you that you would really take a draft of a novel apart and completely rethink it?

CT: Well, it's happening now, my friend. For this new novel, I'd given myself a year for just reading and research, and I started writing at the beginning of the year. I had a structure and this voice I wanted, a character. I'd written twenty-five thousand words in her voice. But during the trip I just realised it actually couldn't be her voice, it had to be the voice of another woman, who's connected. And you just have to wear it. But it's not even a matter of 'wearing it'; I'm actually excited about writing in this other voice and it will be better, I think, for the novel.

CW: So are you just holus-bolus chucking all the existing work out, or are you reworking the existing draft into a different voice?

CT: Well, there are elements of the story I'm keeping, certainly, but because it's a perspective of another person, I felt it would be a wasted effort to try to salvage what I already had. There are certain things we've learned by now, Charlotte, and I know that I could try to do that, but because there's maybe five lines that are precious to me, it's not worth it. It's much more exciting to begin again, I think. And to just think, well, part of the process of getting to this point was actually doing what I did.

CW: Absolutely. I think it's one of the hardest things to convey to new writers in mentoring or teaching—that chucking stuff out is progress. How it can absolutely re-energise a project to throw it all away.

CT: Well, that's what I feel about what's happening now. Yeah, it is really hard to convey that to someone who hasn't got the excitement of where they want to go next with it. So just saying you've got to chuck it without having an idea of what to write instead—then that's more difficult.

CW: But sometimes it's only when you chuck it that you can see what's needed next.

CT: Brian Eno had those cards in the seventies—*Oblique Strategies*. I don't use them, but he created this body of ideas, these cards that have aphorisms like, 'The thing that is most treasured for you in the work, throw it away', or 'Begin at the end', and he would actually just shuffle them and pick one up. I think there is something about the happy accident that we shouldn't be frightened of. Sometimes that's how you can free yourself up. Because we do need certain limitations, otherwise it's all too huge.

CW: Oh, Emily Perkins told me about those. She quoted one about 'honouring thy mistake as a hidden intention'.

CT: Yes, that's beautiful.

CW: So poetic—and liberating as well, to think that actually your mistake is something purposeful that you just didn't know about yet. Still on structure, one of the things I really marvelled at with *The Slap* was how you managed these eight points of view about the same event, but how every perspective absolutely propelled the story forward in that incredibly compelling fashion. How difficult was that, to wrangle those points of view and not keep repeating the same sort of material? It seemed to me that at the start of each chapter I was running to catch up. Everyone was moving, all the time. It was such an achievement.

CT: Thank you. The honest truth is that because it came after *Dead Europe*, which was a novel in which I really, really wrestled with the devil in order to write it, *The Slap* felt effortless. So it started in Hector's voice, and then I had the idea that came from film, of taking the perspective of the different characters. And of course there was a lot of work in getting the timeframe right, getting the voices right, having to forgo some characters. I have some regrets—I wish I'd written in Sandy's voice, for example. It wasn't that it was completely easy, not at all. But it felt like such a joy after *Dead Europe*, because I really battled with that.

One of the great joys of writing a novel for me is working out and playing with and discovering structure. And the other thing for me with *The Slap* was what I was talking about at the beginning, about those obsessions, those old wounds, and yet not wanting to repeat myself. So after *Dead Europe* there was an element of thinking, 'You know what? I don't just want to write in the same voice. I want to write as a woman, I want to write from different ages.' And that felt really liberating because I'd been scared. I don't know if you've talked to other men writers about it, about the fear of writing in another gender . . . but I found freedom in that.

CW: Well let's talk about *Dead Europe* now, because man, oh man, you went to some scary places in that book. You really were brave in that story, I think. Did you feel you were brave?

CT: Look, yes, I felt . . . I knew I was doing a dangerous thing, particularly in taking anti-Semitism as a subject. In trying to explore that racism. There were two points at which I had to give it up for a while because as I was investigating it, I was blurring my involvement with it. And to be naked about what it is, suddenly you're giving yourself over to the most ugly thoughts . . . I mean, that's what racism is, you know.

But how I tried to anchor my relationship to it was to remind myself that racism is just part of the way I want to understand the world. It's one of the things that has made me angry from a very, very young age. I'm not even talking about personal experiences, though I had that, but particularly about seeing how Mum and Dad were treated at times. And also just as an ethical being at a young age, I was wanting to object to the instances of racism I saw.

And just now, what I was seeing in Greece and in Europe recently, the treatment of the immigrant and of the Muslim immigrant, felt as vile and as ugly and as dangerous as the history of anti-Semitism.

Dead Europe is a strange book because it was written before the crisis, but it's only fucking got worse.

CW: There's something frightening about entering into this kind of material. Because you're not standing outside racism and judging it, you're entering into it. You're becoming racist in order to explore it in your fictional world. I felt like that when I was writing my novel, that I must be misogynistic in some way that really scared me. So was *Dead Europe frightening* for you to write?

CT: Completely frightening. Frightening because when you unleash certain thoughts, they feel like you can't control them. That is the book where I learned that there are certain limits to what you should unleash. I mean, you can go so many places in fiction, and into the darkest places, but I think with that book, I learned that . . . I'm hesitating, because the only language I have is a religious language. It's this question: do you want to allow evil in? There is a certain experience of that I felt with *Dead Europe*. I learned that I had to rein myself in, and that not all is possible for art's sake. It's a really good lesson, I think. And I learned it with that book.

It's hard to talk about because I haven't read it for a long time, partly I think because I don't want to go back to those places. There may be readers who think I didn't make the right ethical choice, that I went too far, but I did actually learn the limit. And learned that there is a moral and right reason to set limits in what you do with writing a book.

CW: Turning to a different subject now, I loved your review the other day of the film *The Lobster*. Something you said about Colin Farrell was interesting: 'He has shed that craving for stardom that has made him previously seem desperate as an actor.' Have you seen this craving, this desperation, in writers too?

CT: Ooh!

CW: I have a theory that the third book is where a writer starts getting real.

CT: Yes. I think the third book is absolutely right. Well, you have your first book, right? You've had this dream for so long, and it's just such a fucking buzz to be published. Unbelievable. And then suddenly it's like, 'Oh, I have to write another one!' And a self-consciousness enters the process that wasn't there at the beginning. Self-consciousness is really difficult to manage and understand. I don't think it ever leaves us because we are conscious of, you know, 'This is what we do, this is how we are reviewed, this is how we are understood.' There are certain expectations from publishers and families and lovers. So, yes, sometimes you read a book and you think, who is this written for? Does this person even know? You find that with a lot of second works, and probably my second work is the same.

CW: And mine.

CT: Yeah, because of that self-consciousness. Once you enter the literary world, you can't un-enter it. That's the reality. When I was writing *Loaded*, I was writing for myself, completely for myself, and there will always be a sense of loss, I think, about that. I mean, don't get me wrong, I feel really fortunate. But there is a little sense of loss. With *Barracuda*, for instance, I felt what I wanted was to get to that feeling of writing the first book again.

CW: That brings me to ask how it was to cope with the success of *The Slap*. I mean, it was obviously a brilliant, wonderful thing, but I imagine there is also a more complex side to that level of success.

CT: It was completely disorienting in reality. Yes, it is a brilliant and wondrous and fortunate thing. I've got this studio, you know. And Wayne and I have a freedom that comes from what that book created, which I will always be grateful for. Also, I'm so glad my dad lived long enough to see the success of that, because it also gave my parents room to breathe. They didn't have to worry about Christo anymore. That was lovely.

So, yes, I've been grateful for that.

After *Dead Europe*, when I felt I'd poured so much of myself into that—it's a really divisive novel, but it also created a certain space for me in the literary world in Australia, and I was actually really comfortable with that. I thought, 'I'm going to keep writing the books I want to write and I will do it from working part-time to earn an income; I'll just keep doing this.' I knew I wanted that, so it's not like the success of *The Slap* changed any of that.

But, man, I was not prepared for the level of self-doubt that can come from success. I wasn't prepared for the greed that can come from success, the greed for more of it. I wasn't prepared for how that self-consciousness can so easily slip into narcissism if you let it happen. I wasn't prepared for any of those things. I'm being really honest with you. I think—I hope—that what kept me rooted back in the real world was Wayne, my friends, family. And going back to asking, 'What is it I want to write, what is it that I want to do?'

I feel a bit . . . this is like when you read those interviews with movie stars complaining about their lives.

CW: But this isn't like that, this is real, it is important to talk about this stuff I think. In one of the articles I read about you, the writer quoted another author saying, 'If one of us had to have a great success, I'm so glad it was Christos.' And I felt the same; it felt to me that there was this huge cheering for you in the literary community, which was a beautiful thing, you know.

CT: I do think that is true. That was lovely. Look, envy is one of the worst sins we are all capable of, in any world we exist in. But I felt quite supported by most of the people I even vaguely knew. So the discomfort was coming from me. It was really coming from me, I think.

CW: You seem to me very connected to a community of writers and creative people. I wondered if you felt then separated from that community?

CT: Look, it's been quite a few years now since *The Slap*. It's queer, that relationship, because I did actually get disconnected from a couple of friends who were part of my world and up until a year ago, I thought it had come from me, that I had changed. But I realised that actually—and this you can't control—there are certain ways people are going to perceive you after that success, and it can poison relationships. With lots of people nothing has changed, there's just great cheer about what happened. I don't think it's changed with Wayne at all either; I mean, it's not like he's wanting me to write *The Slap II*, you know. [*laughs*] So with most people I don't think it has changed.

But there are some people, I think, who . . . why am I hesitating? I'll just be honest. I think there are some people for whom the envy has been so hard for them to contain it just makes it impossible to have the old working relationship together. And there are also some people I've known who are important to me but who take a very old-fashioned view, that success does mean 'selling out'. And in both situations it's impossible to navigate your way back to those old relationships.

CW: I think envy should be talked about more, in general. I mean, to pretend we don't have the odd stab of envy when as a writer you work so hard and you often see so little result, well, it's silly to deny it. But that's what I thought was so lovely about your success. I didn't see that in anyone I knew. There was just joy.

CT: Envy is a bit like misogyny or racism: a human emotion we are all prey to, you know. And, in fact, even more than misogyny or racism, because it's so embedded in our sibling relationships, in our schoolyard relationships. Not to acknowledge it is dangerous.

CW: So now, a few years on from that explosive success, do you feel you've come back to some sort of equilibrium, or did you just have to develop to a new way of being with your work?

CT: One of the great things that *The Slap* has afforded me is that you get invited to places overseas. And one of the great things about going to places overseas is you realise that if there is a totem pole, really, you're pretty far down it. [*laughs*] You keep shifting, you know. So I guess I feel like I'm coming back to that space I was in after *Dead Europe* which is . . . this is the space, a really good space, where I want to work from—and fuck the rest.

One of the most destructive elements of being a young man for me was wanting to be liked. Now, one of the good things about that was that I learned to be a good person in the world, which is not unimportant. But it's tiring wanting to be liked all the time! I mean, I just turned fifty, and that's one of the things I'm looking forward to, the older I get. Alright, maybe the body will fall apart, but it's going to be nice not to care that much about it. Still to try to be a good person, but not having to please everybody. As you get older you realise that people are going to make decisions about you, they're going to make decisions about your work, that there's nothing you can do about those decisions, and that's alright.

CW: Let's talk about some practical things now. Why do you have this studio away from home rather than working where you live?

425

CT: Because for a long time I worked from the study at home; we moved around until we got the place we have in Preston. But for me, there's something good about marking the end of the working day and going home. I'm walking home and thinking, 'This is what I'm going to cook tonight', right? Just the simplicity of that, when you've been in your head all day, is wonderful.

Wayne is incredibly supportive about what I do but there were times when I was working from home and the poor guy would be coming back from work and he just would put his head through the door and go, 'How are you?' And I'd go, 'Fuck off!' Terrible, terrible, selfish, ugly thing—but when you're locked in your head, that can happen.

So I've been working out of home for a while now because I just realised I didn't want to damage my relationship. Before here, I was in an open space with filmmakers and other writers and that was great as well. When I'm sitting down to work, I'm quite diligent.

CW: It wasn't distracting, being around other people?

CT: Look, they were pretty focused people. So, no, it wasn't distracting—but controlling the social aspect is harder for me. There's the temptation to go out for a coffee and then, you know, you like these people, and then it's like, 'Why don't we have a drink at three?' [*laughs*] And before you know it . . .

CW: And you can justify it because you're talking about your work!

CT: Yeah, exactly. So this has been great. I don't have internet here and that's a really good thing. The other thing is the walk between here and home. It's about half an hour each way. Walking is all about breathing. I think it just gives me a space . . . I walk here and I walk back but often in the middle of the day I'll do another walk for an hour. It's not that I'm thinking really about what I'm working on, sometimes I just want to escape what I'm working on. But there is that great Doris Lessing term, have you heard it? 'Fugging.' She talked about a writer's fugging time. The time where other people around you would think you're just sitting back or you're just taking a walk. But Lessing wrote that it was central to the writing process and I think that, for me, is what walking is.

Also, because you're sedentary as a writer, I like the experience of being active and physical. So, fugging is a beautiful little word that describes something very hard to put into words, about the process we all need to go through. Sometimes it is stillness you need—I'm talking about it in the emotional sense—and I find stillness in walking as much as I do sitting back in this chair.

CW: I think walking's really central to so many creative people. The movement, the oxygen, something about breathing and moving unlocks things in ways that sitting doesn't do. So when you get here, do you have a certain number of hours? A number of words? How do you know when you're allowed to go home?

CT: For me it's words—fifteen hundred. It's an arbitrary number, I chose that years ago and now it's just a tool I use. Depending on other work—for example, *The Lobster* review I had to hand in last week, when I'm working on something like that I don't think about it in terms of words, I'm just thinking, I've got to get this done.

Occasionally I'm alright on the computer with the novels but when I was in a moment of real fear and confusion with *Dead Europe*, I started writing longhand and that freed me up in a particular way. So half of *Dead Europe* and *The Slap* and *Barracuda* were all initially longhand, and then I put them on the computer. So part of my process will be to go have a coffee, a couple of coffees, and write for an hour or an hour and a half, and then come in here and put what I've done on the computer. Then I'll have lunch and a walk and then I'll come back and then probably write from the computer or just edit the work I did in the morning.

And now—there was a short story in *Merciless Gods* that I wrote first in Greek and I translated it into English. And I'm going to try that again now, with the new voice I want to write in, because the character is a young slave, she's fifteen and has been born into slavery, has never had any education. So how do I create a language for her? I thought maybe if I do it with my limited Greek, maybe that will get me somewhere. And, again, as the Greek keyboard is so hard to navigate because it's a different alphabet, I'll do that in longhand and then put it on the computer, translate in the afternoons. I'm really looking forward to that.

CW: How interesting. What a lovely extra tool to have at your disposal! Now, a couple of years ago I was lucky enough to be in the room when you launched the UTS student anthology, and you gave a most beautiful speech to those young people. One of the things you told them was that they needed to understand, if they were serious, that there are sacrifices and decisions to make. Like not living in the hippest suburbs, like choosing a partner you know will be supportive. Do you think beginner writers can understand the level of material sacrifice required? Is it just material?

CT: I think it becomes harder, because I think we have become more consumerist over my lifetime. This is not just a fifty-year-old man saying, 'it was better in my day' at all. I actually think it's about the speed of capitalist globalisation; what we think is necessary to live a good life now is huge, in terms of material stuff. Of course it's very hard to understand that when you're a young person. But look, I have a sense that the real artist, not just the writer but the real artist, knows this stuff. I remember very, very clearly working in the State Film Centre—which was a great job—and saying to Wayne, 'I'm not happy.' I wanted to go part-time and see if I could make this writing happen.

So even before I was published I knew certain choices would have to be made to make that possible. I was very lucky that Wayne just went [*clicks fingers*]: 'Of course I understand.'

CW: It's such a gift, to have the partners we have, who just demand that you do what you want to do. I have also felt quite guilty about it at times.

CT: Look, all we can say is that we are lucky, and you have to trust your partner. I don't get any sense from Sean that he's resenting it. And one of the lovely things about the partners we have too is that they're not avaricious people; that does make it easier.

CW: I've heard you describe writing as a vocation. What's the difference between a job you love and a vocation?

CT: For me, it feels like what I have to do; that if there was a purpose to my being on the planet, this is what I was meant to do. I can't think of what else I'd be doing. I've had jobs I've loved, I've had jobs I've hated, and the difference is that it didn't feel essential that I was in that job. I knew there would be other jobs I could do. One of my favourite jobs was working at the vet clinic—partly the work, but more that I worked with an amazing group of people. Whereas writing feels like I have to do it. That's what I mean: it's a vocation.

CW: Film is so important to you, and you've made films. Why are you a writer and not primarily a filmmaker?

CT: Film is another language, another tool, you know. Cinema has its language of editing that can be really useful for us as writers. One of the great pleasures in my life is the three weeks I take off in the middle of every winter for the Melbourne Film Festival. I go and see films every day. You get inspired by stories, and how people tell them, but you're also getting inspired by the language filmmakers are using to tell stories.

But I've come to realise that there are certain skills I've learned as a writer that were formed so early on, through my love of reading, that they made writing possible. And there are skills a director has that I just don't think I have. I have patience when it comes to writing, but I have no patience when I'm on set. It feels really boring. That ability directors have to manage their creative vision and be able to manage all these people around them to fulfil that vision, I just don't have it. As well, I've realised through my experience with filmmakers and the adaptations and all that, that I can write a book like *Dead Europe* that goes to where it goes because I can do it in here [*points to head*], but to get the financing to write that kind of work on screen would be a very, very, very hard ask. It can be done, but one of the things I find hard in watching my filmmaker friends is how long they have to struggle to get a film on screen. And then also you're asking actors to do things which . . . I can create these characters, I can make them do anything I want. But with actual human bodies you have certain ethical responsibilities.

I do love film, and I think there is a way for me to make film, but I've given up on the big idea of the feature film. If I do something with film it'll be more essay-like, you know? And that's the great thing about the new camera technology—I can pick up a camera and shoot and it won't be a big film, but it will be a way of exploring film language.

CW: What was your involvement in the productions of *The Slap* for television?

CT: In the Australian one, I had three weeks in the writers' room. It was staggered in two blocks so it was a fortnight initially, where we met at nine in the morning and worked till six in the evening and it was fantastic being in a room with these really bright, intelligent, passionate, creative people. Because I'd known Tony Ayres, one of the producers, for a long period and he knew about my love of film, he was very welcoming. I'd been quite clear that I didn't want to write it, but he said, 'It would be great if we could use you, just to be there for the writers to ask questions.' In the first ten minutes they were all really diffident; I think they thought I was going to not let them change anything. But I just said, 'Look, I'm here, you can ask me whatever you want, just use me. I don't want you to rewrite *The Slap*, I want you to do something else.' Very quickly, I knew that I trusted them and they trusted me. In a funny way it was harder for them to let go of the book than it was for me.

CW: I have a question for you that I was asked recently when I was out promoting my novel. A woman said to me, 'Look, I used to write short stories, and then I decided that I'd rather do something useful and practical to actually *help* people. Have you ever considered doing that?' I sort of laughed, and then I gave her a bit of a lofty lecture on the good of art. But you alluded to this earlier, when you said you sometimes felt you should be doing more politically. So I'm asking it of you: what is the good, the social good, of what we do? Is there any?

CT: Well, your feelings about that are going to depend on what you believe about pleasure, and whether pleasure is something good. And I'd say there is a Protestant inflection to that question that is worth thinking about. I'm caught between two answers: I know art is useful in that very political, ethical way, in the sense that I don't think I'd have survived the self-loathing or self-hatred or confusion of my younger years if it hadn't been for certain works of cinema and certain books that answered something for me, expressed a voice that made me feel that there was a future for me. That's why, in *Barracuda*, Danny discovers literature in prison, and he discovers a very old-fashioned, humanist kind of literature. What am I trying to say in response to the question? Yes, I feel it sometimes; I do ask, 'What's the point of it?'

But I do think we are deeply suspicious of pleasure in this society: really, *really* suspicious of pleasure. There are a lot of complicated reasons that Greece is in the turmoil it's in at the moment. This is a discussion that would last another two hours, but there's something being played out between Western and Southern Europe that's also about pleasure, and what a pleasurable life means, I think. So I think there is a value in what we do, even if it's just to give pleasure. Right? But there is another side of me that understands there is so much shocking stuff happening in the world, you want to do something more. I mean, I'm not a very good activist. I just get bored in meetings.

CW: I can't imagine you being very obedient . . .

CT: [*Laughs*] No. But, the thing about growing up with a sense of the evil eye is—I wasn't in that room with you but there's something about the audacity, that a person wants to ask you that question, which I think says a lot more about them than they know. What I mean is that you want to protect yourself from those people, because there is malevolent intent that underlies a question like that. And—this is the oogy-boogy side of me that I haven't managed to escape—when I get a question like that, immediately in my head I'm going [*whispers*] M'ashallah, M'ashallah, M'ashallah [*laughs*] which is, you know, the Arabic for, 'God protect me, God protect me, God protect me.' I mean, it's not that her question isn't a good one, because clearly you and I are asking that of ourselves all the time—but why is it coming out in this particular way? In this way that feels ugly?

CW: Well, I admit it went in pretty deep. I think you're right about protecting yourself. Can I ask you about your new work in progress? In some ways it sounds like a major shift into some whole new territory—but with familiar questions at its heart.

CT: It's about St Paul. It's a book about a man who changed his whole life—I mean talk about an outsider, this is a man who was persecuting Christians, and then he abandons his clan, his tribe, his people, his family, to pursue the divine, to seek truth. Of course it's connected to what I'm always doing. But the challenge of writing in such a different way is something I've wanted to do because it's a bit of a leap. I think historical fiction is really freakin' hard, and there's so much bad historical fiction out there. But it's a leap worth taking.

CW: So exciting to leap. To jump.

CT: Yeah, it is. It is. And I haven't thought about it in quite this way, but maybe part of the process of coming to peace with everything that happened from *The Slap* is having that whole year just for reading. I set myself this regimen, really, where I was only going to read works written between the third century BC and the second century AD, or I was going to read history about that period. And the Bible. It's been a form of discipline. But it was really inspiring, in thinking about language, the language in which people were writing and speaking at that time. And another really good thing was that I knew there were all these great books being published now that I did want to read—but I realised they'll still be there, they're not going to disappear. If they're good, they'll be there, waiting for me.

ACKNOWLEDGEMENTS

My thanks to all the writers who spoke with me during the three years of *The Writer's Room Interviews* magazine: Amanda Lohrey, David Roach, Margo Lanagan, Kim Scott, Janine Burke, Craig Sherborne, Joan London, Malcolm Knox, Debra Oswald, Lloyd Jones, PM Newton, Wayne Macauley, Sue Smith, James Bradley, Tegan Bennett Daylight, Emily Perkins, Fiona Wood, Christos Tsiolkas. I learned something profound from every one of you.

Special thanks to Ali Lavau, who for three years proofread and edited these interviews with unstinting commitment, precision and generosity, and to Alex Forbes, who transcribed many long hours of meandering conversations. Thanks also to Jenny Darling, Jane Palfreyman, Siobhán Cantrill and all at Allen & Unwin for making this book possible.